D1190782

Unreliable Narrator

Unreliable Narrator

ME, MYSELF, AND IMPOSTOR SYNDROME

Aparna Nancherla

VIKING

VIKING
An imprint of Penguin Random House LLC
penguinrandomhouse.com

Grateful acknowledgment is made for permission to reprint the following:

"Could That Be Me?" from *No Land in Sight: Poems* by Charles Simic,
compilation © 2022 by Charles Simic. Used by permission of Alfred A. Knopf,
an imprint of Knopf Doubleday Publishing Group, a division of
Penguin Random House LLC. All rights reserved.

Photos on pages 35 and 172 from the collection of the author.

LIBRARY OF CONGRESS CATALOGING-IN-PUBLICATION DATA
Names: Nancherla, Aparna, author.
Title: Unreliable narrator : me, myself, and impostor syndrome / Aparna Nancherla.
Description: New York : Viking, [2023]
Identifiers: LCCN 2023003558 (print) | LCCN 2023003559 (ebook) |
ISBN 9781984879806 (hardcover) | ISBN 9781984879813 (ebook)
Subjects: LCSH: Nancherla, Aparna. | Women comedians—United
States—Biography. | Actresses—United States—Biography. |
LCGFT: Essays. | Autobiographies.
Classification: LCC PN2287.N26 A3 2023 (print) | LCC PN2287.N26 (ebook) |
DDC 792.702/8092 [B]—dc23/eng/20230423
LC record available at https://lccn.loc.gov/2023003558
LC ebook record available at https://lccn.loc.gov/2023003559

Printed in the United States of America
1st Printing

Designed by Alexis Farabaugh

To all the versions of ourselves the
world never gets to see [hold for applause]

That is the funny thing about being an artist, it might sound one way in your head but when you make it into the physical thing, you're like "Wow, this is horrible!" [laughs]

JEAN DAWSON

In the artist of all kinds I think one can detect an inherent dilemma, which belongs to the co-existence of two trends, the urgent need to communicate and the still more urgent need not to be found. This might account for the fact that we cannot conceive of an artist's coming to the end of the task that occupies his whole nature.

D. W. WINNICOTT

Contents

Unreliable Narrator

Now That I Have You Here

I wanted to write a book about impostor syndrome, because it's an identity I've embraced without question my entire life—like being a Leo[*] or having brown eyes.[**] But there's no wiggle room on this one, as fun as a wiggle room sounds. My scammer-identifying roots go way back. On my mother's telling, I was born with jaundice and suctioned out via vacuum, so I showed up unwillingly with a cone head and yellow eyes, perfectly styled for my *National Enquirer* cover photo shoot. Even then, I arrived in the manner of someone who wants everybody else to understand I wasn't thrilled about my whole deal either.

Fast-forward four decades and on the heels of moderate success as a comedian, I still only warily accept I've accomplished anything or that I ever could again. I'm relieved I don't consider my continual breathing itself a fluke: "Eh, my lungs got lucky. There was an extra opening for oxygen intake." I'm aware that my self-image is distorted, but does it matter if I fully buy into it? Hello, fringe religions and small-batch cults! Sometimes it's almost like my impostor syndrome is the majority of me, and the rest is my shadow. A therapist once told me something to the effect of "So what if

---

[*] I'm right on the cusp, but it's the more fun, flamboyant one! My pragmatic Virgo heart unenthusiastically understands.

[**] I used to think they were black—you know, like a meerkat's?

you're a fraud? Is that the worst thing? At least you're getting away with it."
She had a point. But I had one, too. "At what cost, Shelley, at what cost?!"
(She didn't take insurance.)

If you need a definition of impostor syndrome, please, allow me.
Merriam-Webster, which added the word to its blessed dictionary in April
2020 (we did it, Team How-Did-I-Actually-Make-This-Team!!!), notes that
it is "a psychological condition that is characterized by persistent doubt concerning one's abilities or accomplishments accompanied by the fear of being
exposed as a fraud despite evidence of one's ongoing success." For some,
perhaps, having this categorization laid out so clearly can rival a spiritual
epiphany. The term is derived from a 1978 article published in the medical
journal *Psychotherapy: Theory, Research and Practice* called "The Impostor Phenomenon in High Achieving Women: Dynamics and Therapeutic Intervention." The authors of the paper, two American psychologists named Pauline
Rose Clance and Suzanne Imes (Clance & Imes: social science's Cagney &
Lacey), write that "the clinical symptoms most frequently reported are generalized anxiety, lack of self-confidence, depression, and frustration related
to inability to meet self-imposed standards of achievement." Ding ding ding!
Cash-pouring sound, but it's just a bunch of bottle caps! Three insecure
cherries across the board—that's me!

Not to brag, but impostor syndrome was initially believed to occur only
in women, although in a 1993 follow-up article cowritten with Dr. Joe Langford, Dr. Clance reframed it as an affliction without prejudice. By and large,
though, women seem to suffer from it with more intensity. It's always ladies'
night when it comes to self-doubt. Or is it?

Since then, the term has been freely bandied about in pop psychology
and business circles, in no small part due to its boundless circulation online,
especially on social media. There are now ample arguments both for and
against its existence. Some academics and journalists posit that it's not

a diagnosable syndrome at all but rather a common human experience. The original researchers themselves did, after all, refer to this set of feelings as a "phenomenon." Others feel it's a corporate shorthand term—if not a fall guy—for a complex interplay of factors in one's life. *New York Times* writer Benedict Carey even argued that it might be a social strategy, rather than an involuntary tendency. Carey wrote that, according to a 2000 Wake Forest University study, people who self-presented as impostors ranked themselves more highly in private. Fully aware of their competency, they still wanted to be perceived as less arrogant in order to come across as more agreeable slash invitable to parties and happy hours. Sorry, Benny C., that ain't me!

Though this may explain why this strategy appeals to some women— everybody knows we're far less likable if we're seen as being full of ourselves (unlike men, for whom more swagger means more, better everything). But it can go too far when the "phony phony" (has a certain ring to it) ends up believing their own humble act, overriding the benefits they'd hoped to reap.

These days, there is increasing pushback against the term, which begs the question: Why did I go and write a whole book about my experience with it? I suppose whether or not it's technically an actual pathology, like many psychology concepts, the suggestibility factor is there. I relate to the experience it describes. And ironically, even this constant parsing and questioning of impostor syndrome is fully on-brand. Does it even exist? Is the whole thing itself a fraud?

QUICK PALATE CLEANSER

Q: What do you call a worldwide symposium of people with impostor syndrome?

A: LongCon.

Right before I got my first big break in comedy—a job as a writer-performer on the late-night show *Totally Biased with W. Kamau Bell*—I turned thirty and was temping by day at a big studio in Los Angeles, doing stand-up comedy by night, stuck in that very human way where time is moving forward, but it sure doesn't feel like you are. Ooh, ooh, also! My relationship with my boyfriend of nearly five years and whom I lived with was irrevocably falling apart. I was staunchly depressed, thanks to my situation and my brain. Thankfully, I could afford to go to pay-what-you-can therapy, where the clinic's guiding philosophy was "Yeah, that sucks you're mentally imploding, but you paid ten dollars, so you see our dilemma."

To cap off the low-grade Greek tragedy, my boyfriend and I had just rid our apartment of fleas for the second time (we did not have pets: the likely culprit was a stray cat who liked to conduct sit-ins on our welcome mat—a form of protest I'd typically respect). To add insult to injury, the fleas left my boyfriend alone and bit only me, leaving me constantly itchy and gaslit in my own home. Conveniently, this is also an apt metaphor for trying to make it in show business as both a woman and a minority. You experience negatives that are clearly at play, but your male or white counterparts don't seem to be affected by them—whether that's being automatically considered for fewer opportunities because of how you look or present (yes, even now), or not knowing whether people value you for your actual ability or just for the fact you make them look more open-minded, essentially as "college admissions brochure" set dressing. Worst of all, you're constantly scratching your feet and weirding out potential employers. Fine! I took it too far!

I was very close to quitting comedy. I didn't know how to move forward in an industry that wasn't even vaguely concerned with making room for me. In the universe's defense, I had lived in LA for only about two years (barely a blip on the hustle-and-grind timeline), but I lacked the inner drive others possessed in requisitely hustling and self-promoting my way forward, armed with the incontrovertible knowledge I deserved to "make it." Still, despite my self-perception that I was lazy and unmotivated, I had what others told me was a diligent work ethic. I regularly did shows and open mics, took acting and improv classes on the side within my budget, and collaborated on projects with others. But I refused to network beyond the bare minimum. I still have two thousand VistaPrint business cards stuffed in an old box somewhere, wheeling and dealing with the darkness.

While I enjoyed writing and performing comedy, I had a tougher time naming my goals. My manager (who I gained only by moving to LA) would ask me what I wanted to do: Act? Write? Tour as a stand-up? Desperate to be included at all, I would say any of it sounded good, whatever chances deigned to come my way. I had no idea what I wanted beyond financially supporting myself with comedy. Even that idea I stole from an interview of a comedian peer of mine because it verbalized what I could not: deserving a place and paying my own way in a competitive field. (Dream plagiarizer—the ultimate artist faux pas.) I hadn't thought past that because it felt presumptuous to ask for more. Not only was I waiting for someone else's permission, I was more than happy to confirm other people's reservations or lack of imagination about me. I was unsure why I was even trying when everyone else was clearly so much more talented and deserving. I was, as any self-respecting (or, rather, non-self-respecting) artist would say, my own worst enemy.

Despite my inner demons' best efforts, little by little—my preferred attack style—my dry cerebral humor gained me fans, at least among other comics who booked me on their shows. Not so much among the suits, though—that is, the people with the power to help me pay rent. To them, I surmised, I was too tentative, too old, too boring, too weirdly specific to equal a lucrative investment in the eyes of the market. I constantly felt like I was flailing both as an adult and a comedian. It didn't help that show business is more than willing to reject you repeatedly and for any reason, such that you quickly realize having any feelings at all is a liability.

For example, the first freelance writing gig I got was consulting at a wildly popular internet clip show—think *America's Funniest Home Videos* but with YouTube highlights and lowlights—where my boyfriend worked. (Nepotism: still going strong!) I was hired on a trial basis as a "consultant," which is an industry term for "writer we don't have to pay as much because the union will never crack our code." My expected role was to pitch ideas for show segments and jokes for the hosts and guests, primarily based on the video clips. On my second day, just as my boyfriend and I were driving up to the security gate that morning, he got a call informing him that I didn't need to come in that day (which he learned later meant "or ever again"). Nothing like a soft firing after one single day of work to get the insecurity calcifying! Oh, and the show? Don't you fret, it's still extremely in demand. It's on back to back for more than twelve hours at a time, like *Law & Order* but for adolescent boys.

This occasional confirmation that I was the worst followed me into my first late-night comedy writers' room, a refreshingly diverse one, both unusual for the time and for the genre. But I still found myself too scared to speak up, because I was convinced I didn't deserve to be there. After all, hadn't I been temping merely a week ago? Even on a good day, the morning affirmation of a temp is "I am disposable." Every time I tried to think of something funny to say at this hallowed job, I'd freeze up, further confirming I didn't belong.

Even when the job started to go better and I appeared in a few on-air segments that went over favorably, I still found myself held hostage by my own anxiety and dread, second-guessing all my ideas and permanently on the hunt for evidence I wasn't as funny as everyone else there. I was so lost in my own head, I couldn't focus on the creative part of creating. And while more career opportunities followed after the show was canceled, the nagging fear that my time would soon be up dogged me, and I hoarded all evidence I was subpar in my abilities. This mindset accompanied me into all subsequent jobs. Every day was Take Your Doubter to Work Day! [Hold for applause.] And when things went poorly, who was to say whether it was a self-fulfilling prophecy or plain old facts?

Tina Fey (of all people) once said, "The beauty of impostor syndrome is you vacillate between extreme egomania and a complete feeling of: 'I'm a fraud!'" She's right. I run on these hopeful fumes of self-delusion and grandiose fantasies, but as soon as anything comes to fruition, I'm suddenly in panic mode because the dupe worked, and I never planned for that.

The better my career has gone, the worse my impostor syndrome has grown. It's not uncommon for successful people to have a fear of being found out. How many of us are truly equipped to deal with the non-airbrushed versions of our dreams? You finally get to sit in first class on the plane, but your neighbors keep looking around going, "What's that smell?" You know it's you, even if you don't know exactly *how*. But what are you going to do? Admit it? I don't think so. You're in over your head, and the further it escalates, the more collateral detritus it takes on, an overcaffeinated tumbleweed propelling toward doom.

For some reason, it reminds me of comedian and actor Steve Rannazzisi, who, for years, claimed he escaped from one of the Twin Towers on 9/11. Only he was never there at all. The fascinating part of this lie is that he used the alleged near-death experience as his reason for abandoning his New York desk job to pursue an entertainment career in Los Angeles. As a comic, I will be the first to admit we often embellish an anecdote to give it more punch, especially the "How did you get started in comedy?" question, which you get asked over and over, though the answer is never that interesting. But this feels less like hyperbole and more like a lie tossing back its feathered boa and crowing, "Hello, world!!!"

In 2015, Rannazzisi finally admitted to *The New York Times* that the whole story was fabricated. "The stupidity and guilt I have felt for many years has not abated. It was an early taste of having a public persona, and I made a terrible mistake. All I can ask is for forgiveness." While his starring role on the FX series *The League* wasn't affected by his admission, he did lose his ad campaign with Buffalo Wild Wings, so there were spicy consequences.

This hyperspecific modern-day parable elucidates the fallout of what happens when you're an actual pretender and you get caught. Impostor syndrome is when you feel like you're Steve Rannazzisi, but you're not. The implications of "being exposed" still feel very real, and so you keep going with the charade. The other option feels even more destabilizing. We all have our own hot wings commercials, after all. Maybe it's reasonable to feel incompetent and undeserving in the face of opportunity and good fortune, especially given how unfair and tenuous life can be?

Speaking of other people, occasionally they may try to challenge your skewed version of yourself. Unfortunately, unlike 9/11, self-esteem is an inside job. (Don't @ me.) Early in the 2020 pandemic, in late spring, when live events had largely pivoted online (apologies for using the p-word), I did a live-streaming show on Zoom. In case you're wondering how well stand-up comedy translates to Zoom, know that comedians were given the option to not do sets at all. Instead, each act could simply chitchat with the three male hosts to try to make sense of their life in that current moment. I chose this route because I had written zero jokes in the past few months and felt about as funny as a whole pizza that's fallen on the street. When I happened to bring up my impostor syndrome, one of the hosts, let's call him Wow, expressed disbelief. Wow thought I was one of the best (his words, not mine—can you even imagine?) and that there's no way I didn't know what I was doing. Like a fastidious detective at the end of an Agatha Christie novel, he presented me with highlights from my own résumé to challenge my claims and thus reveal me as the true villain of my own story.

This was a fascinating rebuttal for someone with chronic self-doubt to hear, mainly because I had always assumed Wow didn't really care for me, let alone respect me. However, in that moment, I was able to step outside myself and think, *Wow is right, I have done those things.* In my head, I could so easily explain them away as lucky breaks and instances of being pitied by others, but I realized how ridiculous those defenses would sound dribbling out of my mouth. That's the problem with mental fixations. They're most potent contained. As their spoken incarnations touch the actual air, their logic falters like a banana that's turned.

FINALLY, I REALIZED it was time to try a different approach. I decided to write about my impostor syndrome. Burrow into its uncomfortable depths— spoon with formative childhood trauma—and see what came up. Fun!

Though the joke's on me, the so-called comedian, because it turns out nothing summons your impostor syndrome like trying to write a book about it. The whole operation quickly escalated, reverse Captain Planet style, into some real mental fuckshit. (Did I use that word correctly, Gen Z angel who is reading this for a research project on elder millennials?) The requisite team members all assembled: Shame, Insecurity, Fear, Sadness, Heart. (Yeah, yeah, Heart got steamrolled on the other team, too.) I couldn't tell where I ended and where the poseur (classy!) began, because weren't the two identities one and the same?

But seriously, my dear pudding forks and salad spoons, I foolishly thought that writing about my own impostor syndrome would cure it—that in interrogating it, I might arrive somewhere more enlightened and, dare I say, reformed. It was the old exposure therapy belief. If you put yourself through the fire, you will come out forged in armor. Who even said that? It sounds like someone's dad misquoting someone else's dad. Save it for the stock poster on the wall of the UFC gym!

Here's what actually went down. First, a bunch of psychic wounds from the '80s and '90s opened in me like a less compelling *Evil Dead* hell portal and threatened to suck my entire sense of self into them, quietly and efficiently, à la Dyson (aspirational product placement, need a free vac). I'm not saying my baggage won per se, but it certainly made some great points. Point A: Me lying facedown on the floor. Point B: Me again, crying smarter not harder. I couldn't help but listen to them. Plus, when you are writing a book, you are spending hours and hours alone with yourself. Who better to keep you company than the gnawing voice in your head, like an AI chatbot set to destroy mode?

The journey itself proved more of a labyrinth than I imagined, and not the cool kind that ends in forbidden treasures or cheese. Early on, my editor commented that I was qualifying all my own views to death. I refused to hold an opinion and stand by it, because I kept coming back to my brain's excellent reminder that I didn't know what I was talking about. But if I did think I knew what I was talking about, I wouldn't be qualified to write a book about my intimate experience with impostor syndrome, now would I? And if the writing process itself didn't give me all the answers, maybe it would at least prove my editor wrong, because isn't the best art created out of spite? Just telling others about my impostor syndrome would be a radical act, a way to finally hurl off the mask and debut the real me. That was the Brené Brown–inspired pitch, anyway.

Of course, one great way to get out of your own head is to try to get into other people's, which offers that valuable "different perspective" that all those therapy memes yammer on and on about. Every so often, I'd mention in conversation that I was working on a book about impostor syndrome, and the person I was talking to wouldn't be familiar with the term. Of course, by "person," I mean it always happened to be a cishet white man with no visible disabilities. That isn't to say that none of the people who identify as such are familiar with impostor syndrome or haven't ever experienced it. Our old friend Dr. Clance assures us it is a feature that can show up in any demographic of humanity. I just happened to have met a handful of the exceptions. And, in all fairness to these guys, impostor syndrome—like probiotic yogurt—does primarily get marketed toward women and minorities. (*Shhhhhh.*)

If you've never had the pleasure, let me tell you, it's a specific kind of painful when you have to explain impostor syndrome to the status quo. That alone is embarrassing. "Oh, well, have you ever felt like you don't deserve anything you've earned, and it's all a huge misunderstanding? In fact, maybe you have no business even pretending to appear competent? What do you mean, *not really*?" There's just no common point of reference.

Out of my own acute curiosity, not to mention a bachelor's degree in psychology, I decided to circulate an informal survey about impostor syndrome among friends, family, and peers in the creative community. I wanted to see whether any new patterns or insights emerged, like maggots from the rotting corpse of my initial findings. No, I also don't know why I went so dark with that simile. As the greats say, I was trying something?

Anyway, these were the questions:

1. Are you familiar with what impostor syndrome is? Could you briefly define it in your own words?

2. Is impostor syndrome something you have experienced or struggled with?

3. Would you say it's something you currently struggle with?

ONLY IF YES to #2 and/or #3:

1. In what areas of your life has it/does it come up?

2. Have you done anything to combat your impostor syndrome, and how has it gone?

3. Do you think your impostor syndrome has any ties to some part of your identity (class, race, ethnicity, gender identification, sexual orientation, ability, etc.)?

The survey hardly constituted rigorous research. Take that, MacArthur geniuses (genii? I rest my case)! My pool was 110 generous guinea pigs with certain demographics such as cis, heterosexual, middle- and upper-middle-class, thirtysomething classifiers unsurprisingly dominating, given my own identity and social circles. However, I found that all but three participants had heard of the term impostor syndrome, and of those three, after looking it up, only one said they'd never experienced it. In line with previous research, the overwhelming majority—92 percent—had dealt with it in some facet of their life, across all demographics, even if they didn't struggle with it as much anymore. As for the other 8 percent, congrats! You believe in yourself without question! Next time, please bring enough to share with the whole class.

Feelings of being a fraud most often came up around work and professional issues in which someone didn't feel they were qualified for the position they were in or the opportunities they got. Frequently, these impostor feelings decreased with age and experience, showing up most often when someone was first trying to establish themselves. Though I did find it amusing that the youngest person surveyed—an early twentysomething with a high degree of success already under their belt—wasn't sure whether they suffered from impostor syndrome or was just actually less skilled than their peers (oh, sugar bear).

Issues around identity and belonging also incited feelings of being a fraud—that is, whether the person felt like a "qualified" member of certain groups of which they were a part, whether that was the comedy community, the queer community, a biracial identity, or even, get this, as a cis, straight, white male. In fact, rather than finding this dominant identity doesn't deal with impostor syndrome at all, I found a number of them have or still do. Though in each case it was someone who works in the creative arts—a field that, by and large, has a lion's share of neurosis.

I also suspect that many cis, straight, white males feel less freedom to express their own self-doubt given heterosexual masculine ideals as well as the narrative that their group holds the most privilege. These dual pressures might make them feel like they have to act as if they're confident, whether or not they really feel that way. As with most human groups, especially ones based on identity, there is a perceived "correct" way of presenting, based on societal expectation. Discomfort and fear of alienation for not fitting in to those ideals is a very real thing.

Interestingly enough, many of the cis, straight, white males surveyed who experienced impostor syndrome rationalized that because everyone is a fraud, why would they discount themselves for being one as well? One even went so far as to dare the universe to give him more chances to experience it! This outlook felt underwritten by the fact that their group is more widely represented in most spaces. Whereas for those of us who are less so, the risk of being found out feels more threatening—the idea you'll be kicked out of the club is substantiated by the visible lack of representation everywhere you turn.

I also found an unsurprising connection between those prone to mental health challenges and the ongoing presence of impostor syndrome. Since anxious-depressive thinking often correlates with negative self-image, this made sense. Not to mention the fact that hai, it me?

BUT THERE IS a different way of looking at the whole charlatan complex. In an op-ed for *JAMA*, physicians Samyukta Mullangi and Reshma Jagsi wrote about the high incidence of impostor syndrome in medicine. They posited that it "might be viewed less as a personal challenge affecting a few than a systemic problem of considerable scale with real, detrimental consequences to those affected."

In reading this, I thought, *Yes, finally*, instead of treating impostor syndrome as a matter of personality or weak will, let's ask, *Why is it so prevalent across so many different demographics?* Otherwise, it makes it seem like your self-confidence just needs to start pounding protein and lifting weights. Let's zoom wider, wider out of the empowerment seminar, and look at the bigger picture.

Because the algorithm is strong, I then read a *Harvard Business Review* piece tellingly titled "Stop Telling Women They Have Imposter Syndrome" and thought, *I can't wait to have self-doubt about my self-doubt!* The authors, Ruchika Tulshyan and Jodi-Ann Burey, argue that "the impact of systemic racism, classism, xenophobia, and other biases was categorically absent when the concept of imposter syndrome was developed." Since I first read it, the piece has gone extremely viral. These systems were meant to engender uncertainty and lack of confidence in those who didn't fit the perceived status quo. By framing impostor syndrome as an individual-level problem through constant, insidious reinforcement, workplace power structures evade accountability entirely.

Because I am a comedian and writer by trade, I am by law committed to the rule of threes. So, yes, I read a third thought-provoking article, titled

"Why Everyone Feels Like They're Faking It"—in *The New Yorker*, no less—which really raised the stakes big time. In it, author Leslie Jamison interviewed both Clance and Imes, the authors of the original study, as well as Tulshyan and Burey, the antiproponents of the concept. My own impostorism came up in full peacock display mode when I read that many women of color don't buy into any of this fraud hoopla. I was relieved when Jamison qualified that many others do still experience these feelings, though the important part is realizing they're not a syndrome, rather they are a function of living in this world. Her conclusion posits "that the impostor phenomenon, as a concept, effectively functions as an emotional filing cabinet organizing a variety of fraught feelings that we can experience as we try to reconcile three aspects of our personhood: how we experience ourselves, how we present ourselves to the world, and how the world reflects that self back to us." For me, this trinity has been in constant battle—negotiating and renegotiating a series of flimsy truces that never hold.

Self-help is so often rooted in the idea that we as a species inherently get in our own way. I don't disagree with this, but focusing so much on the individual takes the greater infrastructure, such as societal messaging and media, off the hook. It creates the unsustainable framework that each person is only in it for and by themselves, and hence, responsible for all their own failings. In that way, we're all fundamentally alone.

I know it's distinctly anti-capitalist and anti-American, but I've always found myself drawn to stories of failure over stories of success. I'm not as interested in the person who got the thing as I am in the next person in line who almost did, or even the person behind them who doesn't know why they're in line but wanted to see what all the fuss is about. That last person's story might be about something else completely, but on the way, you hear about a goal of theirs that didn't work out. So much more of life is lived in the process rather than the result—but we insist on bolding the latter. I strongly suspect that most of us end up being just as affected by our failures as our wins, even though everyone wants to hear only about the wins. But influenced for the better? The science is in: not necessarily right away!

A 2019 University of Chicago psych study found that people are less likely to learn from their failures than their successes in the short term. In five separate scenarios involving different kinds of test questions, a number of participants were assigned to a "failure" condition, where they were told they had answered questions incorrectly. Others might be assigned to a "success" condition, where they were told they had answered answers correctly, or to a control condition, where they received no feedback on their answers. Time and again, the failure group participants underperformed when retested on the same material compared with the success group and even the control group. The researchers found that the reason failure impacted affected people's performance was that it threatened their self-esteem.

It's not just us though. A different study used monkeys doing visual tasks and found that the monkeys who made mistakes performed worse later than the ones who had not initially messed up. And if you thought experimenting on monkeys made you uncomfortable, another unconscionable study found that dieters who were fed pizza and then told they had ruined their diet goal went on to eat more cookies than those who were not told any such thing.

But what are we supposed to take away from these findings? That none of us is ever supposed to fail or make mistakes? That, if they happen, we should never speak of them again and should hurriedly move on? I think failure, especially in the moment, hijacks our brains, and we get lost in our heads, which then negatively bears on our behavior. But that doesn't mean we have to internalize these instances as inextricable parts of ourselves. We're capable of shifting what a failure could mean for us going forward (just as soon as we aren't so emotionally triggered by it). The stories we let failure tell us about ourselves can be revised in line with who we want to be. Sure, winners might have the confidence-boosting edge of victory, but defeat builds character and grit, right? May I draw the court's attention to every sports movie ever?

Have faith, though, Mighty Ducklings, there's more to the story. The idea of failure itself is not necessarily a deterrent. The UChicago study did find that subjects learn just as much from both other people's failures and successes than personal failures and successes, because the threat to their own self-esteem is removed.

But given that all their test groups were in the United States and the United Kingdom, culture may play a substantial role as well. Indeed, the researchers cited another study where individuals in Japan persisted longer after a failure than a success. Other cultures may have varying attitudes when it comes to the idea of bouncing back from mistakes. All to say, inner Oprah aside, I still remain unconvinced that reducing stigma around failure is a bad thing. Clearly, from the research above, it won't lead to some kind of societal Loser Takeover, which, by its own logic, would be Just Big Enough to Fail. Maybe part of the reason people often react more poorly to failure, especially in the moment, is that there is still so much shame attached to losing, especially in the good ol' can-do attitude of the US of A. There's nothing we love more than a rags-to-riches tale of overcoming.

This mentality sounds like more of a bummer than it is. The times we're forced to adapt and reassess and strategize differently end up telling us far more about ourselves than coasting on the highs ever could. I'd even go so far as to say that success itself isn't even as simple as it looks from afar. Usually after the initial thrill wears off (which is always far more quickly than one would hope), the novelty of success translates to a host of new worries. We're built, on a primal level, to anticipate future problems and look for the cracks in the castle.

Just as the histories of oppressed people are erased in favor of amplifying the legacies of oppressors as unassailable triumphs, success stories made up of one win after another don't capture the full truth of what it is to be alive. It's not only that we grow from failure but also that losing is an opportunity to reframe our priorities and values—who gets to take up space where, the goals we want to aspire to in our own lives, and the impact we want to leave behind.

We need to name our rejections and our doubts as much as we need to name our accomplishments. Being alive is about holding the truth of who you are as dear as any imagined reality of how a person could or should be. Impostor syndrome doubles down on the myth that there is a rigid, finite image of winning and, whatever its constraints are, you aren't it. The nonbinary, nuanced truth is that we are all an imprecise product of our failures and successes and are just figuring it out as we go.

True to my own undergrad major in psychology, I wanted to not only interrogate my self-directed ambivalence but also reflect on its varied societal origins. That's my way of saying a liberal (arts) degree of research and intellectual curiosity lies ahead, delving into the bountiful pickle that is human nature. As you may have gathered, I'm a fiend for an outside source. After all, I deeply believe real impostors aren't born; they're made. (So many people to thank!) And yes, as I collected my thoughts and committed them to the page, more often than not, I questioned my own intentions. When you are writing a book about self-doubt, the main order of the day is realizing the inner critic, despite best efforts to the contrary, is your cowriter. Symbiotically, she is the Statler and Waldorf to your show. You both need each other.

Suffice to say that talking about, writing about, and parsing my own impostor syndrome has been an extremely agitating and disorienting process. But being completely, painfully honest is the only worthwhile place I know to begin.

Life can so often be a grotesque maze of smoke and mirrors. It's vital to take every chance you get to walk out of the illusion, if only to reach up, touch your own face, and remember what has always been yours.

Be Free, You Wrinkly Ghost!

Content advisory: *This essay discusses disordered eating and exercising, body image, and weight.*

I've never been fully on board with my face. I know that's about as revelatory a statement from a woman in this world as saying, "Sorry! Totally my mistake!" when there's a global recession. Still, you would hope, you would expect, you would (eat-)pray(-love) that a reasonable gal ankle deep into her forties would crow, "Take it or leave it, suckers!" as she shimmies unapologetically down the street, the unforgiving rays of the sun her only contouring agent, rocking a Jamiroquai chapeau (aka the top hat that's also a furry).

Instead, I've found social media plus time (spent on it) equals tragedy? Wearing the same expression as a stock photo of a frazzled paralegal unable to find her morale-sustaining grain bowl in the office fridge, I can't stop, won't stop, stumbling onto accounts of Insta-fluencers. And not the "please buy my line of designer cocaine" kind where she is so unrelatable to you, she may as well be fiction, but the "OK, she gets it" kind where she is just a very cool smokeshow. The coda is always the same—I find a gorgeous snap from one of these Ideal Idas displaying the least-problematic skinny genes. She is almost always a twentysomething who is conventionally beautiful, cis, and white. This affront is then topped with a caption displaying an upsetting amount of self-awareness of her privileged, rare position, selfishly grabbing away my only weapon—the attempt to write her off as out of touch—leading me to further spiral like a hair down a drain: poorly and grotesquely.

Can my rumination really be helped? If you ask implicit bias, a woman's looks are the staging for so many morality plays regarding the measure of her life. And like the Hunger Games (which, if you aren't familiar with the young adult novel franchise, could also very well pass as the title of a mommy food blog), the odds are never in our favor.

I already knew that working in food service is one of the most thankless jobs imaginable, but I learned of a new low in a segment of *This American Life* called "The $25 Tip." A server in Arizona named Shelly Ortiz related how, during the COVID-19 pandemic and on more than one occasion, she was asked by customers to pull her mask down so they could see how attractive she was before they tipped. Are you screaming? Feel free to join me as I do so for the rest of my life.

Despite the endless soul enema that can be existing as a flesh-and-blood woman, I find the amount of space that aesthetic fixation takes up in my brain entirely unacceptable, especially given how steadily my neurons are dying off—though I prefer to call it early retirement. I imagine each one giving a brave salute to the others, barking, "She's your problem now," before jumping down the closest nose tube. (Did I mention I'm not a doctor? My parents will helpfully remind you of it.)

If there's anyone to blame besides the societal stew in which we all chaotically bubble, the foam finger of judgment would clearly point at me. I chose to be in an industry where the beauty standard can be neatly summed up as "Fuck you!" It's continually thrown in one's face, so much so that even those at the tippy top are rushing to the mirror, investigating what now, to them, might look like a fresh crime scene. Whenever I've been at a promotional event—say a photo shoot or press panel—I'm once again astounded by the amount of hair and makeup people sit through to look "presentable." For TV and movies, "camera ready," particularly for women, can frequently translate into a dolled-up, straight-off-the-assembly-line version of yourself that sort of looks like you, but don't worry, way better? Show business has long been ground zero of the unattainable, so any signs of relatability must be erased.

It's a huge beacon of hope for me whenever I see a close-up of an actress on a big screen (and not in one of her "brave" roles where she's donned every manner of prosthetic to look "plain") and see a crooked tooth or a visible pore—a protest rally front and center. I acted on a show where the director wanted everyone to keep their look natural—that is, little to no makeup. To my dismay, I immediately found myself thinking, *Are you sure that's a good idea?* But ten minutes later, I was relieved, even verging on proud. *This is me, people! Hollywood said it's OK!* Granted, I was playing "a janitor who goes to space" and in space, no one can see you smize, but still. I looked at my unadorned face staring back at me waiting for my move and thought, *Well, the secret's out: I'm brave!* Wearing my actual face as my face let me focus on what felt more important to me as a comedian: landing my jokes. As a performer, for myriad reasons, I have never led with my appearance other than in the self-deprecating sense. Being too glam has always felt a bridge farther from my funny's POV.

Of course, I realize, above and beyond the escapism of entertainment, women versus body image has likely been a battle predating history itself. Picture it: a moody Neanderthal artist photoshops (with berry juices) bigger boobs and butt and a teeny-tiny waist onto one of the cave wall portraits and, from that point on, all the cave ladies must add the anxiety of bodily insecurity atop the anxiety of unrelenting, imminent death. And this was way before teeny-tiny waists were even in—the nerve!!! Things haven't much improved. Just as then, nobody is winning, but now everyone thinks they are only a few savvy adjustments away from contentment. There's a makeup product called concealer—as in *cover that up, you goblin!* And there's an app called Facetune for editing selfies so your pseudo-candid self-portraits look like you, minus the horrific idea that you have an ever-decaying corporeal form. Seeing as we're now all products, we must endlessly improve our packaging.

Not even beautiful people get to escape this abominable system. Of course, they do have incredible, undeniable advantages. In her essay "Being Pretty Is a Privilege, but We Refuse to Acknowledge It," writer and trans activist Janet Mock writes, "People who are considered pretty are more likely to be hired, have higher salaries, and are less likely to be found guilty and are sentenced less harshly. Pretty people are perceived as smarter, healthier, and more competent, and people treat pretty people better. Pretty privilege is also conditional and is not often extended to women who are trans, black and brown, disabled, older, and/or fat." To those points alone, can you really fault anyone for wanting to improve their looks, to whatever extent is possible for them? Of course, with this privilege, there is also often veiled resentment toward the hotties, an assumption that everything is easy for them and handed to them, and often, whether they can see it or not, it is. But also, built on a foundation of white supremacist colonial heteropatriarchy, capitalist structure is built to fuel distrust, insecurity, and competition—incidentally, the holy grail of reality TV.

Even the counterwave of body positivity and acceptance we now have, originally pioneered by radical intersectional fat liberation activists in the

1960s, has been co-opted by brands and framed in ideals of conspicuous consumption. What was once outright defiance of the status quo has now been massaged and warmly lit into Dove's latest pitch for soft soap. Am I really buying the rose quartz neck roller (what am I, a piecrust?) or the anti-aging serum (a very old piecrust) for self-care, or has the virus of capitalism cleverly mutated yet again into the guise of monetizable empowerment? That's the essence of the beauty industrial complex. You're never done. Your self-esteem is never full. Your online shopping cart is never empty.

FOR SO LONG, as a kid, I was remarkably unaware of how I presented physically. As far as I knew, I was a floating orb of light in the mirage of a human form—I know it *sounds* sexy, but picture a starburst in Coke-bottle glasses and a bad wig.

Intellectually, I knew I was South Asian and my parents had emigrated from India. But, especially at school, I truly believed that I was, if not white, then in a nonthreatening neutral zone adjunct to it—Almost White (like a fake Chanel bag, so close, and yet not at all). Let's call it racial purgatory, an assimilationist DMV where you're perpetually hoping your number will be called. Whiteness, of course, was the undeniable top of the pop charts for social status in my upper-middle-class northern Virginia suburb; it meant everything from one's name *not* eliciting a teacher's uncertain throat clearing during roll call to upholding its Eurocentric standards as the only accepted currency of attractiveness. I might not look white, I thought, but I'd be damned if I didn't blend in so well that white people wouldn't see "other" when they looked at me. In fact, they wouldn't see anything at all—other than a reflection of their own inherent superiority.

It didn't escape my attention that a few lucky minorities were "traded up," closer to the top tiers of whiteness. For whatever reason, be it class status or looks or inherent virtue, they were allowed into the cool club. They became the exceptions to the rule that help perpetuate the myth of meritocracy within a rigged system. As sociologist Tressie McMillan Cottom writes in her incisive book *Thick*: "Indeed, any system of oppression must allow exceptions to validate itself as meritorious. How else will those who are oppressed by the system internalize their own oppression?" It's the model minority way—there's no one to blame but yourself!

In terms of looks, there were certain femme beauty standards that were understood to be the objective—which were all very much in line with white conformity. The big one was fair skin, but not *too* fair—somewhat tanned was even better, but let's not go too wild; medium or big boobs, though with a petite waist and flat stomach; slender, fit, perfectly proportioned body— curves are OK, but nothing that would upset the cult of Lululemon (which didn't even exist yet, but the blueprints were there); a small or smallish dainty nose without any bumps or breaks; rosebud lips; big eyes; shiny, straight hair; and the appropriate gum-to-tooth ratio. So yes, what I'm saying is Jessica Rabbit, if you could, please.

It was hard to even come up with that list because most of my beliefs around beauty standards are so deeply ossified that I have trouble not registering them as automatic reflexes of yes and no, the same way people argue that they can't help what they're attracted to. According to McMillan Cottom, "'I just like what I like' is always a capitalist lie. Beauty would be a useless concept for capital if it were only a preference in the purest sense. . . . If beauty matters at all to how people perceive you, how institutions treat you, which rules are applied to you, and what choices you can make, then beauty must also be a structure of patterns, institutions, and exchanges that eats your preferences for lunch."

Of course, children are keen observers of race, class, and gender, and of the idea of beauty as leverage. I observed the reach of its power early on. When I first went to private school, I saw the ski lift tags on everyone's coats from their most recent winter vacations, and I listened to classmates talk about the ballroom dance classes they were taking in preparation for their debutante parties, and realized somehow, *Oh, these are not my people.* I covertly observed the girls with glossy hair or noses too perfectly proportioned and wondered if they knew how lucky they were. To my impressionable eyes, they floated through every situation with ease. Even in gym class, they managed to look coiffed.

I figured it would be helpful to accrue some of this cachet for myself. But how? Unfortunately, before I could brainstorm anything resembling a plan, adolescence came for me, bearing nothing but confusing, upsetting news. (If Death wears a black robe and wields a scythe, then Puberty wears Hot Topic and wields a Bic razor.) I craved validation for my outer appearance. But like many a heterosexual girl before me, I chose to seek it in aspirational attempts for male approval. Whether this was learning to shave my legs (why yes, I did think I would accidentally slit a major artery) or poring over teen magazines like *YM* to decipher how girls™ behaved, I figured something would get me noticed. If I used the right key, the door would unlock to a speakeasy world where I was both beautiful and cool. At the very least, I could wedge my foot into that doorway and refuse to budge. In the meantime, I toggled between resenting my budding sexuality and trying to honor it—always on my own—because I was too shy and embarrassed to broach it with anyone else.

What are bodies after all but needy, slimy water balloons? The balancing act of wanting to be seen while also not wanting to stand out left me frantically soft-shoeing in the middle, arms windmilling in desperation. Oh, and speaking of dancing, I wasn't asked to. In middle school, I remember attending classmates' coed bar and bat mitzvah parties with their requisite embittered DJs, and standing on the sidelines during the slow jams, plaintively thinking, *Is this like hailing a cab? Should I do something with my arm?*

There were unexpected fireflies in the darkness. At an academic camp (I know, I know, so on the nose, it *is* the nose) hosted on a college campus and that I attended the summer before seventh grade, there was a very popular girl named Kelsey. It's stunning how quickly we as humans pick up on social hierarchies, no matter how brief the time we share together. A sun-kissed California blonde who played lacrosse, Kelsey was an exact prototype for Dawn in the Baby-Sitters Club books combined with a hybrid of the twins from Sweet Valley High. It felt like a cosmic oops that she was even at an East Coast nerd camp. She was clearly sent there as an Ambassador of Coolness to help raise our cumulative average for relevance.

I hardly expected Kelsey to acknowledge me as a person, let alone a peer. I was content to simply bask in the periphery of her natural glow. But one day—my flip-flops on, my glasses off—I was squinty-eyed and squeakily padding back to my room post-shower when I ran into her. She stopped short and said, "Wow. You are so beautiful without your glasses."

Um, am I dead? was my first thought. I couldn't believe it. She didn't even use the p-word, she went straight for the b-word (er, the good one)! Plus, this was the first interaction we'd had one on one (and the last, as I recall). "Th-thank you," I said in disbelief, ending it there, lest there was a qualifier, and clomped off, giddy.

I internalized that offhand comment as though she were a fortune teller looking into the hazy crystal ball of my head and divining a triumphant brown thumbs-up emoji. When this forecast was then co-signed by my closest friend at camp, a cosmopolitan, bookish Brooklynite (as far as I was concerned, a mythical creature!) named Janet, I thought, *Well, it's official: Your face has been approved! Your Fairy Coolmothers have spoken.* The way I figured, as soon as I got contacts (LASIK was still ten long-term studies away from be-ing a Groupon option), I could finally join the hotterati!

Much of this logic was hormone-fueled behavior, but I also just desper-ately wanted some sign of acceptance from my peers. Simply picking out the right thing to wear felt like an excruciating hedge maze of decisions that could lead to salvation. Or not. Peers of all ethnicities seemed privy to man-uals on how to mature with more chill than me. Eyebrow threading was to South Asian women as Victoria's Secret thongs were to white women. Meanwhile, I sat off to the side trying to sleuth out clues like a horny Harriet the Spy. My guidebook may as well have been a block of cheese titled *How to Age Alone and with Distinct Odors*. Yes, that is an oblique reference to "Farmer in the Dell," you're welcome, one person who got it.

My fixation with looks was born out of practicality as much as vanity. I knew even then that attractiveness is an express route to the world's good graces, overriding less desirable traits like shyness and lack of cultural fluency. Good looks bestow something of a free pass, a means of avoiding overdue scrutiny. Innocent until proven guilty, you are deemed acceptable until proven otherwise. There is the unfair generalization that beautiful people don't need good personalities because their looks do the heavy lifting. I wanted the op-tion of having a bad personality, at least while I was still figuring mine out.

I was quizzically intrigued by the story of the ugly duckling. What an inspiring tale for all, to become a babe after a real "rough on the eyes" youth—because that's what children should focus on, right? A revenge bod and face? If I could just figure out how to up my game looks-wise, I knew it would mean taking up more space in the world in the best way.

Faces are undeniably harder to revise, so I made my body my first guinea pig. I just needed to narrow the gap between my mental vision board and the mirror, while widening the gap between my thighs. The foundation was helpfully already there. Skewed messaging around close regulation of food, diet, weight, and exercise, all crowded under the umbrella of "healthy" and "good" and "clean," bombards Americans (though I know we're far from the only ones), and my parents were no exception, especially given that they are both doctors. They joined a gym when my sibling, Bhav, and I were young, and became militant about going, often bringing us along. As a tender tween, I learned how to surreptitiously use a StairMaster until one of the employees kicked me off (I wasn't old enough to use it). In high school, I became fixated on working out. This started with going to the gym every day followed by basketball and tae kwon do drills at home, willing my body to become more coordinated. I'm not sure what I was training for with that combo platter. I was the Rocky of fights solely based on roundhouse kicks, elliptical movement, and that exercise where you figure-eight the ball between your legs. Eventually, I started running on my own and joined my school's cross-country and track teams. When I got a plaque for Most Improved Runner my senior year, I knew my self-improvement plan was working . . . literally! Given that running is more or less "walking while in danger," I felt triumphant to somehow have gotten better at it.

In college, though, I really went for it. My sophomore year I picked up an eating disorder—anorexia. I know what you're thinking. In an arena typically dominated by white females, I am a trailblazer! *Representation matters!* As with many people who restrict their eating, the rigid discipline afforded me a sense of superiority. It also took up so much of my attention and energy that I had none left to worry about anything or anyone else. At first, it felt incredibly empowering—like I'd discovered a cheat code for life. My nervousness around others receded; I had no sexual or romantic urges whatsoever; all I thought about was eating. My mind became an assembly line of food emojis past, present, and future. Everything became simple, methodical, predictable.

Maintaining an eating disorder meant keeping myself guarded from other people, which, no big deal, came naturally to me. None of my college friends knew I was struggling with food, not even my roommate. In fact, when I'd newly lost weight, I was running faster than ever, which led my cross-country coach and teammates to give me more praise and recognition than ever before. The ugly truth was that my body disappearing made me more visible—in a good way. The line between wellness and unwellness blurs depending on whom you're asking. While I was reaping short-term gains from my behavior, the bottom was about to fall out, as it so reliably does. My after-school-special lesson dragged out slowly and without editing. First, I stopped getting my period, and coming from a medically inclined family, I knew this wasn't a good sign. I was cold and tired all the time, and my schoolwork and mental health began tanking.

But first, still high on my "new body," I had rashly entered a local pageant for the coveted title of Miss India DC (who then, naturally, goes on to compete for the chance to be Miss India USA, duh). Now, beauty pageants make as much sense to me as a bunch of million-dollar lotto winners competing to decide who is the luckiest. However, my shrinking weight convinced me that if there was ever a chance to be deemed a stunner, this was it. I realize how tragic that sounds, because it was—it came from a lonely place, a desperate attempt to matter to others. So, while everything was crumbling around me, I also went home to pretend I knew how to walk a runway (apologetically and with condolences to the audience). To be clear, anyone could enter, you just had to be OK with being judged on your looks.

Like many subjective competitions, the winners were decided via politicking and insider trading—and I walked away without a rose. It was just further proof to me that no matter how hard I tried to fit in, I never would. My consolation prize was that, barely six months later, I found myself at an all-expenses-paid spiritual retreat, where I was given all the time in the world to find myself. Sorry, I said that wrong, I meant an eating disorder recovery center not covered by insurance, where I had a month and change to snap out of it.

I was relieved to find I wasn't the only minority in residence, but while the majority of other women were there because their families had encouraged or forced them to be, I'd had to explain to my parents what such a treatment center even was. The brochures were particularly unhelpful, with their horses and soft, beige pillows like some extremely pricey, avant-garde version of spring break, girls gone mild (all the centers I looked at were women only). It didn't help that I wasn't technically a severe enough case to qualify for the residential program, but because the center was not within a commutable distance, they made an exception for me. For much of the time I was there, I kept waiting for one of the "sicker" women to expose me as a fraud. Even at a center for dysfunctional behavior, I didn't think I made the cut.

Thus ended the body experiment like many before it—with me moving back in with my parents and working at the mall until the next school year started. One disturbing truth is in getting back to a healthy weight at the center (they wouldn't let you see what the number was), I put on more weight than I ever had before. I then found myself obsessing over it afterward, though not to the same degree as before. I'm not proud to say it, but I felt like I was being punished. This thought is brought to you by fatphobia, which is still something I actively fight to deprogram within myself. But between competitive running and attending a college where there were helpful bathroom signs to please flush your vomit, I didn't have the most open-minded thinking about it. The early aughts still treated body acceptance as a range from thin to thinner. I bought into it all.

Since my default setting is "good student" despite my best efforts to rebel (I once didn't use the sign-in sheet at a doctor's office), I worked diligently on implementing what I'd learned at the treatment center by challenging my distorted thoughts around food and body. But given the onslaught of toxic messaging society slathers on us today like so much skin-tightening cream, which was even more pervasive and unapologetic back then, this wasn't easy. Eventually, though, it stuck. I tried running track again but realized it no longer brought me fulfillment, so I quit the team and ran whenever I felt like it instead. Because I didn't feel as pressured by athletic performance, I didn't obsess as much over what I ate. Soon my life filled up with other interests I previously hadn't had the time or energy to pursue, like writing for my college literary magazine as well as our requisite satire rag. Plus, I don't know if you've noticed, but food makes some wonderful points?

But way back when, since the body experiment had royally crashed and burned, I lay low and re-strategized for a decade, like a born-again cicada wrapping up her late twenties. Eventually, I figured out the real problem to solve. It had been on front of me the whole time: my face. While I can and will blame all societal messaging for this idea, I'm also picking up on notes of self-absorption tastefully paired with a pipe dream of eventually sneaking my way into show business, whose standards for a healthy self-image are, as discussed, dystopian apocalyptic. I assumed, should I ever actually audition for anything, that, as things currently stood, I wouldn't even be allowed to read for the part of a human female. Even if I was going to try for roles like "CGI lemur" and "tumbleweed," I still wanted to put my best anthropomorphized foot forward.

If you ask Hollywood, I am "quirky," which can mean one of two things: (a) "gorgeous person trying out bangs for the first time" or (b) "What do we do with it?" That said, I will fully admit Kelsey the lacrosse-playing oracle's words echoed through my brain well into adulthood. Maybe if I just made a few tweaks, everyone would see that I too could be a looker. I experienced a constant seesaw between the incontrovertible conviction I was hideous based on however many overt and covert signs, and the burning, fairy-tale desire that one day the spell would break, and I'd be seen for the dazzling cupcake I had been all along. I would eagerly squirrel away the rare compliment as proof of the latter idea and the usual lack of attention into the former. At this point, nearing thirty, I knew in which direction the far less ambiguous answer swayed, but like a frenetic little lab rat who keeps pushing the lever that no longer dispenses the sugar pellet, I kept hoping for a different result.

First things first, I had an underbite. It wasn't a hugely noticeable one (from space), but it also wasn't one of those cute ones everyone's rescue dog has where you think, *Feel free to poop directly on my heart, you toothy angel!* My lower jaw crossed in front of my upper one, and my chin stuck out, and it looked incorrect to a dentist and to anyone who's ever watched a toothpaste commercial. I consulted an orthodontist, who informed me it was a type of hereditary crossbite. If I ever did a 23andMe, I'm sure I'd learn I'm 15 percent broken stapler. The corrective procedure was as follows: braces for two years, then oral surgery where both your jaws are broken and reset with screws, and then braces for another six months to a year for fine-tuning. It was the "wait for it" version of cosmetic improvement—a slo-mo unboxing video of bandages dramatically being unwrapped from someone's face.

While my orthodontist said there was no rush to get the surgery, he did recommend that I get it at some point, or my bite would eventually wear all my teeth down to nubs. My main takeaway from this speech was "nubs," while tellingly, my parents' takeaway was "at some point." The surgery was only partially covered by insurance as it wasn't deemed medically necessary (tell that to my future nubs!), so I was extremely lucky to be able to get some financial assistance from my parents. (If this is the audiobook, you will hear a little ding here for an instance of privilege. Just kidding, it would be too many dings. This whole book would just be the sound of a rush hour elevator.)

The irony about wanting to "fix" your appearance is it gets much worse before it gets better, and you are forced to truly battle with your own ego. I never had braces as a child because, what a hoot, I didn't need them at the time. But now, in preparation for jaw surgery, all my chompers had to be shuffled around like a deck of bony cards. My orthodontist didn't do Invisalign because he was a traditionalist—which is a nice way of saying heartless sadist. So yes, I got the version of braces that makes it look like all your teeth are in old-timey jail. In my doc's defense, he only ever called me "young lady," so I am pretty sure he thought I was a tween the entire time I was under his care. It probably didn't help that every single one of his other patients was a kid—evidenced by the gigantic stuffed bear in the waiting room. Before every appointment, I would sit there staring the teddy down, daring it to say something to me.

Getting braces in my late twenties also had an unwelcome side effect: I had to address them when doing stand-up onstage. I was once performing at a bar show, and my set was going particularly poorly. One way my spidey sense picked up on this is that a guy in the audience was heckling me through most of it, talking back after my jokes and being what we (meaning me, just me) in the biz call an "anus portal." After I got offstage, the well-intentioned host said, "If you think you're so funny, guy, why don't you come up here?" And because some people get all the confidence casserole while the rest of us have none, that fine gentleman not only did but proceeded to make fun of my braces for a whole long hour of a minute before the host finally wrested back control. All I'm saying is that there is more than just a fiscal cost in trying to fix your looks. People are going to have things to say about your face, often delivered directly to it.

Finally, two long years later, it was time for the surgery, incidentally my first ever. It took place at the same hospital where my dad, an anesthesiologist, worked—because how fun for no one! The oral surgeon was one of his colleagues, which frankly felt a little too *Sopranos* to me: "I'm breaking your daughter's jaw in two places, but you understand, it's just business." Of the surgery, all I can say is I'm happy to report that anesthesia works (for me)! In case you're wondering, no, my dad didn't do mine, because that's just not a father-daughter event I need as a rite of passage. One second, I remember counting down to zero, and the next I was waking up with a swollen face I couldn't feel. I was on several strong intravenous pain meds that I controlled with a clicker in my hand. Think *Jeopardy!* buzzer, but the answer is always "What is Valium?" My dad kept encouraging me to press it as much as possible, which is definitely the most high-yield version of stealing office supplies I've encountered.

A small detail I neglected to mention is that post-surgery, my jaw stayed wired shut for another two weeks to allow the bones to heal and the screws and plates to set. That meant I was on a liquid diet, which taught me the joys of water poop, and I don't mean diarrhea. There's diarrhea, and then there's when you just pee clear out of your butt. Why am I telling you this? Honestly, why not? You're old enough. (I really hope you're old enough.) Here's another fun fact. Due to a nerve that gets severed when the lower jaw is broken, a longer-term effect of the surgery is that I lost most of the sensation in my chin. To this day, I still don't have all of it back. Even when I kiss someone, I don't register much from the bottom half of my mouth down, and if that sounds weird, it is. I also can't tell when I'm dribbling food out of my mouth or drooling, which is a great litmus test both for finding out who my real friends are and how skilled I am at keeping the bottom half of my face presentable (answer: not very).

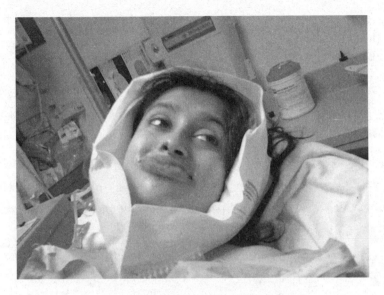

Uh-oh, she's a star! (Me, post-surgery.) [Credit: Mom.]
Ice pack wreath by Nurses™; off-the-shoulder hospital gown: model's own.

As my swelling went down, I eagerly awaited the results, as if my face were a home pregnancy test. Disappointingly, I just saw my mostly same self, now sans underbite, looking back at me. I felt cheated. All that lukewarm soup for nothing! (This was before bone broth had its comeback.)

After most appearance changes, humans become the neediest creatures we are wont to be. I demanded immediate and specific feedback. Unfortunately, I got it. For example, when I asked my friend Kim what she thought about my "new" face, she said, "Interesting." Not content to stab me once, she followed that up with "It's not better or worse, just different than how you looked before." (Hint: This is not the desired response after getting both your jaws broken.) Though it wasn't always as excruciatingly spelled out, this ended up being the popular consensus. It's facepalm-inducing how much in life we go through under the guise of "Once this is done, everything will work out." Then you realize, no, everything is more or less the same, and you can't even take it on the chin because you no longer feel yours.

Still, when I go all in, I go hard. Cue *Face Surgery 2: Judgment Day.* When I was a year or two out of college and pursuing comedy in DC while working a day job, a former coworker asked if I would be in a satirical video for *Slate*, where they were then working. In fact, you can still watch it because the internet forgets nothing and never will! The video was a mockumentary sketch about a new app called Flutter, which allowed for twenty-six characters, a concise upgrade over Twitter. I played a conniving intern (typecasting at its finest). This was the first comedy video I'd been in on YouTube that got some eyes on it. It racked up a good number of views, at least for those days—a hundred thousand in the first week. Thirteen years later, it's just over 850,000 views. Now anything under a million isn't even worth mentioning, so forgive me for wasting your time. (But then again, you're reading a book. You're a rebel, aren't you?)

Even back then, I knew not to read the comments. I believe these days that's taught in public schools. Instead of the Pledge of Allegiance, children put their hands over their hearts, and say, "I will not read the comments, with liberty and justice for all." However, what I didn't know was also don't *skim* the comments. So my curious finger scrolled right on through, and there were a lot of nice or random ones, but of course, that's not what my self-destructive little brain was looking for, was it? "What's wrong with [the intern's] eye"—ooh, there it was.

Now, I knew from looking in a mirror every day of my life that one of my eyelids drooped a little more than the other one. I self-deprecatingly nicknamed it my "lazy eyelid." It neither affected my vision nor was due to neurological issues, so I considered it a nonissue. In fact, it hardly seemed worth commenting on, except online, where everything gets commented on. Seeing that unsolicited feedback was when I decided, yet again, that if I was going to pursue a career where people are constantly evaluating your face, I better make mine as neutral and immune to judgment as possible.

Little did I know that there is no such thing as immune to judgment when it comes to strangers. If you have a face, there will be opinions about it. If you are a woman with a face, good night and good luck. What made it even worse was that I considered a certain strain of trolls to be truth tellers— the ones who specialized in snarky, petty, hyperspecific observations, of the ilk I regularly hurled at myself. For instance, "She's like if a boring story that will not end was a person." So, despite having an impending jaw surgery, I decided to also fix my eyelid. Get 'em all done as close together as possible and come out a walking, talking avatar, that's what I say!

I felt some guilt knowing that I would be paying out of pocket for this surgery because it was strictly a cosmetic procedure. But I was living at home rent-free, and I considered the decision mandatory at the time. I was pursuing a medium in which women are nitpicked and evaluated for everything down to their least significant parts—their ideas (heads up for the anvil of sarcasm). The more I looked at my right eye, the less I could stand the imperfection, especially knowing it could be corrected.

This surgery was far more straightforward. I went in the morning and got some local anesthesia (lurve multiple needles near my eye), the surgeon put a little stitch in my eyelid, and that was it. There was barely time for extended small talk, which was good because I threw up just as my anesthesia was wearing off. Getting my wisdom teeth out was more of an affair to remember. The eyelid healed up over about six to eight weeks, and that was that—no more signature droop. *"Notice anything different?"* I'd purr to friends, chillingly batting only one set of eyelashes, like a broken baby doll.

I sincerely believed I'd get my two procedures and live the rest of my life as a triumphant After Picture. With my new mug, I'd sashay down the street, unstoppable, but for crosswalks. Cue the non–spoiler alert barbershop quartet: "Nope, nope, nope, nope" (in harmony). If anything, I felt chastened by the reality that I'd changed two highly visible aspects of my appearance, at least to me, and experienced very little acknowledgment of it at all. I felt less self-conscious in photos, but it was only because I had convinced myself I had gotten rid of two glaring facial typos. Once I'd decided they were wrong, they were all I could see.

Getting two face-altering surgeries before I hit my third decade made me a one-person version of that unconscionable 2004 Fox reality show *The Swan* (not to be confused with MTV's barely self-explanatory vehicle *I Want a Famous Face*, which was essentially *Pimp My Ride* for heads). As far as I can tell from having seen only the trailers for *The Swan*, the producers took women they found irredeemably unattractive and made them over into their purported dream images using major plastic surgery. Do worry, it gets worse. After narrowing down the contestants to only those most deserving, the finalists competed in a pageant (like me!) for the chance to win a modeling contract, because why stop at "train wreck"? Luckily, it was the only major American misstep that year—well, other than continuing that tiny baseless war we Kickstartered. Here's the feathery twist! No one's deep-seated issues were resolved with the superficial Band-Aid application of a new chin. (You can read more stunning insights like this in my forthcoming self-help pamphlet, *Stuff You Definitely Already Know, in a Clean, Accessible Font*.)

Still, the fact this show existed for two (!) whole seasons demonstrates the extent to which women will go to alter themselves under the promise of societal embrace and the rottenness of the foundation upon which this scam is based. Not to mention that altering your appearance via plastic surgery still comes with plenty of stigma, as if you "cheated" for giving in to the pressures of wanting to look a certain way. Sure, more people are getting work done, but no one is exactly triumphantly showing up to brunch sporting their "I Was a Very Good Botox Patient" sticker. Considering that so many beautiful people did nothing to earn their looks, you'd think the people who put in the time and effort to achieve theirs, despite whatever nature gave them, would be more respected under the "bootstraps" mentality of the American dream. But no, Kardashians notwithstanding, women are conveniently iced out for either not accepting the cards they're dealt without complaint or not enhancing their appearance in some arbitrarily sanctioned "pure" way.

Until now, I've never talked about my surgeries to anyone unless explicitly asked. I was embarrassed. That's on par with the cultural messaging for most people, especially women. Fix yourself so the rest of us can look at you without feeling bad, but don't fix yourself too much, or we'll be able to tell you care what we think, and that's embarrassing for you. There's no winning. Though on a hopeful note regarding human superficiality, there's now a dating show on Netflix called *Sexy Beasts* where both parties wear heavy creature prosthetics on their first few dates so they can each judge each other based on personality alone. I'm sorry to say watching the Loch Ness monster flirt with a gnome is far less deeply moving than one would hope. Ah well, progress is weird.

IF I COULD GO BACK in time, I'm not sure I'd still have either surgery. Few wishes ever end up having the earth-shattering significance you think they will. Of course, it's far easier to say that on this side of the fence. Still, I sometimes wonder about the alternate-universe Aparna, with her sleepy eyelid and gummy underbite of niblets. I doubt she'd be all that different, but with the perspective of time and experience steadily accrued like the interest on a mortgage, perhaps a hair more accepting of her unspeakable flaws. On some level, I'm resentful I didn't give myself the chance.

Another small epiphany came to me after reading "Vanity Project" by essayist and poet Elisa Gabbert, in which she cites that we prefer our mirror images (reversed) compared with our actual images (unreversed), because they're the ones we're most used to seeing. Apparently, selfies have taught me nothing. In a study conducted at the University of Wisconsin–Madison in 1977, participants were presented with two sets of photos: mirror images of their faces as well as true images of their faces. While they themselves preferred the mirror images, their friends and partners preferred the true images of them. So not only has my face consumed way too much of my attention, but I'm literally not even seeing myself the way other people see me!

As I've gotten older, however, I have noticed a comforting shift. I don't even relate to that specific vein of regret espoused in the saying "Youth is wasted on the young." I appreciate myself, external form and all, more now than ever, despite the changes that are rarely fun or sexy, like pulling a muscle in my neck from trying to put on a sports bra or farting without my brain signing off on it first. Not to say I never experience insecurity around aging or don't still struggle with food and body image issues, because as I mentioned before, I definitely do!

Even now, when I am stressed and overwhelmed with my life, I notice myself controlling my eating or my exercise to a rigid, unhealthy degree. On the outside, I'm not doing anything extreme, but on the inside, it's a different story. For many people who have identities where undue focus is put on their bodies, obsessing over what you do or do not eat feels like a means of control in an unpredictable world. It's one way we've been told we can be "good" in a tangible, visible way—and it's why I can't fully shake the mentality. Still, I've come a long way.

And I've also gained more perspective about what my body does do for me, both physically and mentally—all the ways it carries my life and emotions and struggles and contradictions inside of it—and how that, in and of itself, is miraculous. I am one complex, exquisitely packaged set of tubes.

Lately, just like when I was a kid, I spend a good percentage of the time forgetting that I'm being outwardly perceived at all. I live in a big city, and I've never had to deal with catcalling the way some others do. Back when I ran cross-country in high school, I learned quickly that the honks came only when I was running with my statuesque blonde teammates. Even walking around New York City through my twenties and thirties, perhaps because I didn't present in an overtly feminine way (mainly put out a vibe best described as "I mean, I guess?"), I gave catcallers a lot less to work with. But hey, they're the pickup *artists*. Shouldn't they be the ones reinventing the form? To that point, one time a catcaller exchanged eye contact with me to confirm how beautiful the woman walking in front of both of us was, so touché, sir.

Still, the question crosses my mind, more often than I'd like to admit: If I am not really getting that sort of attention compared with other women I know, nor have I ever, what is it about me that's different or unappealing? Is it ugliness? The word itself feels visceral even to say—there's such a strong ingrained reaction to it. It's the worst fate to so many, and yet I've been called it plenty of times online. Some people think I'm pretty, but a lot don't. Like many people, I fall somewhere in the middle, neither conventionally "hot" nor conventionally "uggo." I remember once after a television appearance on Comedy Central, a random guy wrote me a message saying how he didn't think I was funny at all but ended his generous verdict by qualifying that "[you're] bangable I guess." Put it on my tombstone! It reminded me of boys at my high school, all Mark Zuckerberg prototypes, who kept a barely secret website ranking the hotness of all their female classmates. I remember sheepishly looking through it, searching for any acknowledgment that I too deserved to be a piece of meat. Despite myself, I find this internalized oppression fascinating. So many of us are captivated or, rather, ensnared by looks and the illusion of deliverance, acceptance, and belonging they promise us.

Invisibility, of course, is the kind blessing society bestows upon all women as they get older. "You can stop caring about what you look like because we don't even see you anymore! Be free, you wrinkly ghost!" Thanks to working in the entertainment industry, I've learned that even when nobody sees you, you can still be invisible "better." Everyone tries to perpetuate their youth, even after the trappings of it no longer serve them. As an actress, I understand wanting to extend career viability as long as possible, but one must stay vigilant to protect their own intuition. Why am I supposed to continue paying my respects to the Fountain of Youth when all it ever gave me was the bait and switch? Looking back, I see more hesitation and insecurity than Confidence Beast Mode. Not that I'm fully self-actualized now either. On my more human days, I'll find *glaring* new errors in my physique—tree ring neck, crone hands, the world's least requested magic act: appearing and disappearing moles—but now I remind myself it's all a distraction. Those criticisms aren't me; they're messages I've subsumed my entire life to keep me small.

Though I no longer see going undetected as a weakness—it's now a superpower I've been honing my entire life, a worthy opponent to "the gift of flight." Time and again we forget that there is a freedom and power in going unnoticed. As Akiko Busch writes in *How to Disappear: Notes on Invisibility in a Time of Transparency*, "Might invisibility be regarded not simply as refuge, but as a condition with its own meaning and power? Going unseen may be becoming a sign of decency and self-assurance." The true strength of invisibility is no one ever sees you coming. You may still be an underdog, but you've gained an upper hand, able to live your life as you please, without the unsolicited scrutiny of society's gaze. Your lack of concern as to others' opinions leaves them, if anything, charmed despite themselves. What do you know that they don't?

What I've learned with time is that no matter how much I change what I look like, there is no salvation in it. Yes, looking in the mirror or stepping on a scale can take up your entire brain, but to what end? A fleeting sense of passing muster, but whose, and is it ever enough? I still struggle, more often than I care to admit, with how both my body and I look and present. But now, I can finally see outside of this perpetual dissatisfaction in a way I couldn't when I was younger and see it for what it is: just another way of grasping at a sense of affinity, a pyramid scheme of acceptance. Because most of this endless fixation is for other people, even if it's often a projected version of them. And why should any system or person have so much say over how I feel about myself? I have committed to this perspective as a practice, because I know I will lose sight of it again. But every new reminder of it provides a respite. As perverse as it sounds, in becoming less visible, I have stopped clinging to my mortal coil so hard I forget who I am beyond that and why it's enough.

As with every crucible of womanhood, aging is a trade-off that can feel harsh, especially if you received acclaim for your looks early on. In that department, I guess I got out ahead. When I was a teenager, I constantly awaited proof that I mattered, aided by the constant Greek chorus of well-meaning adults: "Oh, but you're still so young—you have plenty of time!" I've long since stopped hearing it, though in that silence, for the first time, there's clarity. Mortality, at last, has become a conceivable milestone. This is it, there's no grand deliverance from the beauty arms race. Having crested forty, I look at my graying hairline (entry-level crone or whatever) and think, "Ooh, you really worked hard for those spots!" In a business that constantly encourages diminishing or erasing your age, it's probably wrong that I'm even talking about it.

I recently found one long white hair in my right eyelid. It's definitely not an eyelash—it's twice as long as any of them, and not in an "ooh, what's your secret" way. It's simply a single wispy white strand that decided, for whatever reason, to pop up in my eyelash area. A rebel of sorts. I plucked it once, twice. It keeps coming back, refusing to explain itself, just happy to be there. I begrudgingly admire the symbolism.

Failure Résumé

To whom it may concern: As a perfectionist, I spend so much time fixating on my failures that I thought it might be a "fun" exercise to make a résumé of them. (As a perfectionist, my idea of "fun" is also extremely questionable.) Usually, the only time we hear about a low is when the story ends with an eventual, hard-won success. I thought it'd be enlightening to frame some lows without the payoff of that assumed catharsis.

During the briefest of internet searches, I discovered a similar idea had already been conceived, which was a poetically fitting way to start an exercise in failure. When she was still a neurobiology PhD student, Dr. Melanie Stefan wrote a 2010 *Nature* article called "A CV of Failures." In it, she advises other postdocs and scientists to make a list of tests they failed, grants they did not receive, applications that did not get to the next round. She writes, "It will be six times as long as your normal CV. It will probably be utterly depressing at first sight. But it will remind you of the missing truths, some of the essential parts of what it means to be a scientist—and it might inspire a colleague to shake off a rejection and start again."

In a similar spirit, I humbly submit the following for your consideration. Be assured, there's a lot more than this, but we don't have that kind of time. I hope you hate it.

Aparna Nancherla[*]

"Comedian"

666 Compromised Personal Data, Mmhmm, YEP 91191[**]

020-234-5467[***]

aparna.nancherla@angelfire.biz[****]

EMPLOYMENT-ADJACENT HISTORY

Sugar Goblin, Washington, DC, 5 years old

Attended first holiday potluck party with my parents. The dessert room was full of all the cakes ever imagined. Incapable of reason, my tiny brain wanted a piece of every single one. When parents rightfully refused my request, threw a full-body tantrum until hosts stepped in for diplomacy, as if I were a tiny dictator with nuclear codes. The next day I opened the box of cakes and everything had congealed into one unappetizing cakeball. Suspecting treachery, threw yet another fit. First sign I will stop at nothing to remain ultimately disappointed.

---

[*] First fail: this font.

[**] I have entered my address online so many times, even a baby with an iPad could dox me.

[***] Wait, was this supposed to be my phone number or social?

[****] This is actually a fax line. No, I can't explain it either.

Woman (You Don't Want) in STEM, Northern Virginia, 14 years old

Halfway through our six-week experiment, one of my two lab partners accidentally killed all the microscopic specimens in our science fair project, so we made up the rest of our data and never spoke of it again. (Surprise, ladies!) Still ended up winning third place in the fair, because America!

Therapy Client in Theory, New York, NY, 31 years old

After being twenty minutes late to every single one of our fifty-minute sessions, karma intervened, and my therapist stood me up. Showed up for my appointment and the building was locked. Texted her, got no response. Wanted to stand outside with a boom box like in *Say Anything* to show her how serious I was about "doing the work." (Therapists live in their offices, right? Like teachers live at school?) Later, she called to apologize and said she totally forgot. The next few sessions wrote themselves. She gradually got too busy to see me, and when I said it was probably best I find another therapist, well, it's hard to read tone in email, but she seemed pretty stoked.

EMPLOYMENT HISTORY (LOWLIGHTS)

Death of a Saleswoman, Northern Virginia, Bright-Eyed High School Graduate

Attempted to sell Cutco knife sets to friends and family after falling for an ad in a coffee shop. Only sold two single knives. One of the customers—my dad's colleague—badly cut her finger while using said knife. Stopped going to the sales seminars without telling anyone. Boss called my house and asked why I wasn't there. After avoiding many, many calls, finally had to tell them I wasn't emotionally capable of moving product aka murder weapons. (But imagine showing up at an acquaintance's house holding a bunch of weapons and demanding money with a smile. It's not right.)

The Job Is Yours to Book & You Will Not Book It, Los Angeles/New York/My Own Home, Midtwenties–Present

What is the quote by the hockey man (see References)? You miss 100 percent of the shots you don't take? Well, you don't get 1,000 percent of the things you audition for, and no one will tell you, either—you just wait for the movie or show or project to come out to confirm, nope, you're not in it. At one particularly memorable audition, had to "act" as though I were being eaten alive by zombie squirrels in front of a very patient man. Another time was told I would be playing a role and then still had to audition for it several times and finally was told I would not be playing the role. Could have done without that first part then, yes? Recently was asked to audition for a part that sounded more or less like an exact description of my real-life self. Did not get a callback.

TV Writer, OR IS SHE?!, New York, NY, Thirties

Learned secondhand from coworker at first late-night writing job that one of my bosses "does not get what it is I do exactly." Hard agree! Let me know if you ever figure it out! Let go from second late-night writing job. Was generously told I could spin it as a "mutual decision." It *was* mutual in that I too thought I was going to get fired from Day One. And then I was! The truth shall set you free. Of health insurance.

Longtime Listener, First-Time Letdown, Chicago, IL, Midthirties

Was asked to be a panelist on a very popular comedic public radio show. Many peers, including a few friends of mine, are regulars on this program. Thought I did OK but never heard from them again. Ever! When my episode aired, someone on Twitter tagged me and commented my laugh was so annoying they had to turn it off and could the show please never bring me back. Wish granted.

Op-Ed Writer but Not in My Editor's Op, New York, NY, Later-Latest Thirties

Was asked to write a regular column for a well-known media out-let. Sent in a writing sample and they responded that they were reformulating and no longer needed a columnist. I understand YOUR CODE. Just love having something taken away from me that I never asked for in the first place.

AWARDS & FELLOWSHIPS

No major entertainment awards (that I know of), but here's some-thing. Got my first supporting part in a movie, and the production company forgot to invite me to the premiere. Here's something else. Went to another premiere for a comedy special I was in, and the door person (is there anyone more powerful?) said I wasn't on the guest list. Would have gone home, except my friend indignantly said, "Um, excuse me, she's IN the show!" Was then waved through. Like a proud boss.

EDUCATION

Bachelor of Psychology *don't know where this is*
Amherst College
*Have barely used degree except to reference during small talk,
and mention as many times as possible in this book, though it has
led to a real weakness for online personality tests.*

High School Diploma *also don't know where this is*
Thomas Jefferson High School for Science and Technology
*(Guess which two subjects I have avoided studying ever since?
Except of course for my psych major—did you know I have
one?)*

REFERENCES

Horribly bad at ones relating to movies specifically. But have also
missed a huge number of cultural touchstones spanning TV, music, you name it, I will not know what you're talking about. For
example, as a thirty-seven-year-old, I asked my boyfriend, without
irony, if Jerry Seinfeld is Jewish.

SPECIAL SKILLS

- Leaving parties without saying goodbye to anyone, because,
  honestly, who even remembers this part? Also, frequently
  not showing up to parties in the first place, so not great at
  saying hello either.

- Eating all the M&M's out of trail mix. I did this once while a guest at someone else's house. My host later came home and, like a waking nightmare, asked if I knew what happened to all the M&M's in his trail mix. Obviously, I said I had no idea. As if either of us was mentally prepared to have an *honest* conversation. I barely knew him!

- Not brushing my teeth correctly (according to my dentist). It's the front back that's a real problem area.

- Habitually late in meeting: people, deadlines, expectations. Triple threat.

- Avoiding confrontation and conflict as long as possible, until I've built up a huge amount of resentment, and then apologizing unnecessarily for a lot of horrible things I've thought about you in my head. Sorry, sorry, sorry. Still sorry.

PS: This résumé is over five pages long. Also, no joke, my editor wanted to cut this piece.☺ So yeah, I'll say it: résumé fail.

Inside Voice

So, you claim you're an introvert, huh? You're hardly alone (even if you don't mind that sort of thing). The type has almost become cool, its lingering whiff of secret society only adding to its allure. Naturally, I must ask for your credentials, if only to compare notes. Mine first? I'll take it from your protracted stare that's both a yes and part of your case.

I was a shy, introverted kid. Not that the pairing of the two is inevitable, but they do complement each other, like that one lost belt deep in your closet that really pulls an outfit together. I was such a wallflower (subspecies: shrinking violet) that I considered our mailperson "stranger danger." My mother, like a Tide pen brimming with utilitarian optimism, brainstormed countless ways to get that giant reclusive spot out of my personality. Several of these covert interventions were presented to me as "worthwhile" and "fun thing most kids would like." There were ice-skating lessons and etiquette classes and a particularly dark Junior Jazzercise chapter (in short, the only kid who would pair with me for partner exercises was the instructor's son, who was barely past toddlerhood). The common through line was toss this girl to the wolves, ahem, I mean other kids. She will learn. They will teach her. Um, excuse me, have you ever met children? One of their claims to fame (alongside constant, self-congratulatory mutiny) is inventing the concept of bullying.

One of my chores, I'm sorry, "growth exercises," was ordering pizzas over the phone. That's right, Sunday evening was Nancherla Family Pizza Hut Night, and my designated job was to place our takeout order over the phone and then drive to the restaurant with my dad to go inside and pick it up. Each time, as I picked up the landline to dial the number, which I had grimly memorized (remember when that was a thing?), I shook with the prospect of communicating with someone who did not know or care who I was. I knew they would be impatient and busy and ask me to speak up, which of course I would not. It was anyone's guess if my words were going to come out in the right order, even though I repeated them to myself over and over like an incantation: "Two medium pizzas, one Veggie Lover's, and one bell pepper and onion." I was also supposed to ask for a side of jalapeños, but I would usually be exhausted by the order itself and hope I could summon my reserves to do it in person.

When we dined at the restaurant, the stakes were even higher. I had to go up to the counter and ask for the check. What sounds inconsequential now—making myself known, briefly, to those outside my inner circle—felt horrific then. I internalized the idea early that I was a nuisance to other people with my aggressive timidity. One of my most favorite things in the world, pizza, tainted forever with the stink of flop sweat.

I don't fault my mother's conviction that the seeds of my temperament were destined to grow into a tree so gnarled and upsetting, kids would point and say, "That one's creepy! It ate my jacket!" When she first came to the States, my mom battled her own agoraphobia. It began with an incident in medical school back in India. While observing a routine surgical dissection, she fainted in front of her peers. In her estimation, the causes were ether fumes, having skipped breakfast, and the sheer bold camp of seeing a cross-sectioned eyeball outside of a face. The experience scarred her enough that she dreaded being in all kinds of public situations after that. She had to take her med school exams in a separate room by herself, telling her professors that it was because she was pregnant (which she was at the time, with my older sib, Bhav, in case you want to know what hard-core multitasking looks like).

To then have a second child who was unable to maintain eye contact and unwilling to even speak to her own teachers, well, I'm sure it felt like the setup of a cautionary folktale. And just like a folktale, Bhav was outgoing and assertive, while I was the weak, silent type. True story: more than one of my teachers got irritated with me for tugging on their clothing instead of "using my words." In my defense, it was an extremely easy system: one tug for "Greetings, respected elder" and two tugs for "I would love to start a dialogue with you, though this is pretty much it." My mother worried how I would make it in the world unless measures were taken, so she adapted the same self-improvement system she used on herself. For example, she watched other parents read stories to their kids in the waiting room at the dentist and challenged herself to do the same. She treated her comfort zone like an escape room and expected me to follow suit.

Until I manifested any semblance of self-reliance, I relied heavily on the capable Bhav for the power of speech. On more than one occasion, I made them come with me to talk to one of my teachers, as if they were my muscle and I was initiating a shakedown for extra stickers. From my assimilating immigrant parents' point of view, I didn't blend in as much as completely disappear. Instead of going chameleon, I went ghost. In my defense, ghosts have incredible backstories and always steal focus in a photo.

Believing loudness and extroversion are irreproachable, best-in-show character traits is a prized American conceit. Not that we're at all culturally alone in these beliefs, but Americans by and large have a fear of pauses in conversations and silence in the company of others. Susan Cain, the author of *Quiet: The Power of Introverts in a World That Can't Stop Talking*, postulates that valuing magnetic, charismatic personalities increased both with our shift from an agricultural society to an industrial one, and with the rise of entertainment celebrity and movie stars as aspirational idols. Reserved, tentative individuals are the notes you don't hear in the jazz of conversation, and guess what? People are always making fun of jazz. I don't think they even know what they're listening for. If they understood jazz better, they might stop yelling over it in elevators. (Who exactly is talking in elevators anyway, besides fiends and prank show actors? Elevators are voluntary hostage situations and should be treated with the appropriate gravitas.) My parents, however, coming from a chatty culture themselves, signed on wholesale to this country's worship of verbal ease and found my own behavior disturbingly not up to code. Getting me out of my padded shell was a must.

Speaking of which, "coming out of one's shell" implies that being shy or reserved automatically equates with a refusal to engage with life. Putting yourself out there means talking and interacting with others, because that's what life is all about, right? Making yourself known needs to be out loud. Reticence implies you are giving up space. It's like when a potential new friend doesn't text you back. The nonresponse starts to generate more concerns than any words could. The lack of a text becomes a question mark of perceived judgment onto which most of us project our own hang-ups and misgivings. In the same way, a quiet person becomes an inadvertent conversational foil for the other person's insecurities. *Does she think she's too good to talk to me? Why hasn't she piped up more? What is she hiding?*

Jokes, I guess? That's right, dormant in many a dreamy loner, like the prize buried at the bottom of the cereal box, is the desire to make people laugh. Unlike the class clowns, quiet or shy kids can be sleeper cells of comedy. Don't get me wrong, I was always in awe of the humor showboats, who could naturally bend an audience to their will. I didn't yet know how to wield that amount of attention myself. Instead, I keenly observed from a safe distance, perpetually terrified of being pulled into the pro bono entertainer's erratic trajectory. I worked diligently to avoid being noticed in a negative way while also questioning why I was never enterprising enough to be featured favorably. It was a strange paradox, but I noticed how humor disarmed people if you wielded it correctly. Making others laugh puts you in the spotlight without annoying them. It was the opposite of when the teacher told me *in front of the class* that I got the most words right on the spelling test, and I saw my classmate Peter make a big show of rolling his eyes at me. Whatever, dude, you don't come from an immigrant culture obsessed with spelling bees for some reason.

My mother, ever on the self-improvement hustle, signed Bhav and me up for a public speaking class when we were thirteen and eleven years old, respectively. Yup, that sweet spot of early adolescence where existence itself is so cringe! Not only would it equip us for the burgeoning second-wave Dada art movement that was PowerPoint, but my mother figured we would be ahead of the curve when it came to effectively talking to strangers. The class was run by an organization called Toastmasters International, whose slogan is "Where leaders are made." I agreed to it because it was always easier to go along with my mom's ideas than not. Though it certainly helped her cause that while I was physically and emotionally a tween, I was intellectually the age of an Easter Island head and figured if nothing else could help me, perhaps adult education would.

Over the two-month course, our weekly homework assignment was to prepare a three-to-five-minute speech on a specific prompt. For example, one was "a hobby I really enjoy"—I did mine on reading because, I don't know if you've heard, it's like the movies but completely different. Each class, the instructor would go over pointers for being an effective public speaker, and then we'd present our prepared speeches. When you were done, the class would give you feedback about what worked ("good eye contact") and what didn't ("monotone delivery"). Like most presentations, we gave ours in a purgatory-like conference room in an aggressively drab business center with a podium and chairs that could best be described as nihilist chic.

Without fail (or rather, with quite a bit of fail), I would write my speech on the day of class, generally at the last possible minute. Hey, at least it was fresh in my mind. And while "performing" my speech felt consistently terrifying, it was also eerily transfixing to have everyone sit quietly and listen to what I had to say. Like a robot learning how to pass as human, I carefully moved my dominant right hand like so to illustrate my point with a natural, fluid gesture and looked around the room making eye contact, "connecting" with the members of my captive audience. The tips we learned functioned as cheat codes for social normalcy, and the stiff formality of effective public speaking strategy was justified because giving speeches was what grown-ups did, and, if all went according to plan, that's what I hoped to be someday. By the way, the rest of our classmates were in fact grown-ups, having enrolled to improve their soft skills and advance their careers. I wonder what they made of the two stoic children learning alongside them. I would have been, as the expression goes, pissed as hell.

When I completed the class and received my official certificate, I had it framed and mounted above my poster of a red panda thriving (my hormones were working their way, very slowly, toward a tween firefighter calendar). Soon after, my mother was delighted to offer me the opportunity of a suburban South Asian American kid lifetime: entering a community youth speech contest via our local Hindu temple. And you thought my life lacked intrigue!

The prompt for my age group—twelve-to-seventeen-year-olds—was "What is one issue you care about affecting the Indian community today?"

This was in the '90s (crank up that time machine) and now "Indian" would obviously read "South Asian diasporic," though I still somehow doubt it would. Every other contestant chose to tackle the salient, evergreen themes of racism, discrimination, and representation. However, my first inclination was to go silly, not to mention I was blithely unaware of identity politics.

Bespectacled eleven-year-old me wrote a tongue-in-cheek manifesto detailing the quality control problems I found inherent in the countless Bollywood movies my parents made my sibling and me sit through. It was a full-on roast. I happily skewered everything from the quantity of movies made per year (Hollywood isn't even close), which I considered questionable in terms of sheer bulk, to common tropes in the movies like how doctors would merely take a woman's pulse to determine whether she was pregnant (I knew this because my physician parents made a point to mock these parts), or how many costume and location and weather changes there were per cheesy musical number. I love Bollywood movies today, but at the time, I had to watch them against my will in the name of honoring my lineage, and I had no one to vent to about my burden. Bear in mind, this was the era of VHS and before standard subtitles, so by "watch," I mean pause every few scenes so my parents could explain what was going on. To my complete bewilderment, my speech went over like gangbusters. In the words of a stand-up, I killed. It was the first time I remember making a group of people laugh in a deliberate and direct way, and I found the experience exhilarating, if confounding. I imagine it's what childbirth might feel like, minus the unfathomable pain—*Wow, that thing came out of me?!* How was it possible that the words I'd written and said had won everyone over, however temporarily? Talk about power. I wanted more.

Despite being one of the youngest entrants for my age group, I won first place. I firmly believe a big part of my success was going funny, because everyone else went serious. That experience forever changed how I thought about comedy. Yes, laughter was transportive—this pied piper sound that united a group in such a seductive way—but it also reached a different, almost primal part of people. I felt dizzy with possibilities, though I didn't yet know what they were, so I sat down.

The occasional five-minute speech aside, though, I remained queen of the quiets. And even as a teenager, I did, against all odds, agree with my mom . . . about one thing. I saw my continuing introversion and guardedness as traits that required fixing. In fact, when I took the Myers-Briggs personality test in high school (though no longer considered a credible assessment in the least), I willed myself to rank as an extrovert on the extraversion-introversion scale. I read each question in that section twice, trying to discern between what I wanted to answer and how I needed to answer. I occasionally looked around at the more obvious E's in the class, wishing I could cheat off them. As if codified test results have ever held the promise of social salvation (INFJ then and now, forever after). Nonetheless, despite my best efforts to "crack the system," I repeatedly scored an "I." The introvert in me shuddered in recognition. The narcissist in me giggled. Once, when I took the test my senior year, I scored almost exactly halfway between introvert and extrovert, leaning slightly introverted, and I considered this a huge win. SHE'S LEARNING! blared the front page of the *Aparna Gazette*.

My self-loathing for introversion wasn't solely due to parental influence, much as I'd love not to take accountability for anything, ever. Discovering that I could have a group of strangers in the palm of my hand felt like both a blessing and a curse. I loved putting myself out there in carefully choreographed segments, but the overall experience overwhelmed me with its sheer magnitude, as if I were a shape-shifter or a telepath. And yet it was neither of those things, it was merely connecting with other people. Finding one way in which I could manage it didn't empower me as much as cause me to naturally fear heightened expectations of me. After all, being funny demands some level of allegiance from your intended audience, and I already felt like too much of an outsider with my early attempts at socializing. Add a couple more layers of otherness as a first-gen immigrant South Asian American cis female, and you have yourself one congealed seven-layer-dip theory of identity.

Also, despite introverts constituting 25 to 40 percent of the population (and, for obvious reasons, I'm positive it's underreported), society still has serious hang-ups about our whole situation. In a piece for *The Atlantic* about the most devoted of our kind, ultra-introverts—those who have shifted to an entirely nocturnal schedule to avoid being around people, journalist Faith Hill (no, not *that* Faith Hill, but dang, that would have been a hoot) mentions the ongoing debate within the psychological community about whether to classify extreme introversion as a disorder. The clinical version of the trait is associated with detachment and an inability to experience pleasure or joy. But it's hard to make as clean an argument when America is such an extrovert-biased country. As Hill explores, social connection has always been seen as a fundamental need in all humans, and maybe that isn't necessarily the case. She writes, "Though the impulse to find some universal traits is well intentioned, it may also be hubristic. . . . The question is where the line is—when another person's way of living or thinking can be invalidated, and by whom, using what measurements." It is encouraging that introversion has at last entered the cultural conversation with pieces like this one and in light of the publication of the aforementioned book by Susan Cain.

Then again, there are still pop culture articles about introverts titled as if it were a strange, unholy revelation—"17 Celebrities You Won't Believe Are Shy, HOT DAMN!!!"; "8 Famous People Who Were QUIET!!!"; "2.5 Hollywood Stars (and 1 Snow Leopard) Who Say They're Loners . . . So

Random." The subtext is some variant of "Um, are you OK?" The way much of American society still qualifies quiet, shy, or more introverted people is typically the same: by explaining our presence to us sarcastically. As I've been told many times by well-intentioned (I think?) acquaintances: "Aparna, seriously, please try and keep it down over there!" A real conversation ender, by the way. Was I introverted because I didn't fit in? Or did I not fit in because I was introverted? These questions continued to nag at me, even as I did become that grown-up and find a distinct way to express myself.

When I first clocked comedy as something that resonated with me, I don't think anyone in my life would have described me as funny. To be a funny person, it helps to have an audience, and for many years, my only audience was myself. I still often find things hilarious or delightful that I can't quite explain to others. Comedy has given me a middle ground between everyone else and myself, a clear, open channel of communication.

I think of stand-up as public speaking's cool, bad-influence cousin, sweeping into town unannounced with her chaotic choices and messy energy. The closest I came to it in high school was opting to write a funny presentation at every opportunity. Though still by no means a class clown, I did receive small glimmers of encouragement here and there. I ran cross-country and went on long group runs with my teammates, one of whom once said to me, "You say a lot of funny things under your breath." My first review!

The summer after my first year of college, a friend and I psyched ourselves up to try a free stand-up open mic at a Best Western just off the freeway (where dreams are made). My first set went well enough that, off that euphoria, I essentially took a four-year break—you know, like how after someone gets elected president, they forget about all the promises they made? But after college, I moved back to DC and finally acknowledged that if you want to pursue comedy, you need to do it more than every leap year. In the beginning, as I was getting more comfortable both in the scene and onstage, I did become more socially capable. But I never quite let go of my reserved, more observant self. An old improv teammate of mine once crudely called me "a grower, not a show-er," as in I turned it on for the stage, but otherwise kept it low-key (if unfamiliar, the expression refers to a penis, since this piece of anatomy is in dire need of more cultural airtime). Sidenote: This same guy also offered to be my life coach. I'll just leave that there.

I'd hear about other comedians who started out as shy, indoor kids and now were bubbly charm parades, and I'd cross my fingers and think, *Any day now, I'll hit personality puberty. . . .*

Surprise! I'm still a raging introvert. If anything, any degree of comedic success has led me to retreat further inward. Finding myself in the public eye even to a minor extent (recognition hovering at about one in every five baristas) has resulted in a very real desire to hide from its haphazard, roving gaze. I've been forced to confront why I wanted validating attention in the first place. Was the craving genuine or did it feel like the only option to make it in a world where being shy is undesirable? I wanted to have it both ways, to coexist in the ebb of retreating and flow of emerging. But there is much about show business that doesn't bend well to these contradictory impulses.

You're inherently a personality when you do comedy, which, I suppose, is kind of like being a rapper or a pop star. It's a package deal—you're never fully off the job. When you're a comedian, it is assumed you will be somewhat funny most of the time. (Though so many of my interviews beg to differ!) When a comedian is not amusing enough, say, on a podcast, you will see it reflected in the comments. It's taken as a whole lifestyle—like we're professional joke mascots who can never take off our giant heads.

But many of us put those costumes on to survive, and there's plenty going on underneath. Research from the University of New Mexico found that professional comedians test lower on extroversion than the average person. And believe it or not, many of the qualities associated with introverts sync up well with a career as a professional comedian. If touring, you generally spend long amounts of time by yourself. And you always need to be hyperaware of situations and those around you to notice and create funny, unexpected material (all the more challenging to soak up the subtleties of an environment when you're always the main character). There's also a unique sense of control and power that comes with trying to make a group of strangers laugh from up on a stage, one that's much higher than, say, trying to make a group of strangers laugh at a party where there is no preexisting unwritten contract to cede the floor to you on cue and listen with rapt attention.

It helps to learn that Bridget Everett, one of the most boisterous, unforgettable, and lively comedic performers out there, is an introvert. And to remind yourself that Martha Kelly, a brilliant comedian, has a very understated energy but is incredibly magnetic onstage, where she exhibits the power to draw audiences into her singular worldview. It's not so easy to guess who's an introvert and who isn't, either—a comedian peer of mine, let's call him Guff, who reads to me like one of the more extroverted people I know both onstage and off, started doing material about being an introvert. It floored me when I first heard it. *But, but, but*—my mind sputtered— *that's not fair, you're operating from the other team's playbook! I smell a rat.* But I knew very well that introverts, especially those in fields like entertainment that value charisma and big personalities, devise an extroverted mode they can inhabit when necessary.

One example of this that completely heartens me is Missy Elliott, the iconic rapper and musician, whose career has spanned decades. She's been very open about her reclusiveness as well as her struggles with anxiety and panic attacks, both of which starkly contrast with her brash, devil-may-care performance persona. In an interview with *Billboard* magazine, Elliott said her shyness has gotten worse with age, as she's felt increasingly judged by others. As an entertainer, you are exposed to an abnormal amount of feedback and unsolicited interaction, especially the higher your profile and the longer your career. The public eye giveth, oh, but then how the public eye taketh away. It's a gaze you can't control.

That such a well-respected musician of her stature has had these ongoing internal struggles felt like a warning to me. It's well-worn knowledge that success and fame don't inoculate you from having problems and usually end up creating less relatable, and hence more alienating, ones. But there was more to it than that. No matter how big she got, Missy Elliott had to advocate for her own sensitivity and needs. Nobody else was going to. She had to draw those boundaries herself. This couldn't have been an easy task, especially given how much her stage persona operated on a different frequency from that of her real-life self. If I am not vocal about my own limits and needs, I realized, no one else is going to be. I need to be OK with retreating as needed without constantly justifying it.

Working against me and other introverts in the business is the reality that the entertainment industry prides itself on spewage. That is, putting yourself out there for better or for worse. I am surrounded by so much performance and performativity that it can be incredibly blurring and draining—like one nonstop party that I would love to leave. Like Guff, I too slapped together my own vehicle of extroversion to cruise around in, but if his is an armored tank, mine is one of those Flintstones cars. The idea is there, but it's hardly solvent. I go to one social event and talk to nine people (a new personal best!), and I expect it to count as my "membership dues" for the next three years. When I squeezed between a column and a wall to say hello to someone at a party once, another comedian walking by commented,

"Wow. This feels like exactly where I'd find you hanging out: hiding behind a pillar." Wow, it turns out everyone can see my dusty bare feet scrambling along, doing their best to keep up.

I have found solace where I've always found it—in one-on-one conversations with trusted friends and positive feedback from respected peers, when both they and I show up without all the bells and whistles. Comedians might be consummate entertainers, but the ones I most admire are also thoughtful and perceptive no-bullshitters. They don't pay compliments they don't mean. There is nothing like a bit of praise from another comedian or artist you admire to set your mind at ease. Am I staying true to myself? Yes, they nod, you are.

That's what I try to remember when I'm yet again the quietest person on a job. I think best on my own, and sometimes being around others hinders my ability to get my ideas out in a cohesive way. This quality dogs me in pitch meetings and on sets and other places, too—wherever turning up the razzle-dazzle is an asset. As an Asian American woman, I fear I inhabit an unfortunate stereotype, and my natural introversion can spiral into bigger anxieties and insecurities about not taking up enough space and not speaking up enough for "my group." I am perpetually convinced my inability to talk for the sake of talking is my Achilles' heel. However, I'm beginning to acknowledge visibility is also about showing up and saying whatever you have to say when you are ready to say it, not on someone else's terms or schedule.

Despite this reluctant crawl toward self-acceptance, I've noticed, to my abject horror, that I have started to resent shyness in others. If they are quieter than I am, if they don't make more of an effort to put acquaintances at ease, well, why not? If I'm at a party and introduced to someone who doesn't work to keep the small talk ball in the air, I think, *You better carry your weight here.* I don't like verbally floundering either, but at least I'm trying. I've been attempting to integrate myself better my whole life, to blend in with a room full of louds. (I'd worry this might sound insulting, but the group in question would have to hear it first.)

It's the same way one might resent an immigrant for not trying to assimilate better or a higher-weight person for not trying to diet. *Why aren't you contorting yourself to fit society's unyielding, ridiculous standards like I am? What do you know that I don't? Do you think you're better than me?* Because I've considered the shy label such a sanctuary to hide within, if I see someone who deserves the label more than I do, I start to wonder if I'm appropriating the term. Then I'll go to a noisy bar and remember, *Ah, the timer starts now.* And I'll calculate how soon I can slip out without being rude. But equal opportunist that I am, I go the other way with it too and resent people who say they're shy or introverted when clearly they are way more social than I'll ever be. *You* don't get to use the term "introvert," you're distorting what the term even means. I envy their assumed ease.

I too get tangled in the common fallacy that just because you're an introvert or a shy person, you can't be loud or outgoing. You very well can—only the performance takes more out of you. While the more extroverted are stimulated by these qualities, you need to recharge. While it can be enjoyable and exhilarating while you're in it—a high of sorts—it's not your baseline state. There is some ramping up and cooling down required.

Turns out, just because you've met one introvert doesn't mean you've met them all. For example, in 2011, a group of researchers at Wellesley College posited that introversion itself is a nuanced characterization with four different subtypes: social, thinking, anxious, and restrained, although they found the least strong evidence for the thinking categorization. Though the research has had mixed support among the psychology community, the variants cover differences like sociability versus introspectiveness versus neuroticism versus simply acting at a more measured, slower pace. The acronym for the four types is STAR. The irony! Imagine the rebranding possibilities: introverts—the *stars* of today's libraries and tomorrow's remote, undisclosed locations. I took the assessments for all types to see where I stacked up, and great news—it turns out I am all four: a full flipping sparkler, Mom! (Predictably, I scored highest for the thinking and anxious types.) But news flash: not everyone is like me; a tidy, empathic reframing of the navel-gazing fear that no one else gets me.

The truth is, I'm using the same hypocritical theory of "performing loudness" as a measure of someone's comfort zone. We're all performing at different points in our life, hell, at different points in our day. There's even a whole school of psychotherapy called Internal Family Systems that posits we are all made up of distinct, separate subpersonalities in conversation with each other.

So why am I holding up performance as an indicator of anyone's bar for internal comfort and needs? Who's to say we don't all have little extroverts and introverts clamoring for space in the same cramped ego chamber? We all perform to integrate better. Some of us were forced to do it more, and others of us weren't or refused to, and I guess, at the end of the day, am I jealous I didn't try less? I know plenty of quiet, introverted types who carry themselves with seemingly little insecurity, and when I talk to my friends, they say I come across just as unflappably. However, like the placid duck floating on the pond, I am "paddling like the dickens underneath." That adds another layer for me (seven layers of identity dip achieved, yum yum)— that the way I present often contradicts how I feel. I think I developed an emotional poker face as a self-preservation instinct. Rather than going in the opposite direction of big and loud, I played it close to the vest.

I too express a more heightened self in my stand-up act, even if this self is spouting into the mic about how I'd much rather be at home. It's a strange line to walk, and I'm sure it confuses both introverts and extroverts in the audience. *Then why is she onstage?* I've had more than one well-wisher come up to me after a show or on the street and say, "I love what you do, but I'll leave you alone now, because I know you're shy!" It's a strange way to be treated, like I'm a person marked off with caution tape. What would it look like if a more exuberant person were treated the same way? "I'm a big fan, but I'll let you do the rest of the talking since you never shut up!" It sounds downright rude when reversed. (Although . . . still worth trying once? Let me know how it goes!) Don't get me wrong, I do appreciate the get-out-quick technique when compared with being trapped in a conversation that will never end.

I understand people don't quite know what to make of me, especially since I am able to turn it on when required or around a few preapproved people (like credit cards but with fewer fees). I don't experience this same condescension with other comedians, because we know we're an odd amalgamation of performance and nonperformance in the starkest sense. Some of us lean into one more than the other, both on and off the clock. Among my peers, there are no cut-and-dried assumptions made about your personality based on how you are "up there" in the spotlight.

What first attracted me to stand-up and later to social media is that I could ask to be noticed in my own quiet way. I've often gotten more attention for my Twitter account than for my stand-up (back when Twitter wasn't solely where one went to abandon all hope), and aside from the level of exposure, I know why. Social media is where I've been my most unfettered, "loudest" self, where I can say all the things that were yelled over or taken credit for by others when I tried to say them to people in actual conversations. I could take up space on my own terms, and the people who liked me could find me from the comfort of their own homes, which is a mentality I understood well.

You did not hear it here first, but the environment of the internet has changed in a way that's no longer as welcoming as it once purported itself to be (even if that too was a false promise), and my tolerance for social media has grown paper-thin. But I still value that there's a place for introverts at that table. It was there that I was able to let go of what was expected of me and dig down into what I could offer with my own words. For the first time in my life, I planted my roots and asked the world to come to me.

For so long, I conflated being funny with being loud. Loudness demands being the center of attention, and so does being funny. Stealing focus in this way feels easier if you're gregarious and undeniably larger-than-life. I've finally come to realize shyness and funniness also operate as two sides of the same coin. Funniness can be loud and announce itself from miles away, but it can also be a sly sneak attack. The best jokes catch you by surprise. I've made my whole package the unexpected twist in the story, sometimes even catching myself off guard.

The few times I've found personal branding inoffensive as a concept is when I remember a brand can fill in the gaps of how to behave and who to be in a given situation. In that way, it can operate like a mission statement, or in noncorporate terms, a value system. So then maybe my brand is uncertainty? Am I unraveling branding's rigidity on a meta level as I attempt to puzzle out my way of being? Or, rather, is embracing my own inconsistencies and competing urges my entire life's work? A strange sort of rebellion has emerged as of late. It's not a neat, wrap-everything-up-with-a-bow sort of rebellion. It's more of a raze-and-burn-as-you-go recognition that I can't operate as a Frankenstein's monster of aspirational qualities that instinctually run counter to mine. For most of my life, I've thought of my personality as "closed for renovation (please excuse our dust)," but the only person I need to apologize to is myself. I should put up a BLESS THIS MESS sign and encourage more people to come over—to where I'm at.

I know why I rejected my own introversion and shyness for so long. They were conflated with a lack of will and an inability to hack it in the world. My mother worried the most, given her own experiences as an immigrant, but I know my blunt, strong-willed dad felt the same way. Now I realize it's not something to overcome, it's what I am. Without this part of myself, I wouldn't see the world the same or have stumbled onto the path I did.

It is to my mother's great relief that I've found my own way to navigate a society unwilling to accept a wide range of being. Funnily enough, my mother said she stopped worrying about me only once I started traveling to different places to do stand-up and doing interviews and performing on TV. Fooling my nearest and dearest? The Little Introvert That Could finally passed the test.

Extroversion is so often seen as strength and power, while being quieter or less willing to take up all the air in a room is seen as weak and submissive. But if an entire personality trait is framed as something needing improvement, what does that do to the person inhabiting it? How do you exist in the world and in relation to others when you're so often fed the message that your instincts are wrong?

The older I get, the more I see introversion as a beacon to bring my ship home. It's like my attempts to thrive and pass in an extrovert's world tired me out, and I'm ready to retire to where I've always been more content. In theory, we're told that being different is good. Meanwhile, from the moment you walk onto the playground, everything about the world tells you the opposite is true. The only kind of odd duck that is palatable is ironically one that presents within the predetermined, narrow status quo margins of what weirdness is allowed to look like. So you spend your adulthood reclaiming your difference and redefining it to suit your evolved sense of self. Perhaps it's not so much that I am now a proud introvert, to hell with everyone else, but that I am now reaching for goals that are my own instead of other people's. And yes, I am fully aware that makes me sound like a Magic 8 Ball who found itself.

I've stopped automatically second-guessing (if not third-guessing and fourth-guessing) my own impulses. If I have something to say, I say it (most of the time). If I don't have something to say, I don't beat myself up about it. If you get too caught up in your own behind-the-scenes (an introvert specialty), you miss your cue to show up in the real world. I try to avoid painting too much of an impression of myself through other people's eyes, because whatever assumptions I make about their opinions never paints them well. For too long, I was stuck in the spotlight effect, a condition most often experienced during puberty in which you think others are paying undue focus to your every behavior and action. I still regularly get stuck in my head in repeated cycles of self-loathing—but then I remember there are no rules on how to show up, only well-worn biases and tired expectations. It's harder to swim against the current without getting any credit for it, but that doesn't mean you shouldn't.

In a field that is ever so slowly telling a wider variety of stories, I firmly believe a shy person's tale can be told in more compelling ways, and not just as a battle to be overcome. Culturally, we are obsessed with the brazen extrovert, even in racialized terms. Loud, difficult women are always seen as more artistically interesting heroines since they're groundbreakers in many ways and playing against the trope of appeasing foils and archetypes. But there's more than one way to fight expectations, and as someone who inhabits a trope as an actual person, I can tell you reticent minorities also have stories to tell. And if those stories don't sound as riveting at first, maybe that's only because no one has bothered to listen to them, really listen, without presuming they know how they go. They don't.

Confessions:
Antisocial Skills

Ninety-nine percent of the people I've had crushes on in the past are not just unattractive to me now, but fully inconceivable as objects of interest. At this point, they collectively possess the appeal of an ottoman. This makes me feel powerful, like a sorceress with bad taste!

There was an unfortunate period of my life in which I was proud of having more male friends than female friends. Then I realized many of them were duds. I was in untenable circumstances, and I woke up. Still, I feel a shameful sense of pride whenever a guy I don't know well (or do) pays me a compliment, as if my worth is somehow refreshed anew. Whew, that patriarchy really chafes, huh?

One of the unexpected challenges of quarantining during the pandemic for me was not getting to "come home" as often. There is no greater feeling than "coming home." I compared it with both "leaving home" and "being home," and it's not even close. In fact, it's embarrassing the other two even entered the contest.

———

Sometimes comedians will test out an idea or a line from a joke on an unsuspecting mark to see if it earns a laugh. This is wrong because they should be compensating the other party monetarily or, at the very least, getting consent. Whenever I do this same thing and don't get a laugh, I know it's karma. Which is an enlightened way of saying "not funny."

A little game I like to play, especially at parties or other gatherings where I generally feel on edge, is to drop a word I made up in conversation. My success rate with this is pretty fernicious, if I do say so myself. On four out of five occasions, nobody asks me what the word means or questions its veracity. And we wonder how rumors spread.

This is better than my other move where I just trail off in the middle of a sentence to see if anyone notices. In LA, everyone is too busy clocking the rest of the room to do so, while in NYC, people are waiting for you to finish so they can start talking. Whereas at family events, at any given moment, everyone is monitoring how emotionally triggered they are, and hence the attention was never yours to begin with.

Being Well

Quick aside: I will go on and on about my experiences with anxiety and depression here, and most likely in other places. But please note this ornery double act currently dominates the "destigmatizing mental illness" societal discussion at large. In truth, they're merely one presence under a roomy golf umbrella that also comprises schizophrenia and schizoaffective disorder, bipolar I and II disorders, attention deficit hyperactivity disorder (ADHD), obsessive-compulsive disorder (OCD), and post-traumatic stress disorder (PTSD), among myriad other classifications. All forms of living with mental illness are just as valid and worthy of our time and understanding.

When I was growing up, people living with depression were rarely the heroes of the story. We were more likely to be the background actors filling out the scene, just going through the motions of living on a surface level. If ever in the limelight, it was only to show someone at their lowest point, in need of intervention or saving, so they could stop being a burden and slip back in with polite society. It's notable, by which I mean hugely insulting to artists and creators whose work I consumed in my youth, that when I tried to think of early depictions I saw of mental illness on TV or in movies, books, and music, the most ready example that bubbled up was a film I watched in middle school health class about depression and suicide prevention. An art teacher suspects one of her students is "in the danger zone" when he keeps painting the same spiraling black void over and over again. Subtle! In a fun plot twist, that student turns out to be none other than the renowned Spanish painter Francisco Goya.

Society lacks a nuanced range of depictions of what a person experiencing depression looks like. An old (but still prevalent) trope is someone who doesn't get out of bed physically or emotionally. Everything around them piles up—the dishes, the emails, the days. Usually, this is in reaction to a situational tragedy or loss. On the quotidian end of the spectrum, getting dumped perhaps, and on the more cataclysmic side, the death of a loved one. Other classic specters include the neglectful, catatonic parent who role-reverses with their child as caretaker, or the desperate, wild-eyed woman with one high heel on, tottering on the edge of a building, inevitably talked down by our worthy lead, well-balanced in both brain and face.

I would come to learn that depression can encompass all these scenarios, but it can also be far quieter, less of a showboat Eeyore,* giving no advance notice of its planned arrival or departure. A "cry for help" can often sound more like a glib aside, or more likely be saved for a private moment.

When I was first diagnosed with depression at the age of nineteen, I was immensely relieved—the smothering fog has a container; the sense of

---

* After a crucial internet deep dive on Eeyore and depression (by which I mean the first page of search results), I found a site really analyzing his condition, and apparently many of his difficulties are pinned, forgive me, to his "detachable tail." Body-shaming much?

burden has a classification; the thing with no clear reasons has, at the very least, a name. *Finally, an answer! I'm medically crushed by the weight of existence!* If you can state the problem, you're one step closer to the solution. (Tell that to the national debt, am I right, ladies?) At the very least there was room for *possibility*—a whimsical euphemism for options like therapy and medication. It was the first time in my life I had ever interrupted my high-achieving path and taken time off from school simply to "get better," whatever that meant. I had felt depressed before, but this was the first time I couldn't keep reading inspirational quotes and carrying on. I got my first B-minus in a class after getting a D on the final, which hardly sounds critical, but up until that point, "the danger zone" for me meant getting a B-plus. It was the first time in my life I asked myself *why* I bothered trying to achieve a certain standard and realized I had no answer. I truly didn't care and hadn't for some time. But until I got a sticky little label I could proudly wear on my chest like clothing marked "irregular," I had attributed it to my own weak will. My knowledge of mental health was paltry, and the only ingrained ethos I had was "Suck it up. Life is hard for everyone."

Since that initial bottoming out, my fallow episodes have come and gone as they pleased, as if through a little doggy door in my brain, one exactly the size and shape of a highly motivated incubus who thinks we're soulmates. The cluster of symptoms manifests in my brain like a person that a self-help book about boundaries would firmly recommend cutting out of your life. You can no longer even remember how you and Brenda met in the first place. That's right, I'm calling my depression Brenda from here on out. (If you're reading this and your name is Brenda, feel free to use the name Aparna instead.)

When I am verging on a more serious stint with Brenda, it's all I want to talk about. My only interest, if you can even call it that, is picking at the wound—admiring its refusal to heal and lack of coherent cause. The question "Why am I such a waste of life?" suddenly becomes my PhD dissertation, in need of endless defense. I stop myself only because I realize it's not socially acceptable to drag everyone around you down into a round of self-centered despair Twister. I don't want to be a burden to others. I've had an abject fear of it since a guy I dated in my twenties broke things off because I was "kind of a downer." (In his defense, he wanted to keep things casual. Nothing is less casual than the other person constantly asking, "What's the point of any of this?")

Depression is a permanently flaccid party horn of a conversation topic, the "describing the dream you had" equivalent of mental health issues. If the other person isn't prominently featured in yours, don't bother. It's the ultimate "you had to be there," except that nobody wishes they were. Hearing myself talk about it, I get sick of myself faster than whoever else is listening does. Before I can even finish the sentence I'm gumming up, my jaw drops open, and my tongue lolls out like a noncommercially viable approximation of an internet celebrity "it dog." Simultaneously redundant and opaque: there's nowhere to go with it, except in eddying circles, down an energy drain.

Over coffee, I once tried to explain what depression is like to a friend who didn't have it. She was the one who asked. It seemed like a conversation that warranted a dinner, at least some light tapas—white bean hummus with pita points, anyone? But there we were. After I barely skimmed the surface of an answer, she paused in genuine incomprehension and then said something like "Geez. That sounds really hard." I know she was relating as best she could, but I had barely gotten past the preamble. It's a riddle to fully convey the intensity of futility and hopelessness to a nonlocal. I did want to gently inquire what she did with all her beautiful pristine brain space—was there a water park in there? Instead, I changed the subject.

The best person to talk to when you're moderately depressed is another person who regularly copes with it. You'll repeat the same infinite loop of conversation over and over, wearily yet somehow tirelessly, like a GIF from a Beckett play. Over the years, I've found a handful of friends with whom I can freely talk about my mental health struggles. While they're not all women, my female friendships are the ones for which I, perhaps unfairly, have the highest expectations for mutual vulnerability. I even had a short-lived podcast with fellow comedian and friend Jacqueline Novak called *Blue Woman Group* about the day-to-day management of being a depressive. Totaling three episodes, it remains a triumph for two souls prone to mental malaise.

And yet, my friend Ed is the one with whom I talk about depression the most freely and in more granular detail, even though we may go long periods without talking at all. It's safe to say it's completely informed the nature of our friendship. Even at some of my lowest points, I've been able to reach out to him, or at least explain myself later with more clarity than with others. We most often communicate via text, sporadically supplemented by email or phone. For years, we forwarded the same Listserv e-newsletter back and forth to each other, highlighting some random quote from it, like a tiny flare of connection—what began as a silly inside joke continued long after it ran out of mileage. It's perhaps less strange to maintain intimacy in digital non sequiturs these days. But our mental health updates have become the equivalent of small talk—an inevitability of life, like the weather or sports. We say things to each other like "The depression has been particularly rough for a while now, but I'm hoping it will level out. I pretty much have stopped talking to anyone else about it." Ed exists as an outside entity from other friends, a blank slate onto which I can paint the rest of my life from a bird's-eye view. Still, our communication slows when either of us is doing markedly worse or better. But I am immensely comforted someone else sees the world through such a similar lens and shares this space with me at all. We're very different people in many respects, but our brains tell us the same lies, and in that way, we share a common dealer.

The other thing that makes the conversational bridge between those who live with depression and those who don't so treacherous is the baseline incompatibility of our worldviews. There's an idea in psychology called "depressive realism," originated by Lauren Alloy and Lyn Yvonne Abramson, which grimly posits that a depressed mind makes more realistic assessments than one that isn't, which operates with a less-accurate positivity bias. While studies of this hypothesis have had mixed results, when I'm talking with another person who lives with depression, we can fully, jealously admit to seeing other people as deluded weirdos, despite also knowing we are both mentally unwell.

On the flip side, when Brenda finally leaves, I want to purge any reminder of her—including others who know her well. If I'm emerging from a particularly bleak period, life can suddenly feel transcendent—like that natural high that fitness fanatics always blather on about. I wake up in an alternate universe where people are nicer, my senses are sharper, and the idea of getting through a single day doesn't fill me with quicksand-like dread. Talking to friends who are going through a tough time becomes fraught. I don't want to be sucked back in—the veil is thin. Social scientist Robert Weiss writes in his 1975 book, *Loneliness: The Experience of Emotional and Social Isolation*, "If [the subject] had earlier been lonely, they now have no access to the self that experienced the loneliness; furthermore, they very likely prefer that things remain that way. In consequence they are likely to respond to those who are currently lonely with absence of understanding and perhaps irritation." My experience with depression is the same. I fear talking about it too familiarly might summon it back, a Beetlejuice of the brain.

Despite knowing better, I even get impatient when I go to my therapist or psychiatrist in a more optimistic mood, as if suddenly struck with the epiphany that our relationship is a sham. With nothing pressing to address or fix, I lose my bearings. The session plays out like a stilted first date in which I do not keep up my end of the conversation: (after a protracted silence) "I like your scarf?" I can hardly stand being inside because the figurative weather is so nice. I should be out in the world soaking up the good times while I have them! Before Brenda's back. I once tweeted, "Wherever my depression is right now, I hope she's happy." The irony, of course, is that it's thanks to therapy that Brenda only works part time.

Well, not only therapy—psych meds also do some heavy lifting in granting me these beautiful reprieves. I've been on them for over half my life now, and they make an incontrovertible difference in my ability to function. I say that knowing antidepressants are a frequently controversial subject, given they can be prescribed willy-nilly and people can be overmedicated. Big Pharma has plenty of questionable conflicts of interest, especially when research studies can be funded or underwritten by drug companies. Not to mention that multiple close friends and family have expressed their distrust in the mental health infrastructure in this country, mostly due to their own twisted experiences with bad therapists and doctors. And yet, without a doubt, medication has saved my life. My first psychiatrist, who incidentally had a thick eastern European accent (closer to Freudian than I dared dream), prescribed me Prozac. After that, navigating a fun round of "Which Side Effects Don't Ruin Me?" it was a switching game from Zoloft to Celexa then Lexapro. Collect them all!

While it usually takes a few weeks for the mood-altering effects of an antidepressant to kick in, once they do, the results can be utterly transformative. Going on meds felt like the first time I tried shrooms. I experienced life in entirely new frequencies, like I got to a new level in a video game. *Wait, there are colors?!* My major side effect with Lexapro was ongoing drowsiness, which is funny, because even when I could show up to my life, I still preferred to sleep through it. A few times, when my life circumstances were more stable, I tried to go off the peace-of-mind pills, but I could never hack it through the difficult withdrawal process. Then, helpfully doing its part, the Lexapro stopped working as effectively.

After that, I was on the meds merry-go-round, as they say, a cheerful analogy for a joyless ride. During this roundabout, I learned Wellbutrin made me clench my teeth so hard at night that I got daytime headaches. I already grind my jaw at night from anxiety, so with the clenching and the grinding it was like my teeth were doing Peloton. I also cycled through Cymbalta, BuSpar, some natural supplements, getting a new psychiatrist— you name it, I tried it! It's not about the destination, it's about the journey! I realize all these drug names are meaningless to most people, so may I suggest imagining me determinedly flying a kite or kayaking or some other acutely inspiring "after example" in a drug commercial.

I then left Team Pristiq with its winning combo of night sweats and cold fingers and toes for Team Trintellix, which offered both bad nausea and constipation. Who's not at their go-get-'em best while also sick to their stomach? And finally back I am on Prozac. It's all a circle. Eastern philosophy was right.

I'm also on Lamictal, which is a mood-stabilizing drug that is used to treat epilepsy. If you haven't noticed, science barely understands what's going on in the brain. Psych drugs are still often throwing paint at the wall. The idiosyncrasies of Lamictal are a real win-win if you're a drama queen. You increase the dosage extremely gradually when you start taking it, and if you miss more than three doses in a row, you have to start over again from the lowest dose. Other than that, as long as you don't get a life-threatening rash, it's just the standard lookout for dizziness, headaches, nausea, drowsiness, suicidal ideation, you know, the uzhe. By the way, what gets me the most is that suicidal ideation is a common side effect of antidepressants. You might feel better about being alive, but also you may think about killing yourself more! Then again, as Andrew Solomon writes so beautifully in *The Noonday Demon*, "Knowing that if I get through this minute I could always kill myself in the next one makes it possible to get through this minute without being utterly overwhelmed. Suicidality may be a symptom of depression; it is also a mitigating factor."

All the med switching was like dating but for my entire outlook on life. I would have a few good weeks or even months sometimes where I felt a jolt of rejuvenation course through me from my latest drug relationship, and I could take on the semblance of a person with hopes and dreams. Then, inevitably, the spark would wear off and the infestation of dark thoughts would settle back in. It's like the depression got smarter and stronger and did not balk in the face of neurochemical alterations. Once you get used to a certain level of it, though, you start to think, *I guess this is all that life is—a gruelingly unpleasant and frustrating exercise in killing time.* Any memories you have of alternate interpretations now strike you as full-on delusions.

The term "high-functioning depression" is thrown around online, and while it sounds like an achievement or a new workout class, I assure you, it's graded on a curve or, let's be honest, a steep frown. I figured this was my calling card because I didn't fit into the more severe versions of chronic depression I'd read about. While HFD is not an official psychiatric classification, the closest medical term was one WebMD scavenger hunt away. According to the site:

> Dysthymia, sometimes referred to as mild, chronic depression, is less severe and has fewer symptoms than major depression. With dysthymia, the depression symptoms can linger for a long period of time, often two years or longer. Those who suffer from dysthymia can also experience periods of major depression—sometimes called "double

depression." In modern diagnostic classification systems, dysthymia and chronic depression are now both referred to as persistent depressive disorder.

What does dysthymia, or PDD if you hate spelling, look like? Well, though meds and therapy exponentially increase my ability to derive more pleasure from my life, I still consistently experience low moods. Despite them, I do my best to show up to work engagements and other obligations. I cancel more frequently now, though always accessorizing with a chic clutch bulging with guilt. I used to force myself to show up, regardless of how awful I felt, because staying at home meant being alone with the same damning mental playlist on a loop, including the hit bonus track "I Am a Flaky Loser Who Constantly Lets People Down." May as well be a loser in public, not to mention that the dance of "doing" can serve as a stopgap distraction from the infinite destructive thoughts. Only when my baseline depression gets worse do I have trouble self-motivating to even get out of bed, talk to people, or do much besides staring into space fixating on how none of this is worth it. Most of the time, to an untrained eye, I am living my life to its "fullest," but I assure you, I am one hollow chocolate bunny (mind you, still a snack).

One of the more cloying things about less severe depression is that you are in a constant argument with yourself about whether it's that bad or not. Even during a recent rougher bout, I still questioned whether I was being overdramatic. I would wake up every day asking myself if I was faking it. *Am I just trying to get out of stuff?* Despite being completely miserable, I could still autopilot myself through exercise, therapy, bill-paying work obligations— all this despite constant crying, zoning out, and a complete detachment from everything and everyone. *A real depressed person wouldn't even be able to look at a to-do list,* I told myself. The judgment would lead to further self-incrimination. You know you're depressed when you can't even express to your psychiatrist how bad you feel because you can't "present convincingly" enough and you don't feel like trying, you know, because of the depression.

This probably explains why, early on in our sessions, my shrink (why haven't we improved on this term and why am I still using it?) told me she couldn't gauge how I was really doing because I delivered everything in the same level tone. When you're a performer by trade, it's devastating feedback to learn you have resting poker face. I desperately want to be the type rushing into appointments with my sunglasses still on, spilling coffee everywhere, throwing myself down on the couch, and exclaiming, "I'm not long for this world!" I've also been in therapy for almost two decades, and yet, talking about my problems week to week can still feel disgustingly privileged. I imagine myself as a Real Housewife of Utopia, the one who lasts only a season because her story lines aren't all that mesmerizing. At times, I low-key dissociate and think of myself as a friend I'm talking about, because otherwise I cannot be bothered to continue. My default is to intellectualize and discuss my depression only clinically, keeping everyone well out of range of the grotesque parts (the emotional "splash zone"), including, for a very long time, myself. When my therapist ends the session right on time, I feel, yet again, as though I've failed in some way. This feeling only gained fuel when I learned from a friend, herself a therapist, that she has "favorite" patients who endlessly fascinate her. *Always a bridesmaid . . .*

According to the National Institute of Mental Health, 1.5 percent of adult Americans live with dysthymia. The one cool thing about being in this exclusive club is we have a secret headshake. But it doesn't look or sound like the more intense image of depression that is most propagated, which can come across as an implicit message that our suffering is unwarranted. Am I one quick fix away from being totally fine? Maybe I just need to meditate *better*? Then how come every time I sit down to do that, it turns into an art film about thought spirals? If no one else can tell I'm depressed, maybe I'm not depressed?

It is perversely amusing to me that the only time other people seem most concerned about your depression is if you're suicidal. The rest of the time, you'll be fine—it's just like a cold, right? Also, not all depressives are suicidal and not all suicides have to do with depression, or mental illness for that matter. I have had plenty of suicidal ideation in my life, but I've rarely felt capable of expressing it or acting on it. My fear of letting others down and being more work for them has always been too loud to ignore, my self-destructiveness capsized by the idea of inflicting it on others. On a morbid note, I also hate knowing others would have to clean up the mess I leave behind. At least if you don't engineer your own death, you can be held somewhat less accountable for the postmortem chores. If you asked my brain, though, it would helpfully pipe in, *See? You're not even good at hating yourself.* I've even had the fear that I call a suicide hotline but then can't sound suicidal enough. As if I am on the phone with customer service and they need my account number, and I can't find my last monthly statement to prove that I am a paying member.

Truth be told, I had another prolonged bout of severe depression in the recent past. At its worst, being awake felt physically painful and I saw no future at all. I only confided this to my partner, my therapist, and my psychiatrist. I didn't have the presence of mind to tell anyone else, neither family, friends, nor a trained stranger. I became so used to inhabiting a different space in my brain around others that my sense of self cleaved into two entirely different people. I hope I am alone in this hesitation to reach out when I most need to.

Though I know I'm not. The World Health Organization notes that around 280 million people worldwide currently struggle with depression. Due to lack of resources and continued stigma in certain communities, it's almost certainly more. Though the exact manifestation of it can vary greatly in each person despite the similar symptom clusters. It's the same way most people love music, but from there, our tastes completely diverge. Maybe you're more of a smooth jazz Kenny G variety while I'm a high school punk band with one listenable song. For example, in *The Limits of My Language: Meditations on Depression*, Dutch writer and artist Eva Meijer names how she manages her depression by throwing herself into her work. "It makes a difference that I'm an optimistic depressive: I have the urge to realize myself and I'm militant and disciplined," she writes. "I usually work too hard, or harder than most people, at any rate, but that's good—it's better to be tired than dead." Nothing sounds less relatable to me than being depressed and losing myself in my work, and yet, (a) I don't doubt her struggle one bit, and (b) I also "do" when I'm depressed, but it's mostly a whole lot of nothing interspersed with erratic bursts of guilt-driven activity slogs and then criticizing myself for all the nothing. Still, this vast difference in internal experience does explain why everyone is full of useless advice on how to manage yours.

People always mean well when you tell them you can't get a handle on your own depression and they offer ready solutions. You clearly aren't eating right, getting enough sleep, exercising—even just a walk (this mythical healing stroll forever torments me), meditation, and cheering up by thinking more positively. *OK, but I've been trying all of those . . . for decades now?* They venture to guess maybe you're doing them wrong, as if I've been sleeping with both eyes open like a fish and I think meditation means joining a club for zipper collectors? It's the same way people feel so entitled to comment on everyone else's appearance or personal choices, as if to prove the obvious wrongness of others in managing their own lives. If something worked for Person X, they're then convinced it will be your magic fix. Though this may come from a place of generosity, if you find yourself doing this, the truth is not only could your advice not help but it may even make someone feel worse. Instead of offering what the person could do differently, offer something you could do for or with them—give them the option to connect, or to decline. The offer itself can be the gift.

At one point, I was simultaneously trying ketamine infusions (horse tranqs, babe—go big or go home!); a TM (Transcendental Meditation) course; fish oil pills; bright light therapy; and something called a Fisher Wallace neuro-stimulation device (sexy, no?), which involves pulsing electrical signals into your brain twice a day, from the comfort of your home. The possible causes of depression can be a complex interplay of chemical imbalances, genetics, life events such as trauma, and other medications or health issues, so treatment is frequently a Choose Your Own Sadventure. It's extremely frustrating that many people still see depression as personal weakness, when many are fighting with every method at their disposal just to get through another day like everyone else. I'm one of the considerably lucky ones, with insurance and disposable income and time and support. Imagine not having one or any of those things and having to cope with it.

I try to do "all the right things," but when my willpower is low, I give into numbing self-soothing—whether that's staying up for hours zombielike, online shopping for another pair of overalls I don't need (the trend is ruining me and not just because of the public restroom plight) or freebasing triggering social media posts and online searches, the emotional equivalent of self-harm. Get stuck in a depressed mindset long enough and you find yourself constantly negotiating what is you and what is the illness, and are those even distinct entities anymore?

In a delicately powerful essay called "How Do We Survive Suicide?," writer Arianna Rebolini captures how hard it is to trust one's own sense of reality when you are constantly being told your depressed self and its messaging are not really you. "How much does my fear of owning this darker voice hinge on a cultural insistence that it's unhealthy, even unnatural?" She asks, "What if I'm all of it?" She compellingly argues that we need a more nuanced understanding of the mind of a depressed person, especially because it's so likely that the depression will recur. She writes, "Survival is continuous; often, it feels like waiting."

While I've been learning to manage my depression better, it too has been exploring personal growth—finding new notes to play. Over the last few years, I've developed premenstrual dysphoric disorder (PMDD)—it's like PDD but now with 100 percent more "M"! All this means is I get worsening depression leading up to the arrival of my period and sometimes during it as well. As I've grown older, I've come to terms with the fact that I'll never be "cured," which was always a far-fetched hope, I suppose. I've spent enough years trying to become a bright sider to realize, *Have I, this whole time, been trying to stare directly into the sun?* I feel even more at depression's whim than I did when I was younger, though I've come to recognize its cyclical nature. Unwavering in its dogged focus, it buys up my entire vision board with advertising. And that's where the money is, sweetheart.

THE COMEDIAN AND TV WRITER Josh Rabinowitz has a very sharp joke I love about the idea of socially adept people gentrifying the word "awkward" for their own devices, making it standard fare to say one is awkward, leaving bona fide misfits in the lurch. Similarly, in recent years, the term "mental illness" has very much been gentrified (and furthermore, in my observation, most often employed solely as a stand-in term for anxiety and depression).

Depression in particular used to be like a period stain on underwear that's still in rotation—best left unmentioned, but we all know it exists in droves. In many places, it's still like that. But it has always been less about causing disgust and more about escaping the intolerable miasma of pity and shame. Now, in today's late-capitalist, end-of-the-world-cosplay world, if you tell others that you are having trouble doing or caring about anything because of your brain, the standard-issue reaction, at least in my progressive-bougie circles, is inevitably "Welcome to the club" with a paradoxical "silence is complicity" aside. Take five for self-care, and then post a meme and "add to the conversation." After all, who isn't sad and scared? Yes, you're suffering, but it's in the zeitgeist now!

In the Mashable article "How Being Sad, Depressed, and Anxious Online Became Trendy," Jess Joho writes, "Sad Girl culture grew up, became mainstream among celebrity and on the internet, then ironically led to an insincere commodification of both sadness and self-care that was the antithesis of its original intent." The inherent complexity is that I'm glad others can relate to people openly talking about their very real struggles. On the other hand, as Joho notes, "The social media hive mind has rushed to express their own genuine emotional distress with the intention of helping to normalize, destigmatize, and relate. . . . In our haste, though, we might've forgotten the fundamental and vital distinction between sad feels and the terms used to diagnose mental disorders, like anxiety and depression."

For example, the reality program *The D'Amelio Show* features the most popular TikTok star with hundreds of millions of followers, eighteen-year-old Charli D'Amelio, as well as her sister Dixie, and their parents, each with their own satellite of multimillion followings. The first episode covers the importance of mental health by depicting Dixie's struggles with online haters. Writes Amanda Hess in *The New York Times Magazine*, "The self-care narrative, with its air of drama and resilience, has an aspirational quality. Prioritizing mental health becomes both a brave accomplishment and a luxury. It all encourages more investment in social media, not less." This despite findings by *The Wall Street Journal* that Facebook withheld Instagram's damaging psychological effects on teenage girls, including increases in rates of anxiety and depression.

Expanding on that notion, in "I Feel Better Now" via *The Baffler,* Jake Bittle writes how the stigma of these mental disorders no longer seems to apply to young, urban, middle-class demographics of the population. He writes, "The same consumerist culture that once shunned mention of depression now also seeks to cannibalize its language for use in advertising and media." Not only is it brave for influencers and those already in the public eye to confess their struggles, but it's made into a generous act of spreading awareness when it could just as easily be argued that it's simply another strategy to get ahead.

I would argue the alternative to stigmatization is not unchecked, unbridled fervor. Like Oprah yelling, "You have depression! And you have depression! And you have depression!" at an eager audience, ready to trust fall into the cultural inclination. I'm in no way arguing the dangerous and damaging idea that anxiety and depression, or any mental illness for that matter, are contagious like the flu, but rather that they are complex disorders that require careful, thoughtful understanding. There is some danger in treating them like a "fun" or "buzzy" identity that can be managed with the right memes. There's a very fine line between acceptance and exploitation.

In the *New Yorker* piece "The Rise of Therapy-Speak," Katy Waldman discusses the rise of mental health and psychoanalytic lingo in everyday parlance and concludes it's not necessarily a bad thing. She considers, "Wasn't it disrespectful to toss around terms—trauma, depression—that can imply so much suffering? . . . The psychologists I spoke to surprised me: steeped in a counter-history of silence about and vilification of mental illness, they could not bring themselves, it seemed, to worry about this particular aspect of therapy-speak's rise." Normalizing forwards the dial on progress, even at the risk of oversaturation, right? I'm not so sure. The terms themselves have started to lose meaning in their prevalence. There is the breezy, monetizable version of depression (cancel your plans, stay in your pj's all day, order GrubDash!) and then there's actual depression (far, far less profit and product placement). It's clear they don't mean the same thing.

In her groundbreaking book *How Emotions Are Made: The Secret Life of the Brain*, decorated psychology researcher Lisa Feldman Barrett argues that our emotions are a result of how our bodies budget themselves. In other words, our physical state determines our emotions, which then determine our thoughts. This is a complete inversion of the widespread and long-understood assumption that our thoughts determine our emotions, which dates all the way back to the Greek philosophers. Barrett argues that both "depression" and "anxiety" are catchall terms for a varied constellation of symptoms, so much so that the two often end up conflated. Her explanation is that "people will use whatever measure you give them to describe how they feel. If someone feels crappy and you give her only an anxiety scale, she'll report her feelings using words for anxiety. She might even come to feel anxious as the words prime her to simulate an instance of 'Anxiety.'" In other words, while one can clinically suffer from anxiety and depression (and so many do!), there is also a degree of suggestibility to both, meaning their leaching into the mainstream could in effect be rippling out the perceived experience of them. For example, when I am depressed, I find I can do little besides steeping not only in my dark thoughts and flattened affect but also in the very idea of being depressed, which then perpetuates it. While this broad shift is assuredly making these terms more accessible and acceptable, could it also be diluting the definitions of the words themselves for the average layperson?

While incidences of mental distress are unquestionably increasing among people, I'd also assume that anxiety and depression have been co-opted by the media and the market at large in response to the increasing terror and hopelessness of the world—the rise of fascism, climate change, mass shootings, genocides—that's all in a day's headlines. Yes, on one hand, the information age has allowed more people to freely share and commune about their experiences, but as we've seen with all aspects of online life, the algorithms operate along the guidelines of what keep the user clicking and scrolling.

When I was first diagnosed, I wasn't at all aware of the cultural implications of talking about my depression or not talking about it. Rather, practically giddy with the new explanation for my unwieldy mind, I liberally mentioned it to friends, family, and even strangers. "Something you should know about me is that I have depression!" I brightly sang like the hero in a musical, threatening to undermine my own truth. After not talking about it for so long, I was trying to make up for lost time. It was the ultimate note from the doctor, not to get out of PE class, but to explain my inability to readily embrace life. For a long time, I thought of it as the most interesting thing about me. Seeing depression's rise in airtime over the years strikes me as less comforting than it should perhaps, but only because of a petty sense of indignation. *I've been doing this for years*, I huff at a headline about how much Gen Z has embraced openly talking about their mental health. My delicate widdle ego demands relevance over appreciating positive social change. Unfortunately, as with all things under capitalism, it's only so long before the brand opportunities step in.

I can't say what the endgame of overly commodifying mental illness is, but it doesn't undo the current reality. According to current statistics, more young people than ever are legitimately struggling, but the potential for abuse is also there. There have always been snake-oil salespeople, self-proclaimed experts, and false prophets (all hail the Dunning-Kruger effect), but the sheer potential reach of social media influencers is a new development. Some are giving mental health advice that isn't always professionally sound, not to mention providing an oversimplification of having mental illness itself. As Barrett noted, if someone is convinced that they have one of the two, they may as well have them.

The teen suicide rate has been steadily increasing in the US since 2007, rising 56 percent in only ten years. Similarly, a CDC study conducted in 2021 found that 44 percent of American high school students reported experiencing "persistent feelings of sadness or hopelessness," the highest number ever recorded. Not only that but the upward trend in worsening mental health predates the pandemic and is true across all demographics: queer, straight, all ethnicities, all genders, both sexually active and inactive teens, every year of high school, and in all fifty states plus the District of Columbia.

In a piece for *The Atlantic* instructively called "Why American Teens Are So Sad," Derek Thompson posits increased social media usage as a significant contributing factor. He cites both the constant onslaught of negative-bias media coverage of the world's ills, as well as young people spending far more time on their phones in place of constructive activities such as sleeping, learning to drive, going out with friends, and playing sports. He also makes the important distinction that "social media isn't like rat poison, which is toxic to almost everyone. It's more like alcohol: a mildly addictive substance that can enhance social situations but can also lead to dependency and depression among a minority of users." However, it's important to note that studies connecting social media use and increased self-harm or suicidality have had mixed results and sometimes contradictory findings, so rather than looking at social media alone, it's more helpful to categorize it as one factor in a world that moves increasingly faster and louder with the technological revolution.

Capturing the full nuances around discussing mental illness in terms of diagnosis and treatment should go beyond the profit-driven algorithms of the internet. I'm not arguing for a moral panic where the broad embrace of living with mental illness online in and of itself is dangerous, but all these disturbing trends do highlight the necessity of further research and analysis, rather than constant back-patting and celebration about how freely we use the words "panic attack" now.

Whether to a clinical degree or not, the truth is that not only teens but more and more people of all ages are anxious and depressed. Perhaps this has always been true and it's now evident only because the stigma of talking about it has been reduced and informational resources are more readily available. But now that the conversation is being had, shouldn't we also be asking why these experiences are so prevalent and what the causes are? Studies have demonstrated that these fraught emotional states are the frequent by-products of industrialization and that they contribute to the stressful conditions of modern life, loneliness being one of these factors. The free market lays all the onus on the individual to better themselves, while the larger, destructive infrastructure remains in place.

In an interview on *The Ezra Klein Show*, author and activist Sarah Schulman commented, "I want to make the work that I want to make and I think other artists should be able to make the work that they want to make. But when your work is seized upon by a corporate society and elevated, then you have to analyze its reception, and that's part of your responsibility to the collective." I don't read this as an artist being responsible for every reaction to their work. I think Schulman means when the sensitive topics you are raising in your work become commodified culturally, as with, say, a different example, the corporatization of the Pride Parade, it's important to think through what exactly you are trying to say and how you are trying to say it in case these developments might change anything for you. Maybe it's not necessarily my job as an artist, but it is my responsibility as a citizen of the world. This can also help distinguish my own message from the mainstream's tendency to seize trends and then sanitize them of any complexity. In their work, artists have been increasingly open about their own mental health, and we're long overdue to talk about it in a more multifaceted, less generic way as a culture. Most especially because we've still yet to open the conversation fully—to the people who most need it, rather than based exclusively on subsections designated by factors like race and class, not to mention overall accessibility.

AS A COMEDIAN, openly joking about my mental health struggles in my stand-up and on social media (before it was *cool*, which is as *Black Mirror* as it gets) has been a push-pull struggle, a constant switch-flip between empowerment and doubt. I've long draped myself in self-deprecating humor like a generous caftan that protects against the unforgiving eye of outward criticism. I began comedy holding everything at a safe distance, converting my insecurities into quips so that I didn't have to fully withstand others' opinions of me. My early material featured jokes about my body and personality, but I soon dug deeper inward.

And though I've rarely been on the pulse of any trend, as of now, the examination of mental health in art is all the rage. Either that or I've gravitated toward a community in which it's perpetually on the upswing, like the return of bell-bottom jeans. But it's hard to discount the current climate, despite the age-old trope of the sad clown. As the bummer of a story goes, all comedians, heck, all artists—if you prefer to think of them as one faceless, sensitive lump—are in pain. Process? That *is* their process. We're in a moment now in which the archetype demands interrogation beyond face-value acceptance. *Yes, show us where you hurt, but don't gloss over it. Really dig in there and turn that discontent into content so that we may relate, like, post, and share.* We're in the "don't worry, because your current torment is tomorrow's cheeky tote bag" phase. This inner turmoil is most often tied to comedians, writers, and artists, as if to instill them and their work with more depth. But health-care and emergency workers have some of the highest rates of both depression and suicide of any professional field—and that was before COVID-19.

A comedian friend of mine once told me he was afraid of going on medication because he thought a more stable version of himself wouldn't be as funny. This isn't a new or rare belief. But as someone who essentially got the courage to try stand-up because I was in the antidepressant "honeymoon" period—that initial burst of euphoria from first going on meds—I'm squarely in the opposite camp. When I'm mired in depression, I can rarely generate any ideas outside of that mindset. Screw self-expression. The attention economy can bite me. (There's your subversive tote quote.)

Are there comedians who struggle with mental illness? Yes. Do all comedians struggle with mental illness? No. It does appear many of us have unconventional brains, though. Being prone to overanalyze or perceive the world to one's own detriment or "outside the box" is likely to be a proclivity of the comic's mind, though I don't think it's a prerequisite. Constantly questioning why everything is the way it is and why any of us are here can be the seedy underbelly of figuring out what is funny about life. Both are dissecting the inherent absurdity and contradictions of existence and reality. As Sigmund Freud pointed out in his book *Jokes and Their Relation to the Unconscious*, comedy is about making the meaningful meaningless and vice versa.

Both the comedian brain and a brain subject to anxiety and depression take nothing at face value. Some of us are lucky enough to have both—a two-headed-monster mind. We're constantly searching, questioning, and foraging some hahas and hehes along the way, but ultimately are left to face the same blank void of nonanswers. Best job in the world!

I have often gotten the question "What made you start talking about your struggles with mental health in your act? Was it a conscious decision?" My routine, somewhat shallow answer is that I started talking about it because the topic was dominating my personal airwaves. I wish the story were punchier, shinier, an enticing slice of kismet, but the truth is I was lost so deep inside my own distortions that I could no longer see outside of them. Sometimes when you are stuck, all you can do is splash around in your own mental mud puddle. The jokes were ripped straight from my headlines. Lucky for me, neither the anxiety nor the depression was debilitating enough that I lost the ability to write anything at all. When my brain is too hostile, I tend to dissociate so that I can write about my experience as if it were happening to someone else. I was so tired of trying to fix this part of my life without success that contextualizing and delivering it to strangers was a way of regaining control. Maybe in that sense, initially tweeting about it and talking about it onstage was an act of rebellion for me. *Yeah, I want to die, but at least I'm creating content.* That could be the motto of late-stage capitalism.

Whenever peers or the media cite me as a comedian who isn't afraid to talk about my own personal experience living with mental illness, I like to quickly point out that many, many other comics whom I look up to have deftly talked about the very same thing both onstage and off. Here's twelve (of countless more): Maria Bamford, Gary Gulman, Sarah Silverman, Hannah Gadsby, Chris Gethard, Naomi Ekperigin, Neal Brennan, Patton Oswalt, Marc Maron, Leighann Lord, Giulia Rozzi, and Liz Miele. There have been multiple podcasts interviewing comedians and other creatives about their experiences with depression alone. Now, it's true that I'm a soft-spoken, self-effacing Asian American woman, so maybe that's the new hook? When I first started talking about it, I hardly thought I was forging new ground. If anything, it was the other extreme—I figured I had nothing fresh to add. There is no worse crime for a comedian than being seen as "hacky"—that is, doing derivative material on topics that have already been covered a zillion times. I had to learn that telling your specific story can be valuable whether it's pioneering or unique or genius or dynamic or not, which is hard in an industry whose tagline is "Gimme the shiny new new!!!"

I do know that the better my career was going, the worse I felt, which, by no small coincidence, followed the exact timeline of when I started talking about mental health in my act. There was a span of a few years during which I recorded an album, taped half-hour specials for both Comedy Central and Netflix, did multiple sets for late night, got cast and acted in multiple seasons of a TV show, sold a script with a friend to Hulu, wrote for my first narrative show and acted on it as well, and sold this book. (Trust me, it was more painful for me to write all that than it was for you to read it. Who do I think I am?!) But through all this, my mental health declined, and because my work achievements reflected the opposite of my well-being, I had the sinking feeling that I was allergic to success. If all the hard work of pursuing my dream was to get to a certain point of self-sustaining autonomy, then why did every new opportunity bring me more self-doubt and confusion?

I was once asked on a panel, "If you deal with both anxiety and depression, how do you manage them enough to not only perform regularly, but also write material about them?" I trotted out some gibberish about listening to and honoring my needs, but even today, it's a question I'm struggling to answer. The truth is, in certain ways, I worry that being so willfully open has been to my own detriment, complicating my relationship with my own well-being.

Strangely enough, this is what I have had the most trouble being transparent about—constantly relaying my experience of mental illness in the abstract, via the clinical remove of stand-up bits or social media jokes to anonymous audiences—all while being unable to share the very much ongoing experience of it in real time. It's the difference between "I am a person who deals with these things in my life, and look at me expressing it all polished" and "I am dealing with this right now, and it's not quippy or pithy or funny or interesting. If anything, it's probably frustrating and annoying to you." When you are physically sick, people are OK with your bowing out of things. When you are mentally sick, but not necessarily to the outward eye, room for empathy is frequently diminished. I often felt too mentally unable to tour or show up to do a friend's podcast, and that was the hardest part—constantly letting others down. When it came to my own increased absences, I began making up excuses and becoming defensive, convinced that nobody wanted to hear the real reasons. The cumulative shame from this deception led to an acute sense of loneliness. The biggest kicker of all? While all of this was happening, I was being praised for openly talking about mental illness and gaining opportunities from it. Whaddaya know, it turns out anxiety and depression don't fit neatly into the bounds of ambition, achievement, and success.

Many times, I found myself actively depressed or anxiously spiraling at a comedy show while making jokes about anxiety and depression. It created a split idea of myself: the comedian who can relate to people on vulnerable topics versus the person who is struggling and operating on autopilot. Even trickier for me is that there's a freedom in not caring with stand-up, but this is also the gateway state to full-on depression for me. I call this mind state "empowered apathy." It's the window between when I first start checking out of the hotel of life and full-blown misery. It's a break from the continual, needy ego roulette that is anxiety, and in that sense, it comes as a huge relief. I conveniently forget that it's also a sign that things are not headed in a great direction.

I finally decided to take a break from performing, which lasted close to three years. Thank goodness for hindsight, right? Nobody wants to hear about your lows until you're on the other side of them, because when you're in them, you're what's known as a wild card. I find it a fascinating by-product of modern life that you're only considered someone worth listening to once you're rational and levelheaded, and able to reframe past life experience into present acceptance and future wisdom.

I still experience the throes of paralyzing anxiety and dread when it comes to performing. I've garnered some explanations via talk therapy of what my fears are: fear of letting others down, fear of being found out as a fraud, fear of facing my true mediocrity, fear of running out of time. But I haven't managed to shift them or rewrite them out of existence, and that's the relentlessness of anxiety and depression: showing up day after day hoping to move the needle even a centimeter. That small amount of space can make all the difference.

Maybe being a spokesperson for anything inherently makes you question your relationship to it. It also turns out that being a spokesperson for mental illness means not always being the most dependable spokesperson, and not just because of the constant second-guessing of self. You may frequently be unable to show up for the job. That's the part of mental illness that isn't conveyed nearly enough. It's not just reposting a list of grounding reminders on Instagram because the experience can vary in specificity from person to person (not to mention I've found not checking social media has been better for me than all the depression awareness posts in the world). There is no one-size-fits-all approach to mental illness, and as much as we want it to neatly fit into a pitch-perfect one-liner or a convenient app or a suicide hotline, it's much too smart for that.

IT'S BEEN MORE than two decades since my initial diagnosis, and I'm now ambivalent about how much I've normalized depression and anxiety as part of my identity. I worry that in aligning myself with them so closely, I have allowed them too much ownership over who I am. Perhaps I should have lawyered up early on and negotiated a more contractual relationship? Only partial custody of my brain?

As disorders that weave together nature and nurture, it's hard to tell what caused what and when. Is it situational or genetic this time, or both? I do know being in a field based primarily on external validation doesn't help my brain's tendencies, that's for sure. Depression and anxiety can resemble a voice that sounds just like your own, as their core messaging feels like it's built into the very foundation of your brain. Insidious in the same way as the internet, they make you think you clicked on something because you chose it yourself, when it's algorithms and manipulative marketing that sent you down this path.

I'm hardly suggesting there's no value in being forthright about one's personal struggles, and not just because of the need for representation of every way of being in this vast, lonely, difficult, frequently terrible world. After all, "laughing about tough topics" is the subject of every other media panel that comedians are asked to do. At this point, I could have a hologram fill in for me. Plus, there is a Rube Goldbergian ease to a joke that skirts the fickle irresolution of life. I write the setup, the boot kicks the tennis ball, the tennis ball rolls into the empty fish tank, the vibration from the tank shifts the lever, and we all arrive at the punch line together, released and born anew. Unguardedly talking about mental illness, even via the deflection of humor, is still talking about it.

But if I'm relating my ongoing experiences with anxiety and depression in my act to be "honest" and "authentic" (alas, a highly trafficked word that's become a parody of itself), aren't I also exploiting my own struggles, cashing in on the fault lines of my pain for professional, often monetary, gain? Am I romanticizing mental illness, as an internet first responder (a tidy euphemism for the "um, actually" variety of troll) once put it, strategically slotting my paradoxically untidy yet polished persona into the latest online catchall ethos? Many (L-U-C-K-Y!) years of resources and support later, I wonder whether I might have exercised some caution in broadcasting painful aspects of my inner experience to others, without considering how opening it up for public consumption might affect me.

I thought I was speaking only of my own real experience, but it's all been subsumed into the slobbering maw of the free market. Against all odds, anxiety and depression became the popular girls, via several VC-backed makeovers that threw off their glasses, de-frizzed their hair, and erased their pores. The messy, unsexy manifestations of mental illness filtered through the Portrait Mode, clean-lined freedom of being an "Anxiety Queen," which, I'm horrified to inform you, is an actual T-shirt. And if we're going to sell that, then where, I ask, are the "Parkinson's Princess" hoodies? While being open in my work felt inspiring and empowering at first, mental illness is a patient foe. However long it's dormant, whenever it returns, Brenda convinces you she drew strength from whatever power you thought you had. She's the main character of the story—not you. There is no sassy mug for that.

I don't regret addressing my mental health in my act because it's true to my experience, but did it also lead to unforeseen complications in my own life and, for lack of a less pretentious term, creative journey? Yes, both are true, which is a great illustration of the reality of living with mental illness.

The actual experience of living with anxiety and depression does not fit tidily into the boxes of profit or buzzworthiness. It's frequently uncomfortable and alienating, no matter how many times a somber talking head in a PSA insists, "You're not alone." No matter how much you share your experience with others, being stuck inside a bad episode of either is still one of the most impenetrable, isolating experiences in the world.

One lesson my skewed brain has taught me time and again is life doesn't tell you what the point is, ever. My depression's favorite line is: *Figure out why you deserve to be here. I'll wait.* The constant negotiating of self can undo you. In fact, even laying out all these doubts and reservations about talking about mental health feels like a snake eating its own poisonous tail—as if voicing them might immediately bastardize my intent. Now, is that my mental illness talking or my own intuition? It's constant improvised choreography simply to get out of my own way. If more and more of us are ending up in this place, we need to figure out what to do now that we're here.

Expanding the conversations about living with mental illness means fully facing the frequently unpalatable aspects of how it manifests and doing that with more than just strangers online. While it's undeniably valuable to open dialogues and reduce stigma on social media, it cannot replace in-person understanding. This can include professionals, friends, family—chosen or otherwise—as well as additional trusted sources. There is no way to undo the experience of living with mental illness, but as a society, we can do better than just blanket posting a crisis helpline number.

In a moment of need, of course, perhaps a thoughtful post or a hilarious video does make a world of difference, but it can't be the sole means of doing the work for yourself or showing up for someone else. Inching in the direction of peace, for me, at least, has meant not falling into the trap of equating my entire existence with what I create and put out into the world. I am still negotiating the impact on myself, and what to do moving forward, and I know I'll never find all the answers. But there's meaning in trying, and meaning can be everything.

Confessions:
The Body Electric

I know we all made an agreement when the modern age started not to scratch certain places on our bodies in public, but hear me out, I think it might be holding us back. Who can be their best self when their armpit is begging for an itch? At the very least, scratch pods? Then nonsmokers like me would have the excuse equivalent of a cool cigarette break. "I'm gonna take five and make things right with my left boob."

All the guys I've dated have been shyer and more discreet about pooping than I am. I didn't get the memo that women don't poop, because all I do is poop. (Peeing is for birthdays and holidays.) Clearly, there was some sort of factory error, and I'm certainly not going to enable the government cover-up around it.

Speaking of which, one time when I was a kid, I ate Count Chocula for every meal for two weeks straight,* and then, for about the same amount of time, I could not poop.

---

* No, my parents didn't realize this was happening. It was a covert-ops mission.

———

About a decade ago, I discovered I pick my nose in my sleep. And now you too must live with this information.

Smells I love that no one else seems to care for:

Gasoline

That's it. That's the list. Considering the impact of this odor on the well-being of the planet, not to mention international diplomacy, my nose may be corrupt.

Without shame, I am a book sniffer. I like burying my nose deep in the crevice where the binding and the page meet each other and flaring my nostrils to get the deepest whiff possible. It's a heady scent and comforting to me in its familiarity, natural but with industrial undertones. When it's a novel, I wonder if the characters are like "Ewww, she's doing it again."

My partner told me there's a known phenomenon that when some people smell books, especially old ones in a library or a used bookstore, they get the overwhelming urge to poop. It doesn't happen to everyone, but it's apparently enough that the Japanese have a term for it, the Mariko Aoki phenomenon. That must be why some people keep books in their bathroom. It's just common sense.

To Do or Not to Do

Could That Be Me?

An alarm clock

With no hands

Ticking loudly

On the town dump

—*Charles Simic*

Caution: *Topics discussed ahead include the behind the scenes of writing this very book, which is to say, those familiar dirges and long, dark nights of the soul that show up with any type of creative work. Proceed at your own risk of eye rolls.*

One shudder-inducing query frequently lobbed at artists and creators is "What's your process?" It's the fedora of questions: unnecessary, overly pleased with itself, and everywhere you don't want it to be.

I wouldn't be so bothered if the subtext weren't begging for a business

bestseller of an answer. Our productivity-obsessed culture* craves an aspirational vision of cheery routines: gently sipped mugs of piping hot coffee, window nook offices with playful slants of light and winky signs like NO MATTER
WHAT IT LOOKS LIKE, I'M WORKING, and regularly scheduled inspiration-
generation activity blocks masquerading as "me time" like midday decoupage
or a twilight constitutional. I know these details not from any personal experience but because I've read them in interviews with those suspicious specimens seemingly designed in military labs. You know the ones, you can find
them all listed on *Forbes Jr.*'s "5 under 5." For the rest of us, though, the truth
hangs limply from a pull-up bar as people aggressively grunt and yell in the
background, like a first (and last) day of reluctant CrossFit (I had a gift card).

Asking someone about their own fraught dance with the muse is essentially saying, "Lie to me and make it pretty."

Don't get me wrong. I understand why artists are asked about process.
It's one part dispelling the spiritual mystique of creation and one hundred
parts garden-variety nosiness. It's the same reason everyone wants to know
what a well-loved celebrity was like if you encountered them in person—you
better cough up that yes, Ryan Gosling's eyes are indeed deep infinity pools
and not that he cut in front of you on line at Trader Joe's (to which one will
reply, *Are you sure it was him?*). In that sense, people like to imagine that the
day-to-day of creating art is "romantic" and "escapist" compared with drier
professions or more thankless types of work.

Then again, everyone's process is of interest these days. In *The New Yorker*,
Rachel Syme refers to our collective obsession with knowing how everyone
else manages their days as "time voyeurism." She writes, "Everywhere you
look, people are either hitting deadlines or avoiding them by reading about

---

* If they were given the opportunity, I wouldn't be shocked if journalists would ask people of interest
who have recently passed on, "So obviously your major project this year was death. What's up next
on your plate?"

how other people hit deadlines. This may seem like a sly way of marrying procrastination with productivity (you're biding your time learning how to better manage your time), but, no matter what, it's an exhausting treadmill of guilt and ostentation, virtue signaling, and abject despair at falling behind." Nestled within this gimlet-eyed curiosity is the Protestant ethos of wanting to better ourselves—we're all one measly life hack away from marrying total optimization with that monkey's paw of an advice cliché: "Find a job you love, and you'll never have to work a day in your life." Whoever said that must have exclusively been on the night shift.

For me, bingeing on other people's schedules is just another form of self-harm—to confirm I am lazy and unfocused and lack passion. But ever the obedient self-help student (if I buy one more pop psychology book, I get a free hoagie), I once optimistically enrolled in an online class meant to teach me how to slow down and reframe my automatic worship of "efficiency" and "doing." Cue the obvious—I never finished it. From a distance, one could argue I graduated with honors. Who eased up more than the person who dropped out entirely? Don't answer that. (I stopped going because my schedule picked up.)

My own creative process is frustrating and grayscale boring. That beguiling form known as inspiration frequently ghosts me. She sees my "U up?" text and not only ignores but deletes. I'm probably listed in her phone as "DON'T." For every work of art "completed" (in and of itself, a philosophical riddle), there are "ten" (lowballing here to preserve ego) that never see daylight. As a self-employed creative (dry heaves), recounting my day pitches me into all manner of defensiveness. My schedule, which is itself a generous euphemism, includes several bouts of MMA fights with my shadow self. As exciting as those might sound, there's no actual action involved. Cue me savagely avoiding starting anything approaching a priority and then immediately second-guessing it after I do start. Elbow strike to my sense of purpose!

I've always had a shaky relationship with getting things done. I zigzag along at an erratic natural tempo, both upholding and resisting capitalism's drill sergeant orders with every pore in my resentful yet guilt-ridden body. My hybrid psyche contains type A fixations (competitive, detail oriented, results obsessed) coupled with type B reflexes (meandering, distracted, hypnotized by the steady passage of time like it's one of those screen savers of sensuous shapes). Exhibit 27: I have started taking daily constitutionals to allow my brain and body time to look at trees and breathe and move. This habit, however, born of visions of self-care, has slowly but surely mutated into power walking through the park while I listen to all my news podcasts at one and a quarter speed, cursing any errant toddlers who cross my path. It remains unclear if this walk is lowering or heightening my stress level at this point. I also compulsively make to-do lists, but they're the same as all the houses I save on Zillow—aspirational to a fault. *She lost me at indoor gazebo.*

On a random weekday during the 2020 pandemic quarantine (i.e., Phase I, so recalibrate expectations as needed), here's what my live-in partner did. Let's call him Tippy to take the edge off what I'm about to tell you, so that you're picturing a talented Labradoodle instead. Tippy put in a full day at his corporate job, filled any spare moments by working on his own small business, reorganized an entire room of our apartment that I've been avoiding for close to a year now, and prepared dinner, which was incidentally my job [flamenco dancer with sunglasses emoji]. The dinner was white bean ribollita, which is a flavorful veggie Tuscan stew with Parmesan-sprinkled toast baked on top of it. Does that sound gratuitously unreal (correct) . . . not just the stew, but Tippy's whole day topped off with the stew, which was itself topped off with cheesy bread?

That very same day, in that very same apartment, mere feet away from this titan of industry, I woke up late because I am self-employed and keep going to bed late because nothing creates a sense of urgency like 2:00 a.m.

for googling "what does it mean if my arm tingles" (which is a real portal to hell, let me tell you). My accomplishments included preparing quick-cook oatmeal (the word "cook" is still in there, thank you); whittling my sense of worth down to a smart little stick—oops, I said that wrong, I mean scrolling Instagram; and spending seven to ten minutes dislodging a piece of apple from between my teeth, relying on no outside help, only tongue! While that may sound like a fruitless activity, it was full of fruit. Upon finally freeing the sliver, I experienced a huge, perhaps disproportionate sense of pride, wondered for a second why my real gifts are so devalued in this world, and then promptly blacked out from the rush of achievement.

Between Tippy and myself, I do wonder how some of us can steadily produce, accomplish, and generate, and some of us can't stop stalling and buffering despite the dogmatic programming, like existential Energizer Bunnies, lying on our sides, beating our little drums in protest, softly weeping behind those sunglasses. For most of my life thus far, I've accepted constant doing as canon. Now I wonder what this lack of imagination has cost me. To come to the realization lately that it's a steadily crumbling facade is hard to reconcile with the entrenched belief that it means I'm not "hungry" enough. It's worth noting the use of the word "hungry" when it comes to work, as if it's an essential human drive without which we as a species would perish. In her book *Do Nothing*, journalist Celeste Headlee questions whether this framing isn't a result of, among other factors, the industrial age, Protestantism, and the self-made model of the American dream. Maybe I'm not hungry because nothing looks good.

THE UNDERLYING EXPECTATION in my family was to be as productive as possible, whenever possible. The only Pledge of Allegiance we made was to the clock. Time was a diminishing resource, visualized as a permanent countdown in the lower righthand corner of our lives. If a "fun" activity was on the docket, like going out to dinner or a movie, it was framed as a justified reward for all the tasks checked off first.

I don't mean to paint my parents as overbearing tyrants. They weren't. Like many first-generation immigrants, they valued hard, high-quality work and familial responsibility. When you're making a life for yourself in an unfamiliar country, the focus is on integration and survival, rather than pondering self-analysis. Work now, figure out the meaning later, or never. The one loophole was going to the library, a sacred place of learning, and the benefactor shepherding me through my entire adolescent nightlife. This hallowed ground for parent and child alike allowed for cover with its wide-armed acceptance of reading. I could sneak in popular cultural downloads such as the Baby-Sitters Club and anything by Judy Blume, as well as the manifold works of one R. L. Stine. Our family crest may as well have been a giant book.

The mentality only propagated as I got older. I attended a hypercompetitive public magnet high school where I was surrounded by overachievers like they were a protective huddle of elephants shielding me from the dangerous belief that I, independent of my achievements, was enough. My driven peers simultaneously won science fairs and debate tournaments, captained sports teams, ran for student government president and won (or angled for some adjunct position to pad their résumés), started their own community service efforts, cultivated interesting hobbies, and still somehow had time to be teenagers on the side. I had a friend who unironically played the harp—you read that right, the instrument of angels. The prevalent idea was that you should be optimizing every area of your life. Otherwise, what was wrong with you? Further evidence the place was a breeding ground for future workaholics and high blood pressure: in one free-period offering called Learn to Relax, we laid down on the gym floor while a teacher led us through a guided meditation. I always fell asleep (me at my most grounded).

Instead of feeling invigorated in these competitive environments, I felt shame. Work was only meant to be enjoyed insofar as it could be achieved and committed to a CV. Accomplishment was an ever-lengthening Hogwarts measuring stick that found me lacking. Despite passing in these environments by getting the right grades, doing equivalent extracurriculars, and being on the same top-tier, college-driven track, I never quite synced up with the motivation to constantly produce results. In school, I stayed in line with everyone around me simply to not unfavorably stick out. But deep down, I knew I wasn't into any of it. I bought into the system only as a stepping stone to the perpetually promised carrot of something better that would come later. You may know it as that timeless logic brought to you by Big Religion? I didn't know yet what that carrot would be, but I assumed it was coming in cake form.

My parents were both doctors, so their work felt unimpeachable because they were literally saving lives. But I wasn't at all interested in following suit. Whatever your parents do, it's pretty much automatically uncool—even if you have unlimited access to textbooks of naked bodies sporting various afflictions and maladies in your home, all with black bars over their eyes (because they'd rather not look at your sorry, gawping face). Instead, I went sprinting in the other direction. My only steady interests were reading as escapism and daydreaming and, toward the latter half of high school, comedy. I felt completely out of step with everyone around me but assumed if I followed the instruction manual, I'd end up somewhere that made sense. That's the promise, after all. But what I mistook for a road was, in fact, a treadmill. What I thought was forward momentum turned into the same chilling loop of scenery over and over again—more strip malls than mountains.

As I got older and retained more control over my own schedule, I was permanently dissatisfied with myself no matter how much or little I did that day. When I didn't get enough done, it confirmed my inherent lack of drive. When I got enough done, it required so much effort in just getting started, I'd be left overwhelmed at the prospect of ever attempting it again. I'd try to envision a fresh start the next day, knowing full well I'd inevitably struggle. This self-fulfilling prophecy of extreme procrastination followed me through life. I wrote my college senior psych thesis in the two weeks before the deadline by pulling back-to-back-to-back all-nighters, despite having months to do it. As a result, I routinely fell asleep in *one-on-one* meetings with my thesis adviser—a truly advanced skill I would not recommend attempting, let alone visualizing. She was kind enough to pretend not to notice. I once had a college gig that required a half-hour original comedic presentation, and I didn't come up with the whole thing until the three-hour train ride to the show. What can I say? I'm very good at what I don't do.

At every office job I had before doing comedy full-time, I busied myself staring down the clock, opening dozens of non-work-related browser tabs and "multitasking," by which I mean rushing to do everything required of me at the last possible minute. When I landed my first showbiz job writing for late night, I was convinced everything would change given that it was my "big break." Cue canned laughter forever. Most comedy writing jobs follow the traditional structure of a full day of work in an office environment complete with a lunch break and weekends off. Over the course of the workday, I'd get mired in my own self-doubt, buck against the structure, and lose any ability to focus. Later, as a monologue writer, I had three deadlines throughout a given show day. After the first month or so of trying to be responsible, I returned to form and put off writing jokes for as long as possible, hastily cranking them out as quickly and shoddily as I could. When it came to my worst fears about myself and my abilities, I was only too happy to prove myself right.

———

WHAT MAY FURTHER muddy the waters, or not at all if you share the trait, is that I was and remain a dyed-in-the-wool perfectionist. That's another side effect of having workaholic parents with high expectations of themselves and those around them. Your own standards become so daunting, it's easier not to start anything at all. Also, if you save everything until the last minute, you can blame your haste for the quality of the work. In his perspective-shifting, anti–time management book *Four Thousand Weeks* (why, yes, the average human life span), Oliver Burkeman calls this type of procrastination "emotional avoidance." Rather than worrying about how long it will take you to get something done, it's more about facing your own discomfort in not being able to create anything good enough. He notes, "Better to cherish an ideal fantasy than to resign [yourself] to reality, with all its limitations and unpredictability."

When you haven't started the work yet, infinite possibilities exist for how great it can and will be—after all, the future outcome is a boundless, hopeful, glowing abstraction. Once you start, though, you quickly realize you are human, the work will be human, and nothing will even come close to your highlight reel of a candy-coated, delusional imagination. Picture a friend reading your first draft and being brought to tears of enlightenment. Doing work as a perfectionist is 99 percent getting out of your dreams and into reality's car, straight into honking, bumper-to-bumper traffic. Enjoy the ride!

Even more helpfully, the amount of resistance and anticipatory dread that comes up is conveniently customized and proportionate to the task at hand—so the longer and more involved and invested I am in the work, the worse the pushback. No matter how excited I was about the project in the first place, as soon as it's time to do it, I'm surrounded by an uncrossable moat

of resistance. There is no reward for crossing the moat but simply a different part of your brain on the other side, tapping its foot, asking, "Where have
you been?"

I assumed I'd eventually tackle my procrastination, but that turned out
to be just another seductive daydream. Rather than chipping away at it one
job at a time, I held out for the possibility that eventually, somehow, I'd wake
up extremely motivated and stoked to do the damn thing. I guess my mind
put that off, too.

YOU CAN IMAGINE what it was like writing this essay, let alone this book. I
know, I know, no one wants to hear how hard it was to write a book, let
alone the one they're reading. Talk about a buzzkill. It's less of a VIP backstage pass and more of a pro bono therapy session. Though hear me out:
Writing anything—even a grocery list—is a process. But writing a book is
not the idyllic woodsy retreat where the manuscript reveals itself to you over
three enchanted nights, despite that one bone-chilling interview I read. It's
a uniquely challenging and lonely task requiring extreme reserves of patience, fortitude, and of perseverance for even an experienced author. It's
like that movie where the guy gets stranded rock climbing and ends up cutting off his own arm (I wanna say *Ghostbusters*?), but the battle is all internal.
So, imagine a first-timer like me, who routinely struggles with feelings of
inadequacy, attempting the task. But why not make something already hard
even more so? I decided to write a book *about* self-doubt. (To be fair, I could
have turned in a completely blank document and it would have felt more
than right.) The resistance was legendary—I scaled new lows, experiencing
a level of avoidance that was awe-inducing even to me, the Chief Executive
Goof Officer. More than once, entire days clambered on top of one another
into weeks, then months, like the grimmest human pyramid, and still, I

couldn't write at all. I'd wake up like a grizzled detective with no new leads on a case I'd been on for far too long.

I had every intention of working on the alleged book. After all, there was a signed contract saying I had to, and so many aspiring authors don't get that luxury. But my procrastination got craftier, cloaking itself in "useful" tasks. I had to ask myself, in the middle of shopping for dowels, "Is this a front for what I actually need to be doing?" (It was always a front. I've never needed to buy a dowel in my life.) I would keep pushing my writing time later and later, and then finally start at 11:00 p.m. That's OK, I would comfort myself, we all have our routines. Toni Morrison used to write at five in the morning. I'd also conveniently forget that Toni Morrison had a full-time editor job and small children, not to mention the helpful wrist squeeze of a reminder that I am no Toni Morrison. Late-night writing wasn't completely useless, but I would frequently doze off in front of my computer, jolting awake to wonder how I had done this to myself again.

Ever one-upping me, my procrastination became a game-changing disruptor. For example, falling asleep branched out from strictly nocturnal occurrences. Even when I managed to write during the day, my eyelids would start fluttering shortly after I began. I wasn't sleep deprived; if anything, I was sleeping more to lessen the stink of another wasted day. But whenever and wherever I tried to sit down and put cursor to Word doc, I'd nod off. This wasn't a form of drowsiness that I could shake off with a quick stretch or splash of water to the face, as with every webinar I've ever attended. This was the unwritten law of artist physics: for every intended creative action, there is an equal and opposite creative reaction. A grim little tap on my memory's shoulder points me to Fran Lebowitz's* utterly perfect one-liner: "Sleep is death without the responsibility."

---

* A procrastinator after my own straggling heart. The last book she was due to write is now forty-plus-years late. Funnily enough, was also very good friends with the late Toni Morrison.

I experimented with odd ways to push through, none of them sexy, in case you're the hopeful type. I'd eat a handful of chips (most of the bag!) or steep a cup of tea (only for it to end up cold and forgotten, just like my partner!) or dance to a song (usually a sad song set to techno to gaslight myself!), but alas, the sandman persisted like he was selling me multilevel marketing leggings. Tippy even acquired a makeshift standing desk, and I discovered (the hard way) I can still go lights out standing up. What a way to discover you're part horse! I alternated prying one eyelid open, Mr. Bean style, with one hand while typing with the other, then switching. Meme-able but useless.

I replaced the work of writing with investigating the case of sudden snoozing. I got blood work done, ready to triumphantly out myself as iron deficient and wash my hands of responsibility. I called my mom and received the frustrating acknowledgment that "Oh yes, that's been happening my whole life as well." I don't need solidarity, Ma, I need answers! I almost did a sleep study. If I couldn't work because I sleep, I may as well sleep so that others could work.

Hitting rock bottom, I went to the place where that's same old, same old—online—and stumbled on a phenomenon sometimes called fear napping. Basically, when the brain gets too stressed out, the body wants to shut down. Sleep researchers have differing thoughts on the why behind it, but the common reasoning is there's a third option to the fight-or-flight response, and that is freeze. While it's not considered harmful per se, it's assuredly not helpful either. I found myself envying those unwitting Ambien users who were still getting things done while asleep, even if those things were sending regrettable texts and buying cinnamon in bulk.

I should also note that I worked on a large part of this book during a global pandemic, the likes of which hadn't been seen in over a century. All of humanity's cultural concepts of ambition and work efficiency were flipped on their heads. Articles on the importance of easing up steadily flowed down the content stream, though there was a constant push-pull debate between those using their new "free" time to finally write their screenplay and those who found their biggest accomplishment in figuring out which pair of sweatpants is best to wear for a month straight. I whimpered when not even six months into the ordeal, Zadie Smith published *Intimations*, a compact, tidy book of essays that spoke to the moment beautifully, not to mention that a good portion of its proceeds went to charity. Barely a year later, multitalented comedian Bo Burnham released *Inside*, a widely acclaimed one-man docu-comedy special about his year in quarantine, which he wrote, performed, directed, and edited himself, and which a critic called "the only piece of art about lockdown that I've actually enjoyed watching" as if it's not outright violence to rank creative work generated during a period of large-scale trauma.

Meanwhile, back at Club Help Me, I completely abandoned checking social media and posted only rarely. This, despite it being the easiest way to get out jokes as a comedian, especially when live, in-person performance isn't possible. Pre-pandemic, people would ask me how I managed to be so prolific on Twitter, and I was always too embarrassed to admit the ugly truth: I used Twitter to put off artistic labor that involved less-instant gratification. My most "productive" years on the platform were entirely an exercise in denial and distraction. Sure, to the content economy, it was fertile, but it was all short-term gains. Eventually, I found myself tiring of it in the way that junk food can't satiate you the same way as a good meal and is more likely to leave you feeling queasy and regretful. The fact that the platform transitioned into a bucket of irate fire ants all trying to unsuccessfully cancel their gym memberships certainly sped up the ill will.

Despite it all, mostly to give myself some semblance of structure and purpose, I very, very slowly kept working on the book. It was like footage in a nature show of some change in an ecosystem, be it growth, maintenance, or decay. To detect any perceptible action requires substantially speeding the video up, but in so doing, the results are fragile, precise, and breathtaking (my words, not those of the viewer).

I employed several strategies, to varying degrees of success:

- tricking myself (Yes, I mean putting my open laptop in strategic locations around the apartment and putting the book document squarely in the middle of my desktop, and then hopefully, I go in just to check one little thing, and, gee, look at that, now I'm working on it.)

- incentivizing ("if you do this, you get ~~one~~ FOUR cookies" [because inflation])

- capitalizing on random, fickle attacks of motivation that come out of nowhere every few weeks (I call these "life swaps"); they last for about seventeen to twenty-two minutes, give or take

- talking myself gently and painstakingly through every micro-step like I was coaching a baby bunny through defusing a bomb

- doing a tangential task that technically counted as "book work," like renaming a bunch of files or whimpering

Because I make all tasks unpleasant for myself and because this one involved unfamiliar terrain, the act of writing itself became ephemeral. I couldn't stare at any progress directly, for fear of scaring the impulse away. Maybe I resent the question about process so much because it's concerning myself with something I dare not investigate too deeply.

Fits and starts abounded, and I clung to any shred of will I possessed, like Jack to Rose's life raft at the end of *Titanic*, even while my chapped hands filled with splinters. "I'll never let go," I rasped as I slowly sunk beneath the surface.

ONE THING I'VE LEARNED, though, is that getting anything done is as much about the not doing as the doing. Culturally, we love to frame everything in relation to doing. We don't like to talk about the not doing, except in a self-deprecating, dismissive way, because it implies something fundamentally wicked and true about us. Not doing is inherently so shameful that we can only name it as a problem to be solved, without exploring its depths.

But I spend so much time in the not doing that parts of it function as a form of the "good" kind of slowing down—like when you realize you've somehow, despite your best attempts, spent an entire day just sort of unapologetically existing. While the origins of my not doing are rooted in procrastination and avoidance, which are distorted renditions of mindfulness fan fiction, I have come to believe that my tendency to meander comes from a deeper desire for ease and stillness, a way of being alive that doesn't rely on relentless productivity plunges followed by desperate attempts to escape. The question is: Do I willingly embrace this possibility, spinning with it in a meadow full of daisies? Or does naming it alone set off a cacophony of car alarms warning me I will amount to nothing? Just guess.

STEPPING OUTSIDE the panopticon of professional work, I can never reliably account for how long it takes my brain to warm up to the idea of, well, anything. It could be answering a scheduled phone call or leaving a party. The more time you give me, the more I'll take. Hesitation is my game plan—

but mine takes the scenic route. In that sense I'm a life procrastinator—though I prefer dillydallier, as that sounds more like I'm wearing a smart little hat and strolling around town, giving mailboxes a little chuck under the chin.

I understand how infuriating these tendencies can be for the rest of the world—it's one thing to take my own sweet time and quite another to take someone else's. I am chronically late. After hearing two friends—both early birds—complain about how rude this behavior can be, I didn't know how to tell them this was so much bigger than them. I've been running late since my mom's period. I am also a last-minute pusher of plans, by five, ten, sixty minutes or days, though I am working on this habit. I think my flakiness and lateness come from the same instinct, namely that I'm never *ready* for anything—even with all the advance notice in the world. I'm on a different timetable and even I am often the last to find out the consequences.

Maybe I dillydally to get in touch with my own intuition, a resource that is often culturally undervalued in the quest for optimized efficiency and relegated to the advice from a best friend in a rom-com. I've gotten so used to resistance being the loudest voice in my head when it comes to "doing" that I have to stop and attune myself to what the resistance is telling me. I've come to question whether this stopping and starting and hemming and hawing is all bad. My general orientation toward the world is "Wait, what?" No wonder I found comedy. It's another means of distraction from the relentlessness of life and the expectations of others, but at least some of those people find respite in it.

IN AN ARTICLE called "The Tyranny of Time," writer Joe Zadeh argues how bound as a species we've become to clock time. He writes of a group of thinkers who argue that the idea of time has been shaped by not only science but also religion, colonialism, and capitalism (much like Headlee's argument about work). Specifically, the West imposed clock time over nature to dominate Indigenous cultures that were more in sync with their surrounding ecosystems. This more integrated form of measuring the passage of time was seen as "irregular and unpredictable."

I am struck by the idea of living a life not so bound to cold, hard numbers, but rather by one's immediate environment. I suppose it would be like living on a farm, waking up and going to sleep with the sun, adjusting my work according to the seasons and the soil. At this point, taking cues from the natural world rather than some man-made conception of our limited existence sounds radical. I wish I could say I've found a way to integrate this mindset into my lifestyle, besides chronic lateness (which is nothing if not chaotic), but I have yet to figure out a sustained solution. As of now, I fantasize about moving to the woods, but unless I leave my brain behind, I doubt that will solve anything. In New York City, you don't even need a watch— everyone around you is ticking, vibrating with efficiency. I attended a Zoom lecture by the novelist and Zen Buddhist priest Ruth Ozeki, whose work often plays with the idea of time and our conception of it. She talked about doing an experiment for herself in which she tried to go two weeks without clocks. She did this by covering all the clocks in her home, not wearing a watch, and not using her phone. Of course, this is a lot easier if people aren't depending on you for meetings or calls and the like, but she said at first it was hard and then she found herself very much going by natural patterns of light and darkness. I tried to imagine doing a similar experiment, and I could hardly see myself lasting a day, if that.

But no matter who we are, our respect of the clock as the ultimate arbiter of the scale of our lives should be questioned constantly. Social media, for example, is completely wedded to when exactly things are "posted" or exposed to the world. Its entire foundation relies on when something is shared, and then seen, read, known, and spread, and by whom. When you consider the attention economy, that is, the marketplace of consuming content and being consumed as content, this is no mere coincidence. The idea of knowing everything exactly when it happens, as it happens, is held sacred above all else. There is no built-in incentive toward moderation, let alone taking a break or consuming less. Zadeh writes, "Capitalism did not create clock time or vice versa, but the scientific and religious division of time into identical units established a useful infrastructure for capitalism to coordinate the exploitation and conversion of bodies, labor and goods into value." He considers how so often processes like climate change are contextualized in terms of clock time deadlines, which has contributed to many people's inability to understand its true impact on our world.

Sure, there are wellness trends like "digital detox" and turning off your webcam and taking ten deep breaths before you return to the pointless meeting, but it's all enmeshed within a web of competitive commodification. It's not as much about slowing down as it is about seeking out apps, products, services, and content in the guise of mindfulness. This is the way the world works, and there's nothing we can do about it. Even the entrenched concept of time as money has co-opted the phrasing "*paying* attention"— another way to translate every moment as an opportunity for further consumption. It's easy to swim along with all these systemic lures because they capitalize on a truism about human nature, which is that most of the time, I am ruled by the pressure to do something, anything, out of an inability to sit with myself. At least if I'm constantly in motion, I won't ever have to face the rawness of existence.

Burkeman also cites this temptation toward distraction as the reason why humans hate boredom so much—it reminds us of our limited sense of control, a state that can be quite intolerable. "You're obliged to deal with how your experience is unfolding in this moment, to resign yourself to the reality that *this is it*." No wonder, then, he reasons, we love the internet so much, a boundless realm in which we can represent ourselves however we want and take in an unending supply of novel stimuli and information. I know this to be true, because whenever I've been online and bored, I find myself doggedly hunting for something, anything, that lights up my brain circuits farthest away from my current experience.

The COVID-19 pandemic was the only time in my working life there was an extended break (and only for a very lucky, very small percentage of us) from this unquestioning adulation of go-go-go, during which, for a few months, the gears in my industry begrudgingly ground to a halt. Indeed, some of us were forced to sit with ourselves and our fragile mortality. All the same, as I retreated further into myself, I was reminded of the words of Jenny Odell in her virtual commencement speech to the Harvard Graduate School of Design: "For someone in a creative field, it can almost be hard to believe that you continue to exist when you're not producing or publicly saying anything."

Any pandemic epiphanies I may have had were further short-lived because as soon as the vaccine came out, it was back to business as usual. As cultural critic and reporter Anne Helen Petersen wrote about our work systems, "Everything fell apart, and we could've put it back together differently, but we just put it back together the same broke-ass way as before?"

Deprogramming ourselves from this mindset rings infeasible for those of us living in the modern, industrialized, globalized world. Showing up to meetings whenever you want or only if you feel like it and treating deadlines like personal attacks (hi) will win you no allies. But maybe there are smaller ways to remove ourselves from the fray. I find it in stopping to distill certain moments: the woman I passed on the street who asked me to help her tie her shoe or when one of my cats gets the zoomies (way more activating than our version of Zoom). There's so much crystallized in these few seconds when we get to share in another's experience. It's the easiest way I lose track of time.

Since the pandemic began, I've built what sound like leisurely activities into my day that require less time management—like going for walks and yoga and meditating. Or afternoon dance parties with my partner, where we put on a song or two and cut loose. In those pockets I can make for myself, I find immense freedom if I'm intentional about why I'm doing them. The crucial part is treating that time as just as vital as whatever task you're returning to, but also not just something to be checked off on autopilot. I have to fight my brain's impulse to tap its watch and go, *Ahem. Back to your regularly scheduled grind, please.* And there's always the meditation session where you end more stressed than when you started because your negative thoughts decide to throw a rager.

The few times I've reliably felt outside the idea of time itself and fully in tune with my environment is when I've taken shrooms (the psychedelic psilocybin, for the uninitiated). On one such occasion, standing in a beautiful rock garden with a waterfall cascading down in front of me and a gentle rain falling, I felt so still and grateful and peaceful that all I could do to express my profound sense of contentment was put my hands in the air and essentially prostrate myself vertically in front of the water. In the back of my mind, I knew it was a temporary state, but for once, I didn't panic about it or skip to whatever was next, the way my brain usually does. As the mindfulness proselytizers say, I was present.

The older I get, the faster my perception of time passage is, and the stronger is my drive to slow down and savor. I'm constantly pushing against the crowd to live this way, but it's when I feel most grounded. Otherwise, I'd be the father I saw at the airport telling his three-year-old to "walk with a sense of purpose." The whole point of being three is not having a purpose and not having any baggage about that!

There are growing multitudes of voices, trends, and movements challenging these entrenched ideologies, which persist despite worsening income inequality and diminishing resources. Thanks to the work of activists like Tricia Hersey and the Nap Ministry, a movement based on the idea of rest as liberation, and sources like those cited earlier as well as *How to Do Nothing* and *Saving Time* by the aforementioned Odell, we are finally and collectively starting to question this work-produce-consume mindset in a deeper way. Hersey started the Nap Ministry in 2013 during a very taxing period in her life. She was a student who was also working and raising a child amid the trauma of both familial loss and seeing countless Black people die from gun violence in the news. She found herself taking naps all over campus and that the practice irrevocably changed her. She envisions this refusal to overwork as a reclaiming of space not often afforded to the marginalized. "We are resting simply because it is our divine and human right to do so, period. There is . . . nothing else on the end of that sentence. It is the end of it."

How to Do Nothing is a call to arms against the 24/7 data productivity expected of all of us and an eloquent clapback against productivity, efficiency, and techno-determinism. Odell's second book, *Saving Time,* picks up on these ideas and reimagines our relationship to the clock entirely. In China, there is a countercultural movement called "lying flat," started by a thirty-one-year-old former factory worker named Luo Huazhong with a social media manifesto that asserts his right to live a slow lifestyle. It's his attempt to push back against China's hypercompetitive work environment, and in a nod to the movement's power, there have already been actions by the Communist government to ban certain internet groups propagating the subversive idea. Culturally, we've embraced the backlash against fast food and fast fashion; it only makes sense that fast life would be next. But as with most societal hugs, let's hope it's not just lip service—I'm envisioning a million iterations of the newest spin on salable relaxation avocado toast interspersed with ads for sandals made out of cubicles from Big Banks right before they got bailed out.

At this point, if I tallied all the minutes I've spent avoiding, hesitating, or distracting myself, it would be the majority of my anytime minutes. I would be a productivity coach's magnum opus in terms of a makeover project. But instead of being disheartened, I've found peace in realizing things I've seen as flaws might not be. Hesitation isn't the worst quality, adaptively speaking. It makes me better appreciate the things I've chosen to do, since I had to go through so many hoops to do them at all. It's frustrating being so constantly consumed with my own fear and doubt, but it does leave me many moments of observing my life in two speeds: that of doing and not doing.

Although maybe there is a third option, just as with fight, flight, and freeze—but without the urgency. Because there is always the doing and the not doing, but there is also the being. I wonder what that could look like.

Instead of being caught in a perpetual dance between seeking stillness and slowness for my brain and body and being beguiled by the constant reminders of FOMO embedded into our culture, I could opt out of the binary entirely—and accept what I do or don't do without the trailing wake of shame. If I stop enforcing such high personal expectations, I can meet myself somewhere quieter. Worst-case scenario, I nod off on the way there.

Case in point: One day while out on a walk, I saw a frowning man with an immaculate-looking corgi in its prime. Every few feet, the corgi stopped and sat down. The dog appeared neither exhausted nor distracted by a nearby fascination. They just decided every so often that they needed a second. A few times, the corgi didn't even bother sitting, they just went ahead and lay fully down, opting out of the pressure to continue. Their owner appeared displeased, but nonetheless resigned to this behavior. They continued this way down the entire block until I lost sight of that hero and their leash-wielding student. *Watch and learn.* The revolution is here, and it will take its own damn time.

A Night in the Life of Revenge
Bedtime Procrastination (RBP)

Learned a very relatable term today: "報復性熬夜" (revenge bedtime procrasti-
nation), a phenomenon in which people who don't have much control over their
daytime life refuse to sleep early in order to regain some sense of freedom during late
night hours.
—Daphne K. Lee

The day is when people who have their act together thrive. That is not me.

I do my best "work" under the cover of night. I'm like one of those little elves who make the shoes. Except instead of making shoes, I craft playlists called "feeb," "jabbo," and "dweep" on a scale of least to slightly less least listenable. (I make my playlists like I make my life: more complicated than necessary.) The hours between 11:00 p.m. and 5:00 a.m. are when the confines of daily life are lifted, and I am free of the stricture of responsibility-infused productivity.

True, these strictures are gentle suggestions for someone like me who is her own boss. But counterpoint, my boss is fickle, impossible to please, and an unsettlingly close talker (try inside my ears). The expectations of what I could and *should* be doing still hinder me. A liberating no-man's-land of schedules, nighttime encompasses the hours when a person can let loose. I'm not talking in the carpe noctem "outlast the DJ, shut down every bar" kind of way. I'm talking a homebody's time to go full throttle with once-hot tea, apartment creaks, and a wi-fi connection.

In twilight, I can scroll through pages and pages of intarsia sweaters, rush order a birthday present for my mom, google people I have no business or pleasure googling, and finally hit the end of the internet, which usually looks like reading email drafts from 2011 to get high on old pain. Only after 2:00 a.m. do I start to feel like I'm breaking a law and getting away with it, even as I am also vaguely aware that the next day will be a bust. There's a delirious, pseudodrunken power in pushing way past "bedtime," whatever and whenever that even means. It's the scheduling power move equivalent of standing the wrong way in an elevator. "You don't own me!" I yell at the system, while simultaneously keeping thirty-seven browser windows open and my arrow hovered above the checkout button in an online shopping cart, very much in the grips of *a* system, if not *the* system.

Even when my energy starts to flag, I refuse to go "gentle into that good night." Yes, I know that poem was about death, but I'm making it about life because, as I've well established, I'm really something else. For the love of bad impulse control, this is not about making good decisions! This is about staying awake until I am fighting for consciousness. When I finally succumb to sleep, it is only after I feel as though I've won a battle of principle. If I went to bed at a reasonable hour—say whenever a person who owns more than two candles that weren't gifts goes to bed—it would be *so* much less of a scene. What can I say? I live for the drama.

How exactly does one of these nighttime quests go down? First off, that's private—rude! But second, I did bring it up. So fine, here's a hazy approximation that would fall apart in court:

11:00 p.m. I have eaten another late dinner despite multiple people and articles telling me, unsolicited, that one great way to monitor your calories is to not eat late at night. I'm not trying to manage my food intake per se (other than the lagging biohazard residue of societal body fascism), but I am trying to "be healthier" because wellness is ever so eager to *mindfully* position itself as the primary raffle prize of late-stage capitalism for a certain set—aka doing hot yoga on a sinking ship. Welp, I guess the rain falls gently on this plain, because I'm in Spain and 22:30 is dinnertime, folks! In the throes of digestion, I want to watch one of our story programs with my partner, who also keeps odd hours, but he has unhelpfully fallen asleep on the couch. Unlike me, he is an involuntary insomniac, so he will most likely wake up again at 2:00 or 3:00 a.m. and then not be able to sleep the rest of the night. Eschewing the unplanned disco nap, I prefer a more traditional night owl routine. I try to watch something alone, but instead, I spend fifteen minutes scrolling through options of what to watch, as gripped by indecision as when I'm in the pasta shapes aisle at the grocery store.

12:00 a.m. Oh, hi, I'm somehow now on my computer, despite multiple people and articles telling me, unsolicited, that good sleep hygiene means no screen time at least an hour before bed. However, I've read most of this advice on my phone during the witching hour, so let's take a wild guess they have not worked their magic. Under the utter farce that "I just need to check one thing" (i.e., the death knell of time you can account for), I decide to visit a clothing aggregator site of small, independent boutiques that I like. I type "jumpsuits" in the search bar. Before I know it, it's 1:30 a.m. and I have looked at over a hundred jumpsuits, a third of them for kids. It's just the options for kids are more fun and whimsical, and I'm sure if I find the perfect one . . . I will still not fit into it. Undeterred, I move on to looking at lockets that hold crystals. Crystals: astrology for people who are bad with dates. Sure, I've spent a frightening amount of money on mental health goods and services, but have I considered wearing black tourmaline around my neck? No? Someone forgot how to *believe*. I end up buying a necklace with several small crystals contained in a small vial. Tomorrow, I will likely email the company, sheepishly pleading my computer glitched and could I please cancel my order? Yes, I've used this excuse before. At the same time, I text with some buddos on the West Coast, where it's a completely appropriate hour for a fun, cazh chat! I realize I am playing with fire when one of these so-called pals wraps things up saying they have to go to bed. Hmm, who do I know in New Zealand? Should I move to New Zealand? Definitely a great decision to think through at this hour. I pop on over to explore Kiwi real estate options.

1:34 a.m. Inspired by my California comrade's toast to honoring the body's needs and high on recently purchased crystal (not that kind), I begin my bedtime routine. This entails a gratitude journal, making a schedule for the next day, a mood chart, and cataloging my daily spending. Yes, I know this sounds like compulsive behavior, and here's a quick peek behind the mental curtain: it is. I get into patterns of doing things supposedly meant to "help me," and then I can't stop doing them even when it's clear they are not helping. Basically, if it's supposed to be good for me, I do it to the extent where it's no longer healthy. It's not a diagnosable compulsion where I think something horrible will happen if I stop doing the tasks, but also if I don't do them, my mind can't settle. Is this my mental illness? My inner quirk monster? Both? Neither? Am I channeling a demon? Anything to not have to take responsibility.

2:34 a.m. I'm unclear how it took me an hour to do all my personal status reports, but on a productivity kick, I try to finish three online articles I started but never got through and have since bookmarked. There are now so many pinned tabs there's no room left to open a new one. The last article is on Boko Haram. I consider why this might not be the right time to read an article on Boko Haram, but if not now, when? This attitude seems to be the mantra of RBP. Nighttime is one big pole swing between "doing me" and downloading the Duolingo app to finally learn French and then undoing me by proceeding to watch yet a third slideshow of Zendaya's best red carpet looks.

3:52 a.m. Well, dang, me. I wanted to leave enough time before bed to "read for fun," but I somehow squandered all my time doing who knows what. (I have the alibi of a goldfish in these instances. I honestly cannot account for any of my whereabouts or doings during these hours, and I have a note from my doctor saying that is OK.) The good thing is I've somehow changed into my pajamas and brushed my teeth. Biggest win of all: I get into bed. This would appear to be a major win for Team Shut-Eye, but alas, I'm hardly ready to throw in the towel. I do a crossword frenetically on my phone. I suddenly pop up like a jack-in-the-box finance bro who's for sure a closer and remember a bunch of stuff I must do during the day tomorrow. There is no way I will get to it anymore, but it does feel absolutely critical to jot those things down RIGHT FRICKING NOW while they are fresh in my oh-so-organized mind. I do this by sending a series of texts to myself, desperately trying to warn Future Me about the peril ahead.

4:15 a.m. All that squared away, the moment has come to read for fun! Nobody gets to take this time away from me. Oh, sure, I can read in the morning, but then it's laden with the guilt of "I should be getting my day started with real work." Right now, I'm still in the gray zone where time is a gauzy sarong of a dream, and I can do whatever the hell I want. The fact that no one is responsive or overtly productive at this hour is a beautiful swaddling respite from daily life—the grind, if you will. I think of my friend who was a night nurse for ten years, but quickly push said thought way, way down until it just feels like gas.

4:23 a.m. I am visibly falling asleep while "reading" a children's adventure series that is not dense enough for me to blame drifting off on the text. I will concede to my circadian rhythms soon enough, but I decide to push through to 4:30 a.m. because it is a nice even number and "I earned this?" When I finally put the book down in a blur, I cue up the end of a podcast to listen to despite already being half-asleep. I refuse not to block out every single one of my waking thoughts. Dead air is the enemy!

10:00 a.m. The first of three different alarms I have set five minutes apart goes off, because for some inexplicable reason I am not a morning person. I hit snooze no fewer than seven times, unless it's one of those mornings when my phone shuts down the alarm functionality for the sole purpose of ruining my life. Either way, I don't successfully wake up until 11:30 a.m. And so the dance begins anew with a shameful grimace and the haunting silhouette of a toddler's romper.

The Agreeability
Industrial Complex

A. Yes, I'd Love To!

For so long, I feared that if I gave myself permission to start saying no, I wouldn't be able to stop. I'd excuse myself from the room, slowly shaking my head. Then, arms up in a preemptive warding-off motion, I'd deny everyone and everything that crossed my path, gaining confidence and momentum as I went. Finally, with muted pomp, I'd bow out of my own death and continue pacing the earth forever, a wraith of firm refusal. *None for me, thanks!*

My standard MO has been to say yes in most situations for most of my life. Notice I didn't say "all situations," and we'll get to that, please lower your voice and sit down. My level of agreeability isn't hugely out of left field since women are frequently socialized to be human doormats, and if you're a woman with any Asian heritage, you are frequently presumed to be an actual doormat. I have been trying to get the "Welcome (Unsolicited Opinions)" stamp off me for years. At the barely formed age of five, I garnered the class superlative: "sweetest" kid. And yes, I went to a kindergarten where they gave out superlatives, because it's never too early to be labeled and then forever haunted by that label.

Like so many women, I'm a people pleaser. One of the key ingredients of this suspiciously warm group is that we say yes when we'd rather not. In the *HuffPost* article "How to Stop Being a People Pleaser and Learn to Say No," which was clearly written as a subtweet to me personally (but it's totally fine, don't worry about it!!!), Kelsey Borresen writes, "People pleasers crave approval and validation, so they'll go to great lengths to keep others happy— even at the expense of their own wellbeing." Often a coping mechanism developed from childhood (aren't they all?!), the people pleaser sees the disappointment of others in them as threatening and something to be prevented at all costs. I immediately contort myself into every variety of shape to address the other party's needs. The only way I am comfortable taking up space is if absolutely no one else has a problem with it. I so often go along with what other people want to prevent disagreement that I often convince myself I wanted what they wanted in the first place. If I asked a friend to help me move (which I would never do in the first place) and they agreed, I would ensure the move worked for their schedule before making sure it worked for mine.

Women are socialized to believe that people-pleasing shouldn't be about the high of recognition but about the mandate to put everyone else's needs (especially men's) ahead of their own. In a piece for *The Atlantic*, Anna Holmes adds a specific caveat: "Successful women of color are expected to obligingly— obsequiously, in fact—say yes as a way to demonstrate gratitude for successes we've earned on our own. If people of color have to, as the old adage goes, work twice as hard and be twice as good to succeed, the women of this cohort must contend with an additional tax: We must also be twice as accommodating, as if to thank others for allowing us our accomplishments."

As a comedian, I most avowedly sublimate myself for any kind of work-related request, because isn't it sooo—pronounced "syoo"—nice to be thought of in the first place? They're doing *me* a favor! What a generous act of community service, no? (This is me saying no at my most comfortable, by the way—as a question, at the end of a sentence, meaning "Please validate me and my parking by agreeing.") In my industry, I am grateful to have a seat at the table at all.

Plus, what if I need something from *them* at some point? Surely, years later, they will remember this moment, and think, *Hmm, well, Arperna [sic] did like and share my web series when I sent her that DM, the first and last of its kind. Of course I can spare her a kidney!*

As a part of both a naturally social species and an industry that primarily runs on networking, I find myself wading through a constant parade of asks, commitments, and negotiations—from small, to medium, to upsetting. My Shonda Rhimes professional ethos of saying yes is hardly rare, especially in a field like comedy that demands "paying one's dues" (though markedly less so since YouTube and other free content distribution platforms leveled the playing field). When you're still an unknown baby artist (this phrase conjures an Anne Geddes moment, so picture me as an infant nestled in a bushel of wild carrots if you must), you're excited to do anything. Delighted in gaining admission to the sandbox at all, you show up stupidly grinning with your brand-new plastic shovel and shiny bucket, ready and willing to dig a deep, deep hole for any self-respect or dignity. There will be countless scenarios of "What have I agreed to?" and "Oh yes, I'd love to bomb at your event" and the evergreen "Why does this keep happening to me?" But many of these realizations will be sprung on you guerrilla style and only once you get there and observe there is no way the setup will be conducive to a good experience. For many of these stand-up gigs, the audience is similarly left in the dark. OMG, twins!

I have a particularly poignant memory of doing a college music festival where the organizers decided my low-key, musing, and brainy stand-up act would best be slated between two punk bands. All I remember of my performance is looking out into a sea of confused coeds and seeing one blissful girl spinning in circles in the back, head tilted upward in delirium. *I didn't realize my jokes were danceable*, I thought, plowing onward. In hindsight, I'd say to any aspiring artists: Follow your intuition when it comes to offers for work or career exposure, no matter how excited you are to be asked at all. You don't have to orchestrate your own suffering to be good at anything. You will still suffer. Nature finds a way. Because no matter what level you're at as a comedian, you're assuredly going to run into stinkers, so you might as well try to be more discerning of when someone is trying to put you in a sorry situation.

Allow me to demonstrate: I once did a pro bono fundraiser for an organization with the important mission of working to end sex trafficking. (Sidenote: I have since learned that there are many instances in which completely legitimate sex work is often stigmatized and made far more dangerous by being lumped into a broad net of scare stories about black market sex slavery, so I should have done more research, full stop. But, at the time, I just thought, *What a worthy cause! I'm happy to donate my time!* Do you already know where this is going? I sure didn't!) At no point did the question "Why is this group hiring a stand-up comedian?" cross my mind. Only at the event itself, once the fundraising dinner had kicked off, did I realize my twenty minutes of comedy was slotted right after a litany of testimonials from both people involved in the organization and real victims of sex trafficking. In the opposite of a twist, my set did not go well. In my defense, I received the same somber, weighted response that everyone else who spoke did. When I sat back down at my assigned seat, the person next to me leaned over and said, "You did it!" which was accurate. I had done it. That was the nicest thing that could be said. While I didn't foresee exactly how unfortunate that gig would turn out, saying yes more carefully reduces your odds of ending up in situations where, afterward, your ego texts you: "We need to talk."

As a full-time comedian, the hardest part about saying no to "help" or appease someone else is the fact I've already said no to so many other people in my life to pursue a dream career. Doesn't that mean, by most definitions of the word, I've elected to be selfish most of the time? After all, I've had to miss nine out of ten gently to aggressively obligatory social events including happy hours, birthdays, murder mystery dinner parties, divorce-iversaries, beatboxing recitals, and the like because I had to "work." Not to mention the fact that stand-up comedy, in and of itself, can be a self-absorbed, one-way conversation of a performance medium. You alone get to do all the talking. People frequently think you are "brave" for doing it at all. Your material is frequently about your life or your opinions about everyone else's. You require one specific reaction from the audience, including where exactly they should pipe in with it. If someone tries to talk back, you are allowed to banshee scream at them, and then put a video of it on the internet with a title like "HILARIOUS Up-and-Coming Comedian with Endless Potential ANNIHILATES Loser Heckler CEO of the Turds!!!" where it will rack up hundreds of thousands, if not millions, of views. It's not even just stand-up—writing, acting, creating, it's all usually in service of myself and my point of view. Sure, it's my calling, but a lot of other people in my life end up paying the phone bill.

Because I have so often put myself and my work ahead of family and friends, I carry around a Costco Apocalypse Bunker–size pack of internal guilt. The least I can do for any success I've reaped is pay it forward whenever possible, however possible. Like the cool aunt who does her own thing and lets them stay up as long as they want to, I value helping newer comics or younger people, especially those outside the status quo. I remind myself how much a kind word or recommendation from a more-established peer meant to me when I was starting out. Plus, then I can follow it up by asking them what it means when something "slaps."

I don't get to every request, though, and these are the indirect, unintentional noes that pain me most. Culturally, we fetishize completists—authors who write back to every reader letter they get, for example. I understand why we do it. Who can't argue that this sort of interaction can be mutually appreciated, particularly if it's a young, impressionable sort or someone else whose own story resonates with you? It's beautifully generous, but it's just not something that everyone has the same capacity for. At best, humans barely have the neural capacity to socially manage the demands of a group of thirty other grunting Neanderthals, let alone a social network of thousands.

But I get it. Nobody wants to hear that someone who succeeded off favorable public consumption of their work (artists and creators) is too tapped out to engage with those who subsequently want their attention. It's not generous. It's not becoming. And it's certainly not womanly. When men don't want to engage with others, they're eccentric geniuses, misunderstood loners, and salty auteurs. If women were permitted the three-dimensionality to not always put others ahead of themselves, the term "curmudgeionne" would exist. Instead, we're branded divas, bitches, cunts, snobs, monsters, spinsters, and oh, let's not forget that perennial favorite, crazies.

Perhaps women have to go to these extremes because they're often ignored the first one to one hundred times they try to respectfully set a boundary. We essentially must metamorphose into full-on Disney villains to be taken seriously when we make a request. *If you really meant no, why weren't you wearing a hooded cape made of puppy fur?!*

In her piece, Holmes speaks to Melissa Harris-Perry, a professor and the host of NPR's *The Takeaway*, who notes, "We shouldn't pretend that if only [women] could muster the courage to [say no], there will be applause, because most often there won't be. Because people hate it. It is completely possible that if you say no, you won't get the chance to say yes. And so that makes the calculation different for us than it does for [men]." There is a cost—and it's one that makes our decision a more cautious consideration. Once, early in my career, I had to back out of a comedy show at the last minute because I wasn't feeling well. The booker then proceeded to email me that if I hoped to make it in show business, I needed to act more professional and that he would most likely never invite me on a show again. Now, I have no idea if this booker would have also said this to a male comedian, but the only lesson I took away from this experience was "You're dispensable, and you have exactly one opportunity to make a good impression."

B. No, but Actually . . .

It occurred to me only recently the extremes to which I've prioritized appeasing people in my "professional network" over those in my personal life. I wish I could blame LinkedIn, but I finally deleted my rarely visited account after years of emails with increasingly urgent subject lines from them. *A cutting-edge web designer you may know is in grave danger!*

Here's how my scale of accommodating people has generally operated: work contacts and anyone I'm trying to actively impress (mortgage lenders, first dates, people on the treadmill next to me) are the first priority bar none; friends, family, and my partner are next, all hastily smooshed into a clump held together by love and guilt, but as discussed, frequently shafted for any job or career opportunity; and finally, way, way, waaay down at the bottom of the list—the boudoir. That's right, oddly enough, the bedroom is liberation central for me. I don't mean sexual liberation. I mean the free, unfettered use of "Nah, I'm good."

As a me once said, people pleaser in the streets, people freezer in the sheets. This should come as no surprise given that if my vagina had a persona, it would most likely channel a stop sign, though one with a fun wig. I should preface: As a cis heterosexual woman who has never experienced a nonconsensual sexual situation, I am undoubtedly one of the exceedingly fortunate ones. According to the Rape, Abuse & Incest National Network, one in six American women has experienced an attempted or completed rape in her lifetime. Globally, the problem is even worse.

I have had partners who were persistent in wanting to do things I didn't want to, and while they might have tried to sway me otherwise, little did they know the iron will and underwear of their opponent. They learned, though. I know, I know, why aren't I naming these stalwart gents? Surely, they all deserve medals for . . . ahem . . . baseline decency and respecting my bodily autonomy. I have had no fear of letting the other party down, so sure have I been of increasingly alienating them the further we continued. If anything, I was saving them future trouble. It turns out bedroom disappointment is my wheelhouse! I was playing a long game without even realizing it.

Before I had ever even had sex, I made out with a guy my senior year of college—where my unfashionably late bloomers at? (Still en route, I'm sure)—who kept wheedling me to go further despite my reticence, until finally I asked him to leave. I had that strange sense of having to play disciplinarian during an encounter that is supposed to be mutually fulfilling. The nice thing about reaching life milestones on your own timeline is you don't have any know-how to pretend otherwise. By the time I first kissed a guy, I was less a churning, hormonal body and more an immersive documentarian, here to bear witness to the mating habits of the North American heterosexual male. Most of my first physical encounters were merely B-roll, and the poor saps were the last to know!

There's a stolid recognition in being socially awkward enough that, despite your best efforts, you can't accommodate the other person. Sure, when alcohol is involved, you might not be evaluated as closely, but I still made sure all gentlemen comrades left our encounters well informed that I didn't know what I was doing. *Sir, let it be known this isn't the Midori sour talking, this is me.* I'd often be so fully misguided in the bedroom that I would repel my trysts without even meaning to. One of my first hookups with a guy, I left him so discombobulated that the next morning, as soon as he woke up from his booze-infused slumber, he physically ran out of my dorm room. It's OK, hon, I also hate goodbyes.

Even in serious relationships, if I didn't want to do things my partners wanted to try, I point-blank said as much. Early on, there was the rare instance where I'd have sex with a long-term partner out of guilt or obligation (praise be the patriarchy!) and remain mostly ambivalent about the whole thing internally, but externally try to get into it once we got going. In her introspective and meticulous book *Girlhood*, cultural critic Melissa Febos calls these situations "empty consent." She writes, "I wasn't at all surprised by how many of the women I surveyed regularly gave empty consent to their primary partners. This is a well-known facet of many long-term romantic partnerships. It is not simply a vestige of legally owing sex to our spouses, but a symptom of genuinely caring for our partners and their needs, as well as a route to emotional intimacy."

I was both heartened and dismayed to learn so many other women regularly engage in this behavior. Despite my general inclination to not want sex, I wanted to provide my partners pleasure out of genuine love for them and respect for their needs. But I learned over time it was better for everyone involved to go with my gut and just say no right out of the gate. After all, my go-to move in the bedroom is to not. I've realized I'm often so uncomfortable in my body that anybody else in my body, for whatever length of time, may end up getting the same trademarked experience. That's the Aparna promise!

I've never ascribed that much power to my sexuality—if anything, I've found freedom in my lack of it. Throughout my life, I've observed how other cishet women frequently and easily got attention, whether solicited or not, and that I never had that experience. Starting with adolescence, unless I bothered trying to be proactive, men typically "no"-ed me before I had a chance to "no" them. While everyone else paired off and made the most of their wafting pheromones, I usually stood on the sidelines. But for most of my teens, twenties, and—shudder—most of my thirties, too, I remained resolutely obsessed with the acceptance and interest of men. But I now understand it for what it really was: seeking love and belonging through society's authorized tropes. So, rather than opting out, I found autonomy in the bedroom early on, even if it originated from a place of discomfort and confusion. *You came home with me? Ha! You fool—I'll show you!*

It's no coincidence that getting my bearings on what I truly want versus what I think I want has taken decades. From a young age, all women, regardless of their orientation, are given a mind-bending series of mixed messages about intercourse. Here is a condensed version of all the messaging around sex I received as a young cis woman, relayed in a dark room with all the blinds closed, naturally:

It's something that might interest you, but whoa, slow down there. Because technically, you should wait until marriage (still one of our favorite answers to what you want to be when you grow up . . . MARRIED!) but still somehow know what you're doing or it will be weird for everyone, so maybe just do it when you're "ready" (or rather, when society is ready to hear about it, which, weirdly enough, is a completely subjective timescale from person to person seemingly based on some incalculable matrix of looks, status, and je ne sais don't even ask), and then make sure he enjoys it (if it's not a cishet he, um, help us understand, we're still extremely lost), but also don't make it seem like you've had too much of it before because that implies you don't respect yourself, and more important, our opinion of you, but if you're a virgin, be careful! Because once you're not, wow, well, we can't even tell you how bad that will be. For us mostly! We won't be able to stop talking about it for no clear reason!!! Also, quick addendum, you might get a disease or pregnant, and that's definitely all on you, not the other person, so don't expect them to clean up your mess. Any questions? Good. We're out of time.

If desire and pleasure even get half a shout-out after all that, it's a miracle. An even bigger miracle is how any woman retains a smidge of intuitive sexuality after all that. (And notice there is absolutely no airtime given to the idea that sex just might not interest you that much now or later, end of sentence, and that's fine, too.)

What young Aparna took away from this talk is . . . *great, well, it doesn't seem to be a lot of work to protect my virginity, so I can check that off my list.* In the meantime, I was happy to explore my physical urges and curiosity on my own with a few foolproof somethings known as my imagination, free time, and hands. But, eventually and given the opportunity, I was ready to see what all the sex fuss was about. I found out during my final semester of college with my first serious boyfriend. Did I enjoy the novelty of it and find it pleasurable after a few test drives? Yeah, definitely! It felt like finally watching a movie everyone has been referencing for years. But was a big part of what I found exciting about it the idea of being desired? Yeah, even more definitely! Positive attention: what a drug. Were there also a lot of parts of it I found kind of gross, tedious, and off-putting, no matter how many times I did them? Yup, for sure.

Over time, I've discovered I don't find sex all that compelling, or even dwell on it all that much, save occasionally. I'll go long stretches without thinking about it at all. Granted, there's a widely held belief that people, especially women, lose interest in sex over time in a long-term relationship, but it's never been a priority for me, period. For the most part, when I'm having sex, I feel halfway removed from what's happening and wonder if the other person can tell or perhaps is feeling the same. I'm not saying I'm a chaste unicorn; I've heard plenty of other cishet women make similar comments about their own sexual experiences. On the flip side, they still seem to have plenty of desire for good sex, even if that's not the sex they're currently getting. I've had plenty of fantasies and I've masturbated to a healthy degree, but once you bring another person into it, it's just always better in my head than in the flesh. And no, it's not my partners, they are all showing up ready for the mission—I'm the one who doesn't suit up. I can't imagine this is entirely relatable, especially when most human beings value touch so much, but I'm more than happy to be your bridge of understanding between people and sentient AIs. You're so welcome.

Society helpfully has a term for women who aren't good in bed or interested in sex: frigid. The idea, as I follow it, is that she's so cold she just lies there. Where did that term even come from? If she's that icy and still, did you check to make sure she's not dead? If she's not into sex, could it possibly be because she's been fearmongered her whole life to not act like she's too interested in sex by society, her upbringing, her peers, you name it? Because there were mixed messages? Or even more radically: could it, gasp, be possible some people just don't care about sex as much as others? You could argue it's one of our basic needs, but I've also met people who "don't drink water" (bless those husks) and others who consider running fifteen miles the same as recharging, so, different strokes (of course pun intended, how dare you).

I have accepted only recently that my not liking sex with other people that much is not a problem. In fact, it's fine, because honestly, who cares? I have tried to explain it away before, and there are, at first blush, cases to be made. For example, maybe it's because of my anxiety or depression. It's true that when my mood is out of whack (hate to brag, but happens on the regs), sex is the last thing on my mind—heck, even acknowledging I have a body becomes a chore. Or maybe it's my psych meds causing low libido and difficulty orgasming (what a sales pitch, huh!), which is also true. But I've been on various combos for decades, and I know those aren't the sole reasons, because my sex drive and level of sexual attraction have fluctuated greatly despite them. Plus, I don't have the option of going off my meds—the noggin don't nog as well without them. It turns out an untreated depressed neurotic is also not going to be a sexual goddess. Or maybe it's the yeast infections and UTIs that I often get from sex—those aren't exactly a selling point—and yes, I do all the tips to prevent them, thanks. I'm peeing right now!

Or maybe I need to work on my relationship more, because yes, there's always sex therapy, which I'm happy to try if anyone knows of a Groupon that takes my fickle insurance. But you know what else? We live in a capitalist, misogynist, white supremacist society, and maybe the need to see everything about us as a consumer-based problem, particularly if you're a woman, even more so if you're a woman of color, is inherently problematic. What if no sex isn't a problem for me, and I am not worried about it? Yes, of course, I want to please my partner, but I also don't want to subject him to subpar, obligatory sex to fulfill a cultural guilt complex—that's neither fair, nor hot. (Although the hopeless baby *Shark Tank* in me does smell a new porn category: SubparObligatorySex™.)

After some scrolling—uhrm, I mean, research—and Wednesday afternoon googling, I figured out that I don't meet the definition of "asexual." I do experience some sexual attraction and pleasure, and so fall closer to the term "graysexual." As with all things, even lack of sexual attraction, desire, and drive is a spectrum. I used to judge myself for not going along with what my sexual partners wanted. Now, I think of it as a tiny spark that's grown into a raging fire everywhere but my loins. And sure, maybe it will change again, and I'll become chair of the board of horndogs, but until then, I'm fine without it.

Existence itself is hard enough without pathologizing every single aspect of it outside the narrowest margins. The more troublesome aspects of lack of sexual interest seem to come, as with most things, from the judgment of other people. In *Ace: What Asexuality Reveals about Desire, Society, and the Meaning of Sex*, journalist Angela Chen explains that "compulsory sexuality" is the societal idea that not having or not wanting sex is somehow abnormal, and even many queer liberation and progressive feminist movements center sex within their narratives. Chen writes, "Life is a continuous process of unlearning for minorities and anyone with less power. These groups—women, people of color, and . . . disabled people—can find it very difficult to claim asexuality because it looks so much like the product of sexism, racism, ableism, and other forms of violence." In other words, learning about asexuality led me to a much more expansive mindset as to "normal" sexual desire, which can mean many different things for many different people and is not, in fact, limited to the reductive stereotypes of cishet and gay cis men who want it all the time and cishet and lesbian cis women who don't. I can't speak to any other orientations or gender identities because, unlike the former examples, I haven't been bombarded with tropes about them over and over again. It's hard to stand firm about what you want in the face of so many arguments that you're the problem. But it turns out I've been doing it all along . . . by not "doing it." (Nope, not gonna apologize for that.)

BECAUSE MY SEX LIFE is one of the few places I've been able to assert my own boundaries, I now see it as an attitude crayon that I can use to color all areas of my life, especially ones where I get to keep my clothes on. In my own considered way, I haven't been "well-behaved" in the bedroom, at least not if we're talking about being a partner who's in it to win it. A strange result of never holding much capital in the physical department, I've found it easier to heed my body's own terms over anyone else's. In this case, showing up late to the party gave me an edge, whether it's always felt like one or not. Though it first came from a place of naivete and hesitance, over time I realized it's a box in which I don't care to fit. Since my sex appeal to others was never something I could reliably bet on, I bet on myself instead. And now I'm finally transposing this philosophy to other parts of my life, too.

In finding this clarity, a tiny coup soon followed. The freedom to start saying no to professional asks arrived without warning and with little flourish—like a tax refund check for two dollars. One baby step forward was realizing that not only would whoever asked me to do the thing be fine if I didn't do the thing, but that I would be, too. If you're thinking, "Yeah, hard duh," then you might not have a PP brain. (People pleaser or peepee, you choose!) Invites and offers are often couched in the gift basket flattery of "We immediately thought of you!" because that's the language it takes to get someone to agree to do something, not to mention a very easy way to get a person with low self-esteem's firstborn child.

But like a targeted ad, that nagging question still popped up in my brain: "What if I'm never asked to do anything ever again, especially by these people?" Until I realized that while that might prove true, it won't matter if whatever is being asked of me is not something I want to do in the first place. My own private no of recognition! I wanted to print it out in five-hundred-point Futura font (look it up, simply gorgeous), frame it, and refer to it in times of need. Better yet, get a prime real estate tattoo that people could ask me about and I would refuse to answer. (Meta!) We love to get invites for gatherings we don't really want to attend, but in the grand scheme of things, isn't it easier if everyone involved is as clear and direct as possible about what they want and, by that logic, also what they don't? Just like sex, it's better for both of you that way.

But how do you know which is which? A tip I once heard on a podcast (is there a more alienating way to start a sentence?) about whether you should say yes to an offer is to stop and ask yourself, "Would I want to do this thing if it were tomorrow?" This led me to the sheepish epiphany that there are so many things I've been agreeing to that sound great in the future and horrible in the present. (One helpful thing about proposals of sex I've fielded? They're never save-the-dates.) If a professional invitation is further away in my calendar, committing is significantly easier. Every time, without fail, I imagine by that distant date, I will be a better, more capable, mentally sounder person who loves to do *all the things*! Many, many thought experiments later, I can assure you that this hypothesis is my worst one yet. I am a pointillist painting of commitment: an idyllic, harmonious scene from afar, a screaming chaos of contradictory dots up close. Thanks to anxiety, on the day of practically anything I've ever agreed to, it turns out there's nothing I'd like to do less. The trick is in narrowing my yeses down to only the events I will mostly enjoy once I get through my standard-issue panic, rather than the ones that will be bad before, during, and after. In doing so, I will, as the business bestsellers say, "optimize" my dread, and for an existentialist living in a neoliberal technocracy, that's not nothing.

By the way, being decisive and being disrespectful aren't the same thing. You can advocate for your own needs while still being cordial, albeit firm, to others. If someone takes your self-respect as a slight, that's not on you. Setting boundaries is rarely a smooth process, but it's worth it if you value your own time and energy. Imagine trying to fit your luggage into an overhead bin that is already jam-packed. (Wow, *very* relatable! Great job, me.) Asking for what you need requires you to take up more space, something women are traditionally conditioned not to do. So, at first, it can feel like you're being extremely rude. In reality, it's a small, firm nudge—a reminder to the person in the middle seat who's all elbows: *Hey, I'm sorry for your loss, but I'm here, too.* (Did I commit to the travel metaphors or what? Gimme my miles.) I've found the less I ask for, the less I get from other people—that might not be intentional on their part, but I'm also short, soft-spoken, and unassuming. If I want something, I'm going to have to step into my ask.

The counterargument would be that saying yes professionally despite your own personal interests or desires is just "playing the game." That's Brand Management 101, babe. It's often not going to be stuff you want to do but is business savvy to do anyway. The consumers are, after all, buying into the polished, two-dimensional product, not the flawed, inconsistent human behind it. But I've realized pretending to be someone you think everyone else wants, based on others' opinions (aka marketing), is lonely. And I am in the fortunate position of not building a career dictated by that. If anything, I've built an entire persona around *not* being able to play the game. What's my secret? (After I deliver this line, imagine me playfully looking over my shoulder as I walk away from the camera.) I don't know how to. And yes, I'm positive it's hurt my marketability as an artist, but I guess I'm OK being less successful, if it means I can stay closer to a true version of myself. The inevitable fun house mirror that translates art to the consumer will inevitably distort me, anyway. Might as well do it my own way. Plus, the whole end point of the game is to get to say no whenever you want. I'm skipping ahead. I've gamed the game.

Despite the loneliness that can result from listening to your intuition over the "obvious choice," there's plenty of solidarity and inspiration to be found in artists doing the same. Michaela Coel, the brilliant creator and star of the groundbreaking HBO series *I May Destroy You*, walked away from a million-dollar Netflix deal because the streamer wouldn't give her ownership rights. In a *New York Times* interview, Coel said, "We go in and out of working with people, and we never quite know who they are, and no one ever quite knows who you are. There's something quite liberating about just letting everybody know." I want to cross-stitch these words directly on my brain like I'm a nightmarish pillow on the dark web version of Etsy.

Lately, I remind myself of the contradictions of my body and my desire with what the world has told me about myself. My body knows when to say no. Maybe if I listen to it regularly like a weird seashell (best for all involved not to picture this metaphor), I'll eventually extricate myself from the broken, hopelessly tangled earbuds better known as the Agreeability Industrial Complex.

I remind myself there is a life cycle to my goals—as an artist, as a social being, as a person with needs and urges—and the same things I agree to or think I want today may not be the same things I envision for myself or want tomorrow. Your self-perception and your dreams change, and sometimes you forget why you coveted certain opportunities so obsessively in the first place. The work is in letting go of old narratives and being aware of and acknowledging wherever it is you are right now. Not only is there relief and breathing room but there's self-discovery on the other side. In a world that's so good at telling people like myself no, it's high time we returned the favor.

Don't Get Mad,
Get Even . . . More Mad

When faced with anything less than open sunniness from someone, I immediately wonder, *Are you mad at me?* It might be slightly reframed—*Am I annoying you? How about now? Definitely now? Don't mind me, I'll just be over here wildly self-sabotaging until my fear is confirmed.*

The bittersweet truth is no one is more irritated at me most of the time than my own anger. At least that's what I would guess. I never quite know where we stand with each other, and that's the whole problem: I am afraid to ask. I'd wager a tidy sum that she's not a fan of my tentative, nonconfrontational ways. So, if you asked her, you might just get hit with "Don't ever say that fucking name to me again."

However, if you asked anyone else, they'd say, "Aparna? Angry? I'd love to see that!" I guarantee some acquaintance will read the previous paragraph and think, "There's no way she swears! That must be a ghostwriter." For the record, I swear a shit ton, but it's mostly to myself.

Starting with my family and trickling out to everyone else in my life, I've always been clocked as "nice" and "even-keeled" and "cool as a cucumber." I've tried letting it out. But, you see, either I back down immediately, like snapping at my partner for interrupting my thoughts and then apologizing thirty seconds later, or I burn most of the anger's fuel off in my head, like when I picture screaming at the driver of the car that nearly hit my pedestrian butt in the intersection, but then I imagine them getting out of the car and deciding I am a great stand-in for all their unresolved mommy issues, and I am filled with relief I never showed my hand.

I know part of me is ready and willing though. Because those rage fantasies burn hot. The counterweight of not giving myself enough space in the world has catalyzed into an internal monologue that effortlessly revs from zero to road rage. I remember once writing something vulnerable on a friend group text (never again) and barely two hours later, one of them distractedly responded with something flippant. I immediately not only questioned her as a friend but also as a human being, let alone how she could be so emotionally obtuse. She became a symbol of everything that was wrong with the world. If you can't even confide in your friends, what's the point?! Obviously, she'd hit a nerve, but if I had addressed it in the moment, it may not have made my feelings go into Voltron mode. I considered talking to her about it, but I found my own reaction so grotesque. I felt like the bigger asshole, despite having done . . . nothing.

In not giving my anger any room in the world, I am the sole audience for any grievances or complaints. And that's how I've become a particularly toxic shit-talking party of one. But, at this point, I've had such mean thoughts about everyone I both know and don't that I'm convinced I'm haunted-doll-level evil and no one can ever know what's in here. Part of what makes emotions like anger so scary is you might say things you can't take back. Sure, you may have a falling-out because you said something you didn't mean to someone out of pure joy, but it's certainly rarer. (I'm thinking something along the lines of *Let's spend the rest of our lives together!*)

———

GROWING UP, anger took a very specific shape in the form of my father's temper. It was a looming threat to be prevented at all costs, or cowed to until it passed. I couldn't imagine ever challenging it directly. But when my older sibling, Bhav, was a teenager, they and my dad would frequently clash. Inevitably, the tension stemmed from the timeless clash of textbook adolescence with parental red tape: how long they could talk on the phone with their friends, how late they were allowed to stay out, when and where they could go and with whom, whether they could date, and later, have a steady boyfriend; the list perpetually evolved with its convoluted, fickle by-laws, clauses, and amendments.

Today, I better understand the complexity of why these dynamics played out in such broken ways, but back then I only perceived these arguments as emotional fault lines in our household's foundation, which could shift at any moment, activated by anger and whoever held it. Whenever Bhav and my dad had a fight—inevitably a disagreement over a stipulation in an imaginary charter it was assumed the whole family had read and memorized—neither side was willing to back down. On more than one occasion, these situations turned physically violent. During one fraught instance, I heard the growing noise of yelling back and forth, then the sound of a dish shattering, followed abruptly by silence, and then the stark bang of the front door slamming. All I could process was that the sky was falling.

To my young, terrified mind, there was no clear course of action in these chaotic situations, in which people I loved became strangers to me. Seeking refuge, I would go into the bathroom and turn the fan on or read out loud to myself or, cringe alert, watch myself cry in the mirror as if in my very own

Lifetime movie. Anything to harness and overhaul the situation, PR style, to myself. I sound glib about it now, but to this day my body freezes and shuts down in the presence of heated conflict, even if just overhearing strangers.

Baked into the very foundation of the spaces it occupies, family drama so often remains behind closed doors (but fear not, publishing it in a book is totally OK). This is even more acutely true for an upper-middle-class immigrant family trying to blend into the white suburbs. Asian Americans, the South Asian diaspora very much included, are still commonly thought of as the "model minority." This was a narrative Asian immigrants created to assimilate better. It was then, of course, co-opted as propaganda by white politicians to paradoxically further both anti-Blackness and the idea of a racially integrated democracy. Is there nothing the white man won't appropriate?

Even in the construction of our own mythos, Asian Americans are supporting characters—in this case, smiling, nodding sycophants. Regardless, this stereotype has only exacerbated the cultural tendency that many AzAm (I see it now and I won't do this again) households already have of prioritizing familial respectability over individual well-being and safety. Part of that identity is keeping any inner turbulence or friction closely guarded. I'm not judging here. I get the motivations, but I also get how it perpetuates a dynamic that doesn't serve us, and often actively harms us.

Many families of every background prefer to keep their dysfunction close to the vest, but when you are already considered outsiders in your community, there is another layer added. Like satellite cults, immigrant families hold their own set of understood beliefs, rituals, and customs that are often out of sync with the wider social strata. Perhaps in holding our own cards so tightly, my family was simply aspiring to be the WASPs-in-spirit we knew we could be. This rings even more true as an assimilationist betrayal given that Indian Americans, as a group, are now the highest wage earners in the US, while the poorest Asian Americans in this country are poorer than their white counterparts.

The other crisscrossing lines of caution tape cordoning off my anger are that, as far as public opinion goes, there is no acceptable way for a woman to express hers. Want to be judged even more than you already are for having the audacity to exist? There's no bullhorn blaring, "Ladies' night! Rage out and emotionally snap, consequence-free!" though I would greenlight that all-female reboot of *The Purge*. The troll backlash alone might destroy the internet once and for all! Cishet men's anger isn't a threat to their likability or worth, nor is it tied to consequences. Whereas women are expected to be flat, smiling cardboard cutouts permanently welcoming you to a car dealership showroom (in hell), men get to be those wildly flailing tubes outside the dealership, drawing attention to themselves for no other reason than that they can, taking up as much space as their unpredictable flopping pleases. Male anger is evidence of passion, investment, and commitment. Women's anger is a dish best served to the trash, because yuck, what even is that? It's clearly gone bad, and what will people say about the smell? Bag it up and disappear any evidence it was ever here.

May I draw the people's attention to the perpetually painful example of Brett Kavanaugh's conduct while being questioned about his alleged sexual assault during his Supreme Court hearing versus his accuser Christine Blasey Ford's? He was rude, red-faced, and barely holding it together. She was calm, collected, and respectful. I'm sure she was enraged, but she was expected to present her anger as a careful, choreographed performance with no room for even a single misstep. And yet, here we all are, watching Justice Kavanaugh now freely weigh in on rulings on behalf of women's lives,

choices, and bodies, including the overturning of *Roe v. Wade*, the case pro-
tecting the right to abortion at a federal level. Since then, it has come to light
that the FBI failed to report or look into the 4,500 tips about Kavanaugh
they received. Now, I'm not a numbers guy, but that's a lot of tips.

The template for what female anger should look like may as well be one
of those vague metal obelisks that pass as art in office buildings. Intending
to evoke stoic power and strength, they end up conveying nothing at all. If a
woman ever falls off her tightrope of neutral deference, she lands in a sea so
teeming with insistence that she "calm down" and "stop yelling," she's likely
to forget she never even raised her voice.

Consider Uma Thurman's statement about other women in Hollywood speaking out against powerful men in the industry, most notably Harvey Weinstein. In an interview clip where you can detect her palpable
rage, she says, "I have learned that when I've spoken in anger, I usually regret the way I express myself. So, I've been waiting to feel less angry, and
when I'm ready, I'll say what I have to say." I can only imagine how well
versed she, as a veteran of the industry, is in her rage being weaponized
against her.

Even when disciplining in heteronormative families, moms get short
shrift when it comes to unleashing emotion. And now, hopefully, post-
global-pandemic-lockdown, we're all on the same page about how much
childcare and care work in general ends up falling on women in these situations. There are countless ways to be a bad mother, especially if you dare to
get frustrated with your three-year-old autocrat in public. The number-one
trait of a bad father? Not being there at all. Fortunately, though, there's that
one day a year moms are favorably recognized with the high bourgeois
honor of chrysanthemums and a single slice of frittata.

And, of course, not all women's anger is treated equal. It's parsed differently based on intersections like race, class, neurodiversity, visible disabilities, sexual orientation, and gender identity. For instance, white upper-class female anger is generally always handled with more priority than that of Black women. In her incisive book *Eloquent Rage: A Black Feminist Discovers Her Superpower*, Dr. Brittney Cooper writes, "The truth is that Angry Black Women are looked upon as entities to be contained, as inconvenient citizens who keep on talking about their rights while refusing to do their duty and smile at everyone." The opposite racial stereotypes can be just as detrimental—for example, the assumed passivity and subservience of Asian women often erases them entirely from the conversation. The overarching commonality is that those who may have the most justification and need for their anger are granted the least leeway to express it. Rather than considering it a standard operating feature of being alive, it's an add-on, a bonus allowance, one that you pay extra for in other areas—whether it's being further othered or treated as though you reacted without cause. The overarching conceit remains the same, however: female anger is always the bigger problem than whatever led to it.

AS A SOFT-SPOKEN, measured woman who happens to be a comedian, I've keenly registered the way my anger, the kind used to elicit a laugh, plays to an audience. For something often treated with outright dismissal offstage, it's both fascinating and destabilizing to see it even tolerated and celebrated onstage. People often delight in seeing me, as an actor and performer, play with an angrier persona where I get upset, yell, or approach belligerence (er, the closest I can get), because it's so incongruous with how I baseline present. I've played salty characters on-screen or rageful personas for sketches where I threaten the audience, though it never escapes me that I'm playacting at a gear I never shift to in my real life. Is the crowd's amusement because they think I have no real business anywhere near anger? Is me enraged inherently ridiculous? Am I betraying myself by leaning into the farce—essentially doing madface?

I've tried out real anger onstage only once. I had a meltdown at a final show at a venue that was shutting down, and because I hated performing there, I figured now was the perfect time to tell the crowd. I don't remember exactly what happened because I entered a part of my brain that exists only under extreme duress, but I do remember knocking over a stool and shrieking at a bunch of fratty bros (who remained, as always, unconcerned). Afterward, one of the other comedians on the show said I should do things like that more often. But the very thought left me shaking. Actually, no, my own anger left me shaking. *What the fuck was that?* I thought upon leaving the stage. *Who do I think I am?*

It's not as though anger and comedy are strangers to each other—in fact, they could be coleads in a rom-com, destined to end up together. Observe the classic specimen of the angry stand-up comic, a ranting misanthrope railing on society's ills and misfires. In an *LA Times* interview, Jerry Seinfeld—you know, from *Bee Movie*—commented, "Well, all comedy starts with anger. You get angry, and it's never for a good reason, right? You know it's not a good reason. And then you try and work it from there." I felt surprised to hear that, I must admit; I don't think anyone would characterize Seinfeld as an "angry" comedian—more like moderately ruffled. His harshest polemic is "What's the deal with . . . ?" But it helps to hear him admit he's channeling anger beneath the surface, too. *All of us* are pissed. Comedians just happened to have found a very specific outlet for the emotion. Hey, it's better than yelling at strangers on the internet. Though, alas, many do both.

Of course, comedians who are more overtly political use raging takedowns as part of their craft. Yet their invective is still delivered via the safe harbor of a practiced persona. For example, satiric news show hosts are generally upset in their segments, but because it's entirely a controlled, joke-laden performance without the consequences of real rage, the audience can feel not only secure but often delighted in this venting by proxy. It's planned, so the audience never has to feel as though they're not in on the joke.

But even when unpolitical, the safety of expressing anger via comedy is that it's done for a laugh, no matter how heightened it gets. When I get mad onstage, I'm still courting the audience's permission above all else, willing to play into their idea of my anger as ridiculous in exchange for their approval.

But genuine, targeted anger is not like that. It demands not only attention but discomfort, without the promise of release. You, and what you represent, made me mad; now I will make you hear me out. And no, there won't be a payoff at the end, at least not for you. This unwillingness to compromise is why true anger frightens me more. There's no concern for the audience at all. If anything, they become the unwilling targets.

One example is when a comedian is especially mad at a heckler and explodes out of proportion to the interruption. Typically, a comic will handle an unsolicited or aggressive comment from the crowd with a pointed, roast-style line, such as "Wow, I guess I get the microphone because I can talk without sounding like a piece of shit." If landed with speed and precision, this kind of barb will be more successful than the rest of their whole act. The power is rebalanced: the crowd is back on the side of the comic, against the heckler. However, if provoked enough, some comedians will unleash rage without the softish cushion of a punch line, at which point the situation can go any which way. As long as the anger is within the guardrails of their persona, the comedian can remain funny and likable, but once the performer relinquishes this control, they can assuredly become neither. The crowd may quickly lose sympathy for them when certain lines of social acceptability and morality are crossed. In clickbait terms, this is known as a TOTAL MELTDOWN!!! And this uncharted territory petrifies me.

Take the gutting example of Michael Richards. In November 2006, rankled by audience members in the front row who persisted in talking through his set, Richards went into a racial-epithet-laden rant, using the N-word multiple times and referencing atrocities such as Jim Crow–era lynchings. Long silence. In the video I forced myself to watch, while some of the crowd laughs nervously at first, the reactions quickly turn to shock and disbelief, and soon enough, beginning with the specific recipients of his vitriol, people start to leave. Finally, Richards, understanding he's gone too far, wordlessly leaves the stage.

In his public apology, he said, "For me to be at a comedy club and to flip out and say this crap, I'm deeply, deeply sorry. I'm not a racist, that's what's so insane about this." His defense was that he was trying to be more outrageous to deescalate the situation. Richards later cited the event as a major reason he decided to retire from stand-up the following year. A decade and a half later, one might argue that voicing those words and ideas in that context out loud does in fact make you racist, though don't worry! It turns out you're very much not alone! We all have work to do in this area, not just the Proud Boys.

This particular strain of anger—both the complete loss of control and the abandonment of any propriety or concern for others—horrifies and titillates me. Regret, disappointment, ostracism, and an embarrassment one can never fully recover from, the unmasking of a rapacious monster within. I suspect it's there in all of us, even me. *This* is why I'm so afraid of anger.

Hannah Gadsby was the first stand-up I ever saw who bridged controlled onstage anger with the discomfort of no punch line so that the audience was forced to bear witness to their own complicity. The whole impetus of their show *Nanette* repositioned those who were watching from entertained spectators to silent bystanders by gradually filling in the context of traumatic life events that happened to Gadsby that they later revised into a comedic story.

I watched *Nanette* live while Gadsby was touring it through New York in 2018, before it aired as a Netflix special later that year. In it, they posit the idea that vulnerable or self-deprecating comedy is always at the expense of the performer. You are baring yourself, but additionally, the onus is on you to keep it light for the audience, hence the term "comic relief." When you are already a member of a marginalized group, are you scapegoating your-self to ensure the comfort of others? There is no joke where something or someone isn't being thrown under a bus.

This idea was revelatory to me. I was putting myself and my life on the chopping block to connect with an audience. My bits where I expressed my anger as essentially a party trick suddenly felt much more uncomfortable. There are long moments in the latter half of the ninety-minute performance in which Gadsby is visibly furious and offers the audience no humor to fall back on. When I saw the show, I can attest that the crowd, myself included, was forced to steep in our own disquiet. We all realized together that, given further context, something we had easily laughed at earlier wasn't funny at all—it was horrifying.

To this point, many critics (and by critics, I mean cishet male stand-ups on my social media feed) of the televised version of the show argued *Nanette* didn't qualify as an actual comedy special. Their justification was that the common through line in comedy specials is jokes, and if you're going to break that structure, it's closer to the specter of a self-indulgent one-person show. Who even determines this distinction—the High Tribunal of Laughter? I strongly disagree, because comedy and tragedy are undeniably on the same spectrum of human expression, not to mention the brain's ability to feel pain and pleasure is deeply interconnected. So it's a discredit to humor's range as an art form to insist on a rigid, static definition of a comedy special. It's just the (predictable) status quo grumbling at the needle of innovation shift-ing over to a new record, playing a song they don't recognize and can't sing along to. Perhaps they were also unsettled by the depth of their own uneasiness when you took away the "jokes." After all, so many of these edgelords like to use that designation as a Get Out of Jail Free card to spout plenty of questionable opinions. In fact, in Gadsby's memoir, *Ten Steps to Nanette*, they write:

> I wanted to distract that very large segment of the world which is prone to devolving into reactive anger when it comes to women speaking unapologetically in public. . . . I wanted to make them experience intensely negative feelings but not allow them any capacity to connect meaningfully with me at my most vulnerable.

Watching Gadsby prioritize their outrage above the audience's comfort in a medium built on spectator approval, I saw hopeful opportunity, an escape hatch for my own.

THESE DAYS, anger courses through me in all its volumes and frequencies—boiling resentment, erratic fury, and mild annoyance to name a few favorites—as if I'm in some permanent emotional cardio boot camp. My proclivities are not just from having lived in New York for ten years, though that certainly didn't help. The fabric of the city is threaded with a simmering discontent that can be tapped into at any given moment. Significant hardships and minor grievances are all stitched together into one impossibly dense, enraged quilt. I would wager the city's entire power grid runs on misdirected aggression—an infinitely renewable resource, constantly at a surplus.

When I lived there, I did my part in contributing to the community. Even now, on any given day, I am irrationally frustrated when my friend doesn't text me back right away when I need counsel. *Why am I never worth anyone else's time?* I am irked at the barista when she gets my order wrong, even though she repeated it back to me. *Why does no one bother listening to me?* I am enraged at the person in line behind me who stands too close, feeling their breath down my neck. *What am I, a fucking ghost?* Each instance builds upon the next until I am ready to scream, but, due to my make and model, can't.

Part of me is unsurprised. Bottled up for decades, my anger was, of course, quietly biding her time, amassing enough resources to initiate a hostile take-over, a personality coup. She wells up over everything now, a sudden boiler room gust of irritation—perhaps foreshadowing eventual core combustion. I know I haven't respected her. She has a right to push back. I treated her like a lurking shadow, when she's simply a pressure valve, regulating the ebb and flow of being human.

Of course, whenever my anger does show up, she feels justified. One of her natural inclinations, after all, is to demand room for herself upon ar-rival, like the person in line. Yet I am constantly talking her down, tenta-tively, like a hostage negotiator on their first day. *Down, girl. There is no real person at fault here.*

What if the stranger is encroaching on my personal space because they're in a rush and they might miss their flight! And the barista is distracted be-cause maybe this isn't the job she wants, but it's the one she has right now because she's hustling and all she wants to do is paint. So maybe she's not listening extra carefully to every order that comes through. Do I want to be *that* entitled customer? And my friend is not available because she is busy, because everyone is busy, because that's the currency of the world we live in, as adults, as worker drones, as flipping automatons in the foosball table that is modern life! How often am I unavailable—most of the time? That's my compulsory inward interrogation: Why am I angry? Do I deserve to be an-gry? Am I considering the full humanity of those around me?

The default answer is perfunctorily always no. Things could always be harder or worse or more unfortunate. I haven't earned this emotion nor do I deserve her spoils. Her arsenal is a privilege, not a right. Right? Then again, am I considering my own full humanity? Also no.

I am reminded of anger's conditionality. From my perspective, my anger is fully warranted, but from yours, the view may be entirely different. The doubt that I may have overlooked your side hinders me every time, even if you did transgress. When people have been angry at me, I couldn't always explain my actions. All human beings are messy, self-involved, and, unfortunately, frequently ruinous mysteries even to themselves. How do I negotiate this truth with what to expect from the world?

I foolishly daydream that if my anger lands, it will be perfect, like the words of Omar Little in *The Wire*: "You come at the king, you best not miss." (Full disclosure: I only finished the show in 2022. Please respect my privacy during this difficult time, but also, *incredible show*.) Yet I still want to make sure no one is caught unawares before I go whole hog, or in my case, a quarter hog. That's why it's easier to see where everyone else is coming from first. It's not like I can plop down safety cones and a tumbling mat so nobody gets hurt, or make everyone sign an NDA for that matter (at least not yet). Rather than just letting 'er rip, I demand that my anger be accurate, precise, and proportionate. But, oopsy daisy, she isn't any of those! She's underdeveloped and green, like when I try to explain a bad work experience in an email and find myself minimizing my own version of events to my former bosses so I don't seem too difficult. They aren't even my bosses anymore! She's petty and nasty, like when customer service is not being helpful, and instead of being mad at the soulless company's policies, I wonder how this specific representative is so impressively stupid. She Trojan horses herself inside other strong feelings, meaning that, frequently, when I am down on myself and sad, I am actually mad at the world but have just directed it all inward.

There are glimmers of progress. I got in a fight on the phone with Bhav and, as with much family tension, I was trying to help by mediating but got overinvolved. Still, when I sensed them getting mad, a weather system that I know acutely well, a newfound rush of exhausted ire burst out, especially because my intentions had been good. I told them that I was tired of always deferring to their anger (something they had never asked me to do), especially because I had already apologized for my mistake. I wasn't going to just sit quietly and be berated. We ended the call there, after which I immediately burst into tears, unused to playing offense. But weeks later, when everyone had cooled down and we talked about it, Bhav expressed a relieved, astonished admiration I had lashed out back at them. They confessed that they had always been afraid I wouldn't be able to stand up for myself when I needed to, and despite the sting of my words in that moment, my pushing back had actually comforted them. This admission alleviated some fear of my own as well. Despite feeling shame for my words in those heated moments, I had to recognize that what I said came from a place of honesty. Our chaotic parts deserve room—if we don't make some willingly, they will take it up themselves. And I remember the flip side of it all. Where there is anger, there can also be forgiveness. If there isn't any room for the anger, there may not be any room for the forgiveness.

I'm finally starting to see my own anger as a necessity. Without it, I'd just be constantly gaslit by the world. Promising me one hand and giving me neither, I'm left wondering if I'm the unreasonable one. Anger reminds us we are justified in asking for what we deserve. While I've focused on the day-to-day microscale of anger, there is also the entrenched macro anger at societal injustices and the age-old, systemic imbalance of the haves and the have-nots—a thorny intersection of every kind of identity and every method of disenfranchisement. I interrogate this type of outrage within my-self constantly, since it can so often manifest as performative gestures of progressivism. When I feel anger on behalf of another group, I know I need to investigate my own privilege and possible contribution to their griev-ances, and while I'm at it, decenter my feelings and ego.

One of my frustrations with liberalism, especially of the moderate vari-ety or from those of us in less directly affected positions, is that there's a "theater of upset" that happens over true crimes against humanity—whether it's children kept in cages at the border, yet another unarmed Black person killed by the police, or corporations shirking the blame for poisoning an entire community slash planet—the deep fury is real, but it doesn't turn into any kind of meaningful action. Amplifying issues and my anger about them on social media is one small step, but I don't want to stop at slacktiv-ism. Another term for this is "virtue signaling," which always makes me think of a nun hiring a skywriter. Of course, people should be enraged about these things and about the extent of apathy of which people in power are capable, and it's valuable to inform others about continued injustice. But the crucial part is converting that immediate gut anger into longer-term action. Otherwise, it stalls out or, worse, catalyzes into jaded apathy and cynicism.

Not that any of it is easy or straightforward. There are so many deserv-ing GoFundMes and their like out there (thank you, broken health-care sys-tem, among myriad other contenders!) that one can easily start out enraged and come out the other end of the activist car wash disheartened, over-whelmed by the sheer scale of suffering and brokenness of everything.

In a world that is literally burning with wildfires fueled by massive cli-mate change and beset with pandemics, in an economy that is consistently and negatively affecting those who can least withstand it, in countries whose governments lie to them time and again to consolidate and further their own corrupt powers, what is left but anger as the fuel of hope that drives us to care and to act rather than to despair and retreat? Stoking my own wrath is a delicate balance of keeping myself motivated and focused without getting lost in the weeds of the amount of impact or the desensitization of overexposure.

I doubt I'll ever get the full hang of my anger; in the same way that the ideal time to learn a language fluently is in childhood, the golden window has closed. A chronic overthinker of everything including this sentence, I can't quite let go the way my anger demands. However, as a performer, I can call myself out on the put-on of anger versus the real thing. And these days, my willingness to express the latter does appear in fitful snatches— and whenever this happens, for a second, I feel a small shift. I sometimes back down immediately, lacking the confidence to follow through. I am off the trail, wandering in circles. But still, there's that moment, the pause of looking over the brink. I feel overbearing and rapacious and dumb and irrational and mean and wrong, but at the risk of romanticizing it, I also feel alive. Impossibly, unpredictably, uncomfortably alive. Because anger, for all its extremes and pain and intensity and bluster, is never boring or rote. It can be simultaneously myopic and careless and vital and important and inextricably bound to what it is to be human.

Confessions:
It's Not Personal(ity)

Whenever I meet a dog or baby for the first time, I have a distinct fear they will recoil from me such that an old woman standing nearby will say in a hushed whisper, "They sense great evil."

Even my computer passwords are insecure.

I enjoy Justin Bieber's music (not so much the rest of him).

Sometimes I will play a new song I like so many times that I will start to detest it and wonder what I ever saw in it to begin with. Fun fact? Also my approach to relationships.

Whenever I really like one song by an artist but don't like any of the rest of their music, I feel like *I've* let *them* down. I even imagine meeting them one day and never being able to admit my horrible secret. Even my people-pleasing has dreams.

———

I've thought lesser of a baby for not handling something the way I would have; a baby, for crying out loud, and believe me, she did!

I will often like a known asshole simply because they were nice to me. I will recall their kindness and I will feel chosen. It won't even be that they were particularly nice, it will be that they weren't a jerk, which is pretty much the lowest standard someone can meet. That's probably the asshole's whole strategy: if you are selectively benevolent, those recipients will staunchly defend you, thinking you see something in them that sets them apart from the rest. Here I go, being fooled by assholes at every turn. Is there a better description of the world as it currently exists?

Ha!ku

The "eye" key fell off

Her keyboard whle wrtng ths

Book. Metaphor much?

Anxiety in Three Acts

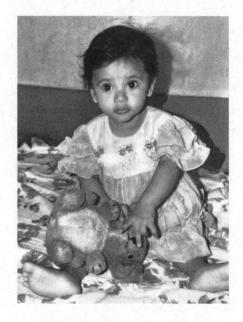

Even as a baby, I was overwrought by the whole existence thing. [Credit: Family photo.]

I. A Trembling Little Thing

Swallowing pills

Lighting a match

Lighting the stove

Fireworks

The car wash

Catching a ball

Any self-maneuvering done on wheels

Ghosts

Big dogs

Small dogs with agendas

Anger

Thunderstorms

Mean kids

Kids I don't know

Grown-up strangers

Strangers who I strongly suspect are mad at me

Authority figures

Authority figures who are definitely mad at me

Drugs

The dark

That's a short list of the fears I had as a kid. My nerves were like the weather—constant and unpredictable. Unlike the weather, they were not the go-to subject for small talk with people I didn't know well (see above: strangers).

I viewed the world as a deceptively benevolent setup with hidden mine-fields I somehow needed to avoid. But, lucky me, I wasn't allowed to play video games, so it's subversive I even went for that analogy. My family had neither Nintendo nor Nickelodeon, so if my '90s nostalgia references are sadly lacking, put it on my therapy tab. My parents ran a sheltered ship. No, not homeschooling, this isn't that kind of book, but their list of first-generation-immigrant rules limited most ways children learn about the wider world: no sleepovers, no trashy books (anything with a suggestive or offensive cover font) or unapproved TV shows, no dating, no coed anything really, and no chewing gum (clearly a gateway to anarchy). While Bhav, my older sibling and the first-born child, diligently looked for loopholes whenever they could, the primary message I soberly imbibed was the world is a dangerous and unsafe place—proceed at your own risk. Or, even better, sit tight and proceed with caution when you're twenty-seven if you make it that far. Good student that I was, my fearfulness was always taking notes, the main one being "Please help me."

During my early years, I never used the bathroom at school. I trusted the toilets at home, sure, but school toilets were stranger danger. Nobody had debriefed me on those sinister sewage sirens with their tricks and poisons, and I hoped in vain for a mandatory Potty Protocol Debriefing (stop here a moment to savor the skill level of this pun). In my defense, we should all be afraid of public restrooms. Nothing good ever happens in them. I was terri-fied I'd lock myself into a stall, not be able to get out, and ergo die tragically before my time in a senseless accident, a suburban legend for generations of girls to come. Not that my kid brain went that far. The fear simply ended in an ellipsis. The yellow tape of my worrying read, "Do not mentally cross this line because it will dot-dot-dot WALL OF RESISTANCE."

One fateful afternoon, my first-grade class had our own version of an En-glish tea party, where, in keeping with tradition, all talk of empire was rele-gated to subtext. Like the early Brits, I hadn't yet learned how to contain my greed—I overdid it on the lemonade. In the plot twist we all saw coming, I raced to the bathroom, and, yes, it did take me far longer than it should have to figure out how the stall door fastened and unfastened. And then I missed my bus home because natural selection is real! Also because I couldn't get my stupid mittens on in time. Try, just try, to imagine a level of helplessness in which mittens are a viable threat. Did I mention they were already hooked to my sleeves? They weren't going anywhere. And neither was I.

When the limited system I was operating within broke, I was bereft. I was dot-dot-dot to the max. I had heard horror stories about kids missing buses, and in response, I'd clutched my evil eye and prayed such a fate would never befall me. Some deep instinct for self-preservation kicked in—likely the same one that revs up now when someone asks for a bite of my dessert— and I thought to ask a teacher for help. I know I was operating at a primal level because I had to talk to a person with power (see previous: authority figures).

I found a viable teacher-victim and, using a combination of squeaks and interpretive dance, managed to persuade her to drive me home. But therein lay the rub, because as a child entirely reliant on The System, if it wasn't pinned to my jacket, I didn't have it—including my address. Where I lived was more an abstract idea than a concrete one. (Sidenote: Yes, there are children who are precocious and well-spoken by the age of six, and to them I tip my hat and say, "With all due respect, you creep me out.") Also, I realize leaving school premises alone with a teacher would never be allowed today, but it was a wild time back then—pretty much Studio 54 with chalkboards.

My teacher drove us out of the parking lot and into the surrounding blocks, as I resigned myself to the state of affairs: (1) I had no idea how to get home, and (2) I was terrified to communicate this fact since it might result in someone getting mad at me. Instead, every few blocks, my teacher would ask, "Should I turn here?" And wanting to be a team player, I would nod. This led to bigger and bigger concentric circles around the neighborhood, all of them eventually ending somewhere we had already been, finally concluding poetically back in the school parking lot. *The first of a series of metaphors for her life*, the author somberly reflects. My parents eventually had to come pick me up and discuss with the school the impressive circumstance of a child who manages to get into trouble in a completely passive manner.

One might think that growing up in an uneventful upper-middle-class cul-de-sac would leave me blissfully unconcerned with the stark truths of the big wide world. But living inside a vacuum-sealed bubble had the opposite effect. Suburbia has its own culture and customs and cookie-cutter template of how to live. And all of it is disturbingly neutered—a Rockwellian diorama of the American dream. It's a phantom limb, torn asunder from the metropolis it feeds off, with no allegiance beyond the concerns of its paranoid moms and youth soccer leagues. Any unknown quickly took on monstrous shape in my imagination.

Of course, we had a neighborhood watch, you know, the analog version of the Nextdoor app, before busybodies found each other online. The logo was a shady silhouette of a ne'er-do-well in a fedora, undoubtedly Carmen Sandiego's evil twin. Once, through our eyes-and-ears patrol, I learned of a suspicious-man sighting. Nothing came of it, but I thought about that guy for months—what was he up to?! Clearly, he was playing the long game. My imagination gave him a five-season prestige TV show. Potential threats weren't a question of if, but when.

It didn't help that my main influx of information was the nightly news my dad watched. Hypnotized by the anchors' somber Gregorian tones and the over-the-shoulder graphics, I absorbed every drop of sensational propaganda, whether I understood it or not. Everything went into my brain's scare blender, overflowing into an amorphous smoothie of things to freak out about. Between the news and my father's other favorite programming, nature shows—which somehow never come with a graphic sex and violence rating—I espoused the Hobbesian credo that life is "nasty, brutish, and short." I was just another unlucky gazelle, who happened to live near a Borders bookstore (RIP).

I was constantly on guard for what would befall me next. I was barely distracted by the promise of a Cinnabon at the mall food court. Children, of course, can smell weakness on each other years before body odor enters the picture. My virtuoso level of helplessness marked me as a prime target, though mostly for entry-level tormentors hell-bent on working their way up the corporate ladder.

In kindergarten, I got bullied during what was supposed to be an uneventful, peaceful activity: reading corner. We sat on the rug in assigned spots and listened to our teacher read aloud. And every afternoon, without fail, the mop-haired kid next to me demanded I pull up the tape from the floor that marked where we sat. (I no longer remember this tyrant's name, another blurry worm for my subconscious's inspo board.)

When I mutely refused, he'd explain that he was going to bring a knife to school and then we'd see what's what. I blocked out what exactly this kid threatened to do with said knife, but I'm pretty sure it wasn't slice up a lovely fruit and cheese plate for two. I had no idea what to do, besides stop going to school and enter the witness protection program. Instead, I fell back upon my strategy of aggressive nonreaction, and eventually he got promoted to bully middle management and moved on.

But I remained a target. PE was already one of my least favorite classes as it involved entirely theoretical abilities—strength and coordination. We were working through the square dance unit (why hoedown etiquette was incorporated into late-1980s and early-1990s American school curricula, I refuse to understand or look up). On the day in question, the dance was a conga line (which, hate to be that guy, but NOT a square dance). The kid behind me, let's call him Mohan because that was his name, kept whisper-threatening me to move faster, otherwise he was going to inflict unspeakable violence on my family and me.

What can I say? I attracted blue-sky menaces who specialized in future possibilities rather than current limitations.

The thing is, there was a beat? And you can only go so fast when there is a rhythm to follow? But even I knew this case would fall apart in the face of bully logic, so instead I pretended I couldn't hear him. Because I was so into the music? That's why I was shaking so hard? I was the first known incident of "dancing for your life" that predates *So You Think You Can Dance*.

One forgets how lonely childhood can be in these moments. It's not exactly like you can ask for help—the low opinion of tattletales being well ingrained early on. But I also gathered there would be repercussions if I narced on another kid to the Feds, as it were. This was yet another example of how I couldn't hack it in the version of the World™ as described in the brochure. I frequently had the suspicion that I'd been dropped into the wrong universe and had to make the best of it. These are the small mental caveats devised by the perpetually overwrought. *There's been a glitch. It's fine. Just make it work until you are safely returned to your soft white holding cube for further evaluation.*

It's entirely apropos then that I was a Y2K high school graduate. Barring a miracle, I figured age seventeen was as far as this whole thing would go. *You had a good run*, I thought midway through my senior year, wondering why everyone was so invested in college applications. When nothing devastating happened at the stroke of midnight on January 1, 2000, I was relieved, but also genuinely amazed. It was yet another sign that reality and I weren't on the same page.

II. Enter Adulthood, with Wary Hesitation

Well past college, I thought of my constant fear as simply me "worrying" about things. That's what I thought was happening. It wasn't a medical condition as much as an idiosyncrasy that complicated my life. My mother was a self-described worrywart, as if constant fretting were a stubborn skin blemish best left to private conversation. Anxiety didn't seem to me like a mental illness anyone could suffer from—it was more like a fancy way of saying you were nervous. Like calling clothes "garments."

It wasn't until years into my comedy career, as my own battle with stage fright snowballed, that I noticed the term "anxiety" being tossed around the cultural milieu with awfully reckless abandon, especially considering the cautious nature of the word. I still didn't think I had anxiety, though—after all, when I'd taken a semester off in college, my official diagnosis had been depression. Why should I get to have all the things?

I saw the way anxious people were being portrayed, and figured unless you were Richard Lewis overanalyzing your way through a Boku commercial (very specific '90s juice reference, but if you get it, *you're so welcome*), you had no right to the identity. At the same time, my nerves about performing comedy were now so disruptive, I had trouble thinking about anything else for hours, sometimes days, before a show. Nor did I realize that my constant worrying about pretty much everything else might qualify as anxiety. I just figured my personality sucked.

I finally started talking about my own anxiety when it consumed so much of my mental space, the only place it could go was into therapy and my work. The strange thing is after I finally took ownership of it—for example, I did a joke about having anxiety in my Comedy Central half-hour special in 2016—overnight, it seemed like everyone had anxiety. We can hugely thank the presidential election that year for the collective meltdown, but it was like the vocab factory made a surplus of the word and suddenly it was being used all the time for everything. Tired? It's anxiety! Mad? Anxiety! Stressed? Definitely anxiety! I don't mean to discount anyone's actual experience of it—after all, it's a complex, very real, very hard thing. But given everyone's overall sense of impotence as to the state of the world, it felt like it became THE only thing to talk about. It's strange to think of a mental illness as getting "popular," but the media was having a field day. They may as well have been talking about Bennifer 2.0—the tone reeked of "Let's dish!"

It's not like the prevalence of discussing anxiety did anything to quell mine. I sometimes imagined my own as the misguided caretaker who has kidnapped my brain and is holding it hostage in an old cabin, forcing me to spin a very specific story against my will, à la Kathy Bates in *Misery*, a movie that I, fittingly, have not seen.

I USED TO get nervous only *before* a show, but then my nerves started leaking over into my actual performance. While I had always been scared to look at the audience too much, I now couldn't bear to look at them at all, convinced that if I did, I'd spot that one vengeful member, making a throat-slitting motion at me.

I found myself performing on autopilot, wishing for my set to be over. Unsurprisingly, this made my pre-performance anxiety worse, turning it into one vicious cycle, albeit one with a bittersweet laugh track. The irony didn't escape me that I had started getting attention for talking openly onstage about mental illness, including anxiety, and now, this exact experience was undoing me. I was passing up opportunities to perform and feeling increasingly ashamed of performing less, ironically even turning down mental health charity fundraisers. My own brand had come to collect, and I was balking. Let's stroll through what had become my dreaded preshow rundown, shall we?

9:15 a.m. I begrudgingly wake up to the familiar pit in my stomach. I'm so used to it at this point that I can almost successfully persuade it to shove off, at least for now. I tell it that I'll deal with it later. In the meantime, I'll just numb out in this coveted window of sweet denial. After all, showtime is still twelve hours away. I could be thousands of miles away with a new name and dye job by then. Plus, I have to worry about more pressing concerns—like an audition, say, or is today the podcast with someone I've never met but find inconceivably intimidating even from a distance? Either way, I'm sure something will happen that will reveal how disappointing I am! I've internalized a system of judgment in which everything I do, even something as innocuous as whether I hold the door for a stranger, goes toward a tally of my being a "good" person or a "bad" person. Stand-up cuts the deepest because it's such an exposed position for someone so debilitatingly concerned with other people's opinions. "I want to make my life as emotionally chaotic and unsafe as possible!" I say every morning into the mirror, having managed to build an entire livelihood around that exact philosophy.

I should be grateful that I'm not touring. On the road, I have to plan my entire days around my anxiety, since I don't have the routines of home to distract me. I did a festival in Australia that was two weeks straight of shows every night. I was in a state of looming panic the entire time I was there. I woke up every morning to my own internal Emergency Broadcast System test: *They are going to hate you, they are going to hate you, they are going to hate you.* Being so far away from home only emphasized the feelings of doom—no matter where you go, you're going to let people down.

The predetermination of failure eclipses the act it's referring to. If I walk myself through what failure entails—having a bad set—it sounds minor. And yet, like bowling pins, it always resets to the same high-stakes, all-or-nothing worthiness as a person. The beginnings of terror clench my stomach and chest, snaking up my throat. My own body is foreign to me, a heavy object. I go about my day, the symptoms coalesce, and a question lingers— *Why do you keep doing this to yourself?*

3:00 p.m. I ride the train back home from a voice-over job, and I vaguely consider the shows later—maybe I should think about crafting a possible set? I try to open the Notes app on my smartphone, where I will dash off set lists, but a wave of nerves overtakes me, and instead I half listen to a news podcast. In the grand scheme of international diplomacy, my shows tonight could not matter less. This is an odd comfort that I still manage to feel guilty about.

4:30 p.m. Four hours before showtime, give or take, and the jig is up. I can no longer deny the two sets I'm doing later tonight. I can barely handle the reality that there is more than one. Prickles of doom hail down on me. I feel as though I've never before in my life done a stand-up show.

I envision myself leaving for the show, walking up to the venue, attempting light chitchat backstage—oh no, wait, there is no backstage at this place, so I have to stand in the audience until it's my turn (a social anxiety spiral all its own)—and then do I hang out after my set even though all I want to do is disappear? Do I try new material? What if none of it works and I freeze up? There are cool, young comics performing in the first show, and they will remind me how irrelevant and boring I am. And what about the audience? The last few times I did this show, I have had fine but not great sets—why am I asked back? All my peers will watch me struggle through jokes without strong endings, and then what? Just like when I was kid, my brain hits that dot-dot-dot wall . . . !!!

5:30 p.m. Because I've had multiple cups of coffee today, my thoughts take on a hyperactive quality. Simultaneously, a heavy drowsiness falls over me, some free swag courtesy of dread. My overwhelming impulse is to sleep, but if I nap, I will wake up disoriented and upset. Having too much caffeine has set the freak-out gears in motion extra early. What I need is water and movement. No, I don't mean appreciatively watching a synchronized swimming routine. I mean hydrating and doing a kickboxing workout on YouTube. I get into it, too—my aggression ratcheting up during the paid ads. Exercise is one of the few things that temporarily gets me out of my head. For a brief period, I transport to a fantasy of myself as the superhero nobody asked for: the Cardio Clown.

But I start working out too close to when I need to leave for the show. Classic! I rush to get out the door and end up running late. *At least I didn't cancel*, I comfort myself. I bring a few tabs of propranolol, which is a short-term antianxiety pill. It mostly swaddles my brain into a gray neutral gear, but it does make it easier for me to slip into autopilot.

By the way, I've tried plenty of other methods of combating anxiety—psychotherapy, alcohol, mindfulness, breathwork, bodywork, power poses, affirmations, meds, and hypnosis. That last one was with the aid of an extremely upbeat hypnotist who was default psyched about everything, the type who makes you realize the glass is neither half-full nor half-empty, it's rigged. That guy's glass runneth over. He gave me several recordings to listen to, but instead of being hypnotized, I'd fall asleep. Unfortunately, my anxiety, like my hypnotist, believes it can manifest whatever it puts my mind to. I am up against a worthy foe.

I can sometimes manage nerves a little better with meditation or some other mind-body exercise like 4-7-8 breathing (four seconds in, hold for seven, eight seconds out; according to the hypnotist, it simulates the respiratory pattern of someone under heavy anesthesia—yes, please!) or tapping (tapping certain points on your body while processing whatever thoughts you're experiencing), but it's all a fickle puzzle of timing and chance. A crapshoot. Sometimes it helps, sometimes it doesn't. My state of mind frequently comes down to a coin toss.

7:45 p.m. I'm now fully freaking out about performing, with a generous pour of running-behind panic mixed in for good measure. The physical symptoms of my anxiety can range from acid reflux to sweatiness to racing thoughts and increased heartbeat. It's always awful, but *how* it's awful is different almost every time. Like those mystery jelly beans, I never know what flavor I'm going to get! But the gist is always that something is going very wrong or is about to—your entire body is convinced you forgot to turn the stove off before leaving your home on a metaphysical level. Frequently my brain short-circuits straight to depressive thoughts of *Why do you exist?* and *What is the point of any of this?* Because it can't handle the full force of the anxiety, my mind defaults to fatalistic detachment.

In high school I ran cross-country with a girl who, all of a sudden, simply couldn't run as fast as she used to. It wasn't clear why, and no one ever figured it out. To my knowledge, she wasn't injured or ill. One day she was one of the top runners on the team, and the next day she wasn't. I am forever convinced the same thing will happen to me with comedy. Listening to an old set often puts me in a better headspace because it serves as a reminder that I've performed before and can do it again. I play a recording of the last show I did—it went OK, but my mind lingers on the moments that could have gone better.

8:27 p.m. My mind is a mad spinning top by the time I get to the venue. They have me going last, which is . . . not great. Firstly, I didn't know I was going last, or I would have prepared appropriately (ahem, tried to negotiate my way out of it). And second, now I have to stay and watch most of the show, during which I will carefully note how well everyone else does and how badly I will do in comparison. This will serve only to ramp up my anxiety since I will become consumed with the thought that nothing about my act is worth watching.

The long period of time in which I will now have to manage my nerves overwhelms me, but what choice do I have? I can't ask to go up earlier. It's a privilege to be the headliner. And there's no way to explain to the show organizers that it's a bad idea for me to go last, not when my only argument is that I'm going to be a letdown. There's the risk too that it'll turn into a self-fulfilling prophecy. Sometimes I have to go up earlier so I can leave in time for another show, but tonight I have a big enough window between spots. I mentally calculate when to take my pills since they take roughly twenty minutes to kick in. I don't want them to wear off just as I'm hitting the stage. If I time it right, they might even last through my second set at the next show. It's a precise calculation of drug timing, and now it's part of my job.

9:20 p.m. To my utter relief, the crowd is generous to the other comics, but then again, not so much that they are laughing at everything. They are piping up where they feel the comic deserves it, which means they may be able to tell if I'm on autopilot. Which I often am these days. *Why do I keep ending up here?* My mind has gotten snagged on this question—right alongside the helpful thought that I'm going to die. *Very chill, brain. Real value-add, thanks.* The only way I know to stop the incessant chatter is to take my pills. Bottoms up!

9:35 p.m. The last act before me is onstage. She's doing great, as I assumed she would. She's twenty-five or something unholy and has achieved far more in her career than I had at her age. She's so likable, too. *Now that's a real stand-up,* I think, pushing myself to feel worse. She should be the one headlining. I saw her going over her notes before she went on, but now she seems to be doing an entire tangent off the cuff, and the crowd is Eating. It. Up. One can always be wrong, but in sizing up the audience, I think I may fare alright. A palate cleanser after the real star.

A decade plus into stand-up, I understand what I'm dishing out and how it will generally be received. But the honesty of live performance is you never quite know what's going to happen. An audience might like you but be full of tepid laughers, and it will be a real slog. A different audience might not care for you, but one particularly enthusiastic person or corner of the room will tide you through.

9:40 p.m. T-minus five minutes to this performance gauntlet, and I have come to terms with my fate. Who really even cares about a comedy show? Nobody! Except these fools. But then again, climate change. Never forget climate change! None of this could matter less. My brain is in "go-time" mode, hitting me with variations on the same theme over and over again: "You don't deserve to be here. You are not funny, and you are not a performer." *Maybe*, I weakly think, *but here I am. Might as well try?* In that sense, no matter how unworthy I feel most of the time, my job is to get up there and show people how my mind works and that's it.

Of course, one of the big reasons, if not the reason, that people think stand-up is so challenging is the possibility of bombing—a complete lack of understanding and acceptance from the audience. It taps into our universal and fundamental fear of rejection and ostracism. Here's the thing: there's nothing quite like bombing. That's true. Here's the other thing: you bomb frequently as a stand-up—maybe not always to the same extent, but bad sets are as regular as crummy moments at any other job.

When I was starting out, whenever I wasn't doing well, I'd try a line like "Oh, you guys are doing that thing where you're laughing so hard, no sound comes out" or "It's OK, I'm fluent in silence. I can tell you guys liked that one." I had enough material to do almost a whole hour just on what to say when jokes didn't work. Bombing is part of the craft, of any performance craft, though it's the most immediately apparent in stand-up comedy. An actor might give a lackluster performance in a play and even garner walk-outs, but it's still not the gut punch of a joke getting nothing. If you're doing enough sets, you get used to the unpredictability of an audience. You realize that even if seven out of the last nine audiences have laughed in one specific spot, they will not laugh the tenth time nor the eleventh or twelfth, but then audience thirteen will somehow be back on board.

According to a 2020 article in *Personality and Social Psychology Review*, researchers cited multiple studies, where "failed comedy tends to elicit disgust, anger, and disapproval." Not to mention the secondhand embarrassment of watching someone bomb can be unduly uncomfortable for all. If the comedian is an experienced one, bombing may still be uncomfortable, but they'll also have built up a reserve of strength; they can handle it. The audience members are the ones who must openly contend with their own discomfort, which they will do—at your expense.

I bombed at a festival show in Ireland. I was the only non-cis-straight-white-male on the lineup, and during one of my set's more protracted moments of silence, someone yelled, "You're shite!" Nothing like a lilting accent to twist the knife deeper. There's something about tanking overseas that really nails home the idea, "Oh, so there's nowhere on the planet I can go where people won't despise my art!" I comfort myself with the notion that this show tonight will definitely not be a repeat of that experience. I just have to get through it. As soon as I do, I know I will be filled with relief, no matter how it goes.

9:43 p.m. At two minutes to showtime, I want nothing more than to press myself into a wall and hope no one will find me. I imagine telling the show organizers I feel sick and need to leave (which I did once and still feel hugely ashamed about)—yep, that's how a natural performer thinks. . . . *Let's just get this over with!*

9:45 p.m. The comedian before me finishes her set to enthusiastic applause. *Hope you all are ready to be bored and angry.* The emcee jumps back onstage for a quick hit of banter and then starts introducing me. All I can do now is show up. Thankfully, everything in my brain is drowned out by adrenaline. In a way, it's as if the show has already happened, and now, I am outside my body, watching it play back. I walk up into the moment.

III. The Ticking Time Balm of Horror Movies

Horror movies get me right where they want me—as a captive audience. I do not enjoy them. They viscerally upset me, burrowing under my skin like a greedy parasite. And yet I am drawn back to them time and again. I am the girl who hears the noise in the dark, creepy house and goes to investigate. Another part of me yells at the screen, "You idiot! Don't do it!!!" But I never learn, because I *want* to be shocked, to experience dread and feel ghastly in one contained, controlled experience. What a welcome alternative to the nonchalant terror that can attack us at any moment, from any direction, out in reality—the kind of frightening that gives no warning and leaves as silently as it came. The outsize feeling of controlled fear in a safe environment is what I'm chasing; I need something, anything, that shocks me out of the weary numbness of the never-ending news and social media cycles. I know I'm not alone—after all, true crime has never been more popular.

I, for one, had to mature into this masochism. When I was a young fearball, even the suggestion of horror was way too scary. The *TV Guide* one-line episode descriptions of the Nickelodeon show *Are You Afraid of the Dark?* were enough to send me spinning out.

My friend Tommy is the Michael Jordan of being scared—the professional who knows what he's doing and adds his own flair to it. He loves horror movies. Halloween is his favorite holiday and he goes all out, dressing up, of course, but also putting pumpkins and fake tombstones in his yard and stashing monsters and ghosts in his trees. Once, he invited me to join him for "100 Greatest Horror Movie Moments" at a now-shuttered Los Angeles theater. I went, and very quickly it dawned on me that the entire event was just a montage countdown of all the parts of the movie that make me squeeze my eyes shut and plug my ears until they're over. That was how I spent most of the evening—other people must have thought I was on a first date that was misfiring on all cylinders. I tried forcing myself to watch a few, but after a guy pooped out his own intestines, I too left my body. I felt like one of those kids whose parent makes them smoke an entire carton of cigarettes to get smoking out of their system. I know why I had agreed to go— because I am someone who watches horror movies regularly! But, as always, I forgot the rest of that statement: with regret.

A few summers ago, I went to see the horror movie *Midsommar*, directed by Ari Aster. Again, I don't know why I thought I would enjoy the experience, given I hadn't many, many times before. I'd watched Aster's first big movie, *Hereditary*, on a cross-country flight because I am unwell as a person. It's deeply disturbing, despite the downright slapstick whimsical direction it takes in the climax, and the overarching goal is clearly to unsettle viewers to maximal effect, with grotesque imagery that was repeated for no other reason than as if to say, "In case you missed the part where I chose to show you the worst possible thing I could come up with, here it is again, you sucker! And again!"

It was an utter mistake, and by the end, I was so upset, I pressed the flight attendant button before I realized they could not help me. I tried to cleanse my palate with a lighter film called *Book Club*, which is my favorite genre: older women up to all sorts of shenanigans with their reading glasses and lived experience.

So why did I watch *Midsommar*? In the trailer, it looked like a movie about a creepy cult of Scandinavian villagers and their "barbaric" practices, juxtaposed with the beautiful imagery of traditional clothing and vibrant flowers. It was a seasonal movie—pumpkin spice for the summer set. But I also knew it was a horror movie, and deep down, I recognized I was making the wrong choice—again, just like a character in one. There was a 110 percent chance there would be no happy ending. One small consolation was I did go to one of those theaters where you can order an adult beverage.

But even my effervescent peach spritz couldn't help me with what followed. Even before the title credits, there was an extremely traumatizing and graphic scene, which merely established the main character's backstory. And as soon as that first disturbing thing happened, I thought, *What in the actual hell?!* as if I hadn't willingly chosen to watch this film. I became one of those irate customers at an airport ticket counter insisting, "I am a loyal Delta customer. This is unbelievable, just unbelievable. I will be canceling my miles membership." Every time something scary happened after that, I had the same reaction: *You gotta be shitting me! This again!* While others around me in that theater may have been disturbed by what they were watching, though some were laughing so who the hell knows, I was the only one acting as if I had bought a ticket to a Pixar movie and then been catfished by Hollywood.

Mentally, I continued my path downhill. The movie had several scenes that achieved their aim in either terrifying or nauseating you. Oh, what's that? That's the whole point of horror? Well, sure, I guess, if you want to get technical about it.

There is that well-known quote (not actually by Albert Einstein, by the way; too bad he has no other claim to fame) that goes, "Insanity is doing the same thing over and over again but expecting different results." That's exactly what I've been doing with horror movies. Going to see them over and over with the expectation something different will happen—this time I will be moved; I will learn something new about the human condition; there will be some kind of happy ending; the liberal usage of the human body as a meat sack metaphor will signify something deeper to me. Instead, I am left grappling with the same unrepentant firing squad of questions: *Do I even like horror movies? No? Then why do I keep going to see them?*

I can't stop asking these questions, because, clearly, I don't know the answers. But I notice the parallel to other threads of adulthood, like, *Why do I keep staying up so late and then waking up late and then doing the same thing the next day? Why do I do stand-up if going into every performance completely wrecks me? Do I find solace or conviction in these patterns, even if they are destroying me? Might there be some hope of salvation, if I can just figure out the why?*

A negative pattern comes with its own comfort and predictability. It's courting mutually assured destruction as a form of control over an unforgiving universe. I'll undo myself before reality does. I'm psychoanalyzing myself again, but I don't think I'm wrong. And that's coming from someone whose love language is apologizing for things that aren't my fault.

There is something about staring into the face of abject fear, whether real or imagined (when it comes to fear, the difference is often negligible) and thinking, *OK, sure.* This is a way of experiencing the world. Maybe the reason I torture myself with horror movies is that they add weight to the idea that being alive is inherently terrifying. Sure, it cakes some makeup on it and plays it up for effect, but just as comedy can be cathartic, horror can be gratifying. There's something distinctly camp about the whole genre—as if all humanity's collective fears got together, rehearsed, and put on the equivalent of a drag show. After all, the pairing is the "comedy" and "tragedy" masks, not the comedy and family drama masks or the comedy and *John Wick* masks. Horror plumbs to the other depths, the tension of being alive and the truest fact of all, the one we exhaust ourselves trying to mask: one day, we won't be.

Though, just like a horror movie, I'll add my own unsettling addendum to the supposed resolution. Horror movies take death and they turn it inside out into a kind of farce. To my mind, the characters who end up surviving aren't necessarily the winners. They are the unwilling observers; they've seen it all, and now they have to go on living. My anxiety plays the same game. I've visualized every bad outcome, and yet, somehow, I return to do it all over again. I press play on the next one. I get back on the stage. Maybe that's the real horror afoot.

Confessions:
Survival Skills

Whenever I choke on a glug of water, I think, "Not today, Darwin!!!"

I have been anemic on and off for most of my life. Being both a vegetarian and a small-voiced far leftist has not helped. Ditto bleeding out every month. At any given time, I'm on one iron supplement or another, as if metamorphosing into a robot in the slowest way possible. The one I'm on right now packs a particularly powerful punch. After I take it, my burps taste like keys, and kissing me is like sucking face with one of those machines that spits out flattened pennies imprinted with the Statue of Liberty on them or, in my case, the words "Beep boop, you're welcome."

When I locate the "You are here" icon on a map, my first thought is *I'm a star!!!*

At my elementary school carnival, I entered the cakewalk and much to everyone's surprise (fine, mostly my own) won a cake. The prize was a cake shaped like a rabbit and covered in white coconut flakes. I wanted to ask if I could get one of the non-dandruffy, more delicious-looking chocolate cakes, but I didn't want to be perceived as difficult. That cake sat in my family's fridge for weeks. And for weeks, I stared into those jelly bean eyes with pure resentment and "what if"–like revenge fantasies. And, wow, did they stare back just as defiantly. I've been afraid of success ever since.

I am an age where it's not considered acceptable to have food stains on my shirt, and yet, I will get one within minutes of wearing a new piece of clothing. There's a 99.9 percent chance it's peanut butter. And a 0.1 percent chance I will not do it again.

I feel an undeserved sense of pride when I fill up the pee cup past a certain line at the doctor's office. I'm helping!

Unboxing My
Real-Life Rom-Com

Presentation of the Package

I have always loved the idea of finding the one, but more as a form of security than making my heart soft and pudding-y for someone else. Even early on, I was very into the idea of the commitment and the sustained promise of attention along with a strong jawline. Because I found so much lacking about myself, I was entranced by the idea that someone else might find something there that I had somehow overlooked.

I didn't think too much about the relationship beyond the other person being in love with me. I didn't care that much about a ring or marriage or kids, but the idea that someone wanted to spend all this time with me, as if I were a human version of the TGIF sitcom lineup. *Hot dang.* The very idea that another human could be so into me just as I was struck me as impossible, and so it became the most beguiling fantasy. Yet, in my fantasies, I was always someone else.

As a cishet woman, none of this feels particularly revelatory to me, especially when you consider that my generation and I were fed a diet of binaries from a very young age—hopeless nerd or effortless cheerleader, virgin or whore, eye candy or ear candy, just one of the guys or girlie girl, wallpaper or centerpiece. I clung to identifiers and labels because I so often had trouble figuring out how others saw me. Perpetually on a scavenger hunt for clues, all I could reasonably conclude was that "my deal" generally did not involve the attraction of other humans.

Even now, when it comes to my physical presence and how I occupy space, I'm most "comfortable" (whatever that means) envisioning myself as a sentient coatrack. I'm here to observe or to learn, on good days maybe both. I'm used to feeling invisible to others. Yes, there's an unmistakable vein of pity in this, but it's how the world has frequently engaged with me. I say that full well knowing I have certain glaring privileges, such as thinness, no visible disabilities, membership in the upper-middle class, and, more recently, a quivering Jell-O sliver of public persona.

And still. I have a strange relationship to attention. I court it to justify my worth, but so often when I get it, I don't know what to do with it. I constantly want to prove I exist to others, but can't handle the implications of getting that proof. After all, exposure is a wide-cast net that draws in anyone and everyone. You don't get the attention of only those you feel comfortable and qualified to engage with, which, it turns out, is only a couple of humans I've known for a decent amount of time. And when it comes to romantic interest in particular, it's been a yearslong game of hot potato, hoping to catch the sizzling spud, but then flinging it away in horror when I do. Am I affable in a demure way? Check and check. But sexy or alluring? Check please!!! (That's a hard no.)*

On occasion, I might live vicariously through a perfume ad, imagining myself as the enigma with the wispy scarf beckoning a handsome stranger

---

* This is where a woman stands up in the audience and goes, "Stop it, you're gorgeous!" To that I reply, it's not just how you *feel* about yourself that determines how the world treats you—would that the world were so obedient.

into the realm of vetiver-laden secrets. For the most part, though, I haven't the slightest clue where that world is, let alone how to even apply for a day pass. The only thing I have in common with the Siren of Scents is I too own a scarf, though mine is bulky and gives my neck the appearance of a shar-pei who teaches art.

To be clear, I no longer consider this a fault, despite society raising its eyebrows at my expense. Sex appeal isn't in my emergency contacts—it's rarely shown up when I needed it, so I've never depended on it. That's the front-of-house story on what I'm putting out there. On the back end, I deep down want adoring companionship—someone to share intricate inside jokes with, to pick up from airports and have fights with that themselves become fond memories. I want to be able to wedge my head into their neck crevice, but for less than a minute because after that it's no longer comfortable for either party, no matter how in love you are. I know some people have all these things with friends and other loved ones, but I know that opening myself up that fully feels feasible with only one other person, and oh, how to find them?

Let's take a quick walk down mammary* lane and find out.

The Box Is Opened: Fascination

My first formulation of attraction was more akin to acknowledgment and coexistence, a model of diplomacy rather than carnal urges.

My first friend who is a boy, though chill historians may allow the term "boyfriend," is a similarly quiet sort named Sam Sutton. He is also five years old, and after school most days he comes over to my house, and we

---

* Yes? Were you hoping for some accountability down here? There will be none of that.

play Memory, the card-matching game, in amicable silence. If this ends up being the extent of companionship for me in old age, I will be legit stoked.

I know Sammy's love is true, because when I pee my pants while standing next to him in the school library, neither of us mentions it or ever speaks of it. This is all I ask for in a potential partner, even now.

My childhood crushes include Macaulay Culkin (but specifically as Kevin in *Home Alone*), the Greek god Hermes (you had me at winged sandals), and the Teenage Mutant Ninja Turtle Raphael ("cool but rude"). Even now, I consider reality a major flaw when it comes to men. My wheelhouse is the gray area between attraction and projection. Deep down, some part of me wants to *be* them, and short of that, settles for the consolation prize of being *with* them.

My fixation comes from a place of coveting their access, their irreverence, and their power. It's funny to think of Kevin in *Home Alone* as powerful, but then again, he is David, and his Goliath is two fully grown male criminals. After all, who can do less wrong than a young, cheekily rebellious, cishet, upper-middle-class Caucasian boy? His every wayward move is dismissed with an irrepressible grin and shake of the head. The world is his oyster to shuck and discard as he sees fit.

As my winking and nudging hormones arrive en masse, I concede that perhaps these guys might be worth more than just intel on accruing social capital. In my tween and teen years, I go to various summer camps and every time "fall in love" with a fellow camper. I then try to win them over with the undeniable strategy of sending them mail they never asked for. When I am at academic camp (yes, I mean voluntary summer school, and no, I will not take further questions), the object of my desire is Nithin, who's in my writing seminar. He lets me know (via third party, as is the twelve-year-old way) that he doesn't like me like that. This information does not stop me from writing him not one, but two unanswered letters about being chill and fun long-distance friends. Nothing says low maintenance like involving the US Postal Service.

At wilderness survival camp, my target is unsuspecting Paul. He isn't in my cohort, and the only interaction I have with him is at the airport, where we exchange two words. I then proceed to walk by his gate too many times (think less meet-cute, more psychological thriller). When I get home, I for sure call the program and lie that he was in my group as a means to get his address. Yes, of course I check the internet first, but this is the late '90s and nobody has a trackable web presence. (Imagine not being able to get the entirety of someone's personal information off your phone in seconds. Inexcusable!) Yet again, Paul doesn't respond to my heartfelt letter, most of which is just me trying to explain who I am. That's right. I invented Teen Missed Connections. Somebody tell my Wikipedia page. Fine, I'll do it.

With the fervor of a men's rights activist, rejection only emboldens me.

I faithfully daydream about eventual fateful run-ins with guys who clearly have said no in every single way: actively with "no thanks," passively with nonresponsiveness, written, out loud, via middlewoman. They'll come around, I tell myself, fate can't be argued with. (Remember I was *really* into Greek mythology.) When my interest finally wanes with one fixation, I update my fantasies accordingly with whatever new prototype I've envisioned. I imagine the ideal male as a composite of things I find appealing, like steely eyes, a smart haircut, soccer legs, "good egg" principles, and a goofy personality. I might throw a career in there—like a fireman—or dream up a role-play where I'm a librarian, and he's returning books late,* but I barely register faces most of the time. My crushes very rarely, if ever, star in my fantasies. I find it easier to picture an idea of a person—the bare minimum

---

* You decide whether this is real or not; I'll never tell.

of someone else being there. I'm still not sure if this is due to shame or an unwillingness to share focus. (Uh-oh, stand-up comedian alert!)

Inside That Is a Box: Hesitation

My senior year of high school, I receive the first indication that I register to the opposite sex as anything other than a walking bookbag. I am invited to the homecoming dance by a very nice boy named Henry, who is also my teammate on the track team. I am a horrible date. I act cold and rude the entire night and then run away at the end to avoid the whole kiss—no kiss scene, a classic hot mess Cinderella. What I think happened is I couldn't believe Henry had the nerve to ask me to a dance, shattering my incontrovertible proof that my desirability was untenable, and so he needed to be punished. The logic is infallible.

For most of college, I do not drink, experiment, or hook up. I still go to parties, though, and if my peers are lucky, I dance like one of those flipping mechanical dogs—in sudden self-congratulatory sequences followed by prolonged periods of stillness. Once, high on my own supply of sobriety, I steal a guy from another girl on the dance floor. That was pure me, baby. I do notice, however, that whenever a guy I'm dancing with is physically aroused, I am horrified. Save it for the stage!

I'm mostly shruggy about the cis-male body's hidden treasures. (And no, there is no attraction to other varieties of bodies either, other than an overall appreciation for the unimaginative aesthetic standards we're all trained to worship.) But I still feel left out of the sexual charms race given how closely it coincides with status quo conceptions of belongingness in society. At a loss of how to proceed with my bodily education given that the old college try has amounted to nothing, I escalate tactics.

Despite having negative game, I start asking out guys—usually ones far above my pay grade. This mirrors my childhood tendency to pursue those whose lives I would like to unpack, as if knowing them more closely will somehow teach me their ease at moving through the world.

I ask out a cool soccer player while he is toasting bread in the dining hall. The plan is flawless—who is in a better mood than someone awaiting hot carbs? Inexplicably, he says yes. Maybe he mistook me for a giant piece of toast. We then go on a stunningly mediocre date, and he does not respond to my subsequent emails. I was big on following up as if I were a growing business circulating a "Tell us what we can do better!" survey. I also go on a couple of "dates" with a bar bouncer whom I hit on after he makes fun of my ID. Our first hangout, he tells me that I "think too much" multiple times. (Read me, Daddy!) During our second and last encounter, he abandons me to go look for coke. It's unfathomable we're not married.

Improving on my letter-writing campaigns of yore, I embark on a new round of cishet male mind infiltration. Using every tool at my disposal— AOL Instant Messenger, Friendster (RIP), my school directory—I begin corresponding with as many guys as possible from a cross section of networks spanning high school, college, and beyond. It's purely a numbers game. Some of these people are fun to talk to but a lot of them are not. It doesn't matter. I am an anthropologist gleaning valuable insights.

In a low point for everyone involved, I meet up with a guy from my high school track and field days (he did not know who I was until I contacted him—as was my way) in the middle of the night. I give him a hand job in his car while thinking, *Welp, now I am a real woman.* Wait, I said that wrong. *Welp,* I remember thinking, *I guess it's a job because it feels like work.*

Now that second base is out of the way, kissing is next. My first one* is

---

* Technically, my first "kiss" was with a not-bad-looking CPR dummy. Fine, not a kiss, but a start!

with a Brazilian guy from a neighboring college. A dorm floor mate and I go out to drinks with him and his friends. It is a Wednesday or, at least, feels like one emotionally. I'm sure we really hit it off because I no longer remember his name. I am buzzed, though not as drunk as he probably imagines I am, since I pour most of the shots he buys me directly onto the bar floor. But still, I am on an exploratory mission for the greater good of humanity, and so, we go back to my dorm room. We make out for a while, the whole time during which I think, *Yes! It's happening! Slimy!* I then proceed to give him very bad oral sex. How bad? Well, he stops me at one point and suggests we go to sleep, which tells you everything you need to know. Nothin' but teeth, babe!

Inside That Is Another Box: Commitment

My last semester of college, I trap my first boyfriend. Let's call him Ethan. Ethan is Jewish and has four lesbian moms, so just try to imagine how highly he values himself. I promptly assume we are going to spend the rest of our lives together. A man who was willing to see me regularly and even, gasp, enjoy my company? My low self-esteem is sold. And I lose my virginity! More important, he buys me my first vibrator—the real missing link! Thank you, sir. Now, truly, I am a woman.

A few months in, Ethan clarifies that our relationship is only until graduation, since we both have big grown-up lives to live. My heart immediately chimes in, "Counterpoint: no." I try to convince him otherwise, my entire argument being "But why?" After we break up right on schedule, I move back home to DC and work very hard on getting over it. Imagine a sports-movie training montage but replace burpees and running up stairs with crying and staring off into the middle distance. I even start another relationship with a wonderful guy named Fred, who's in town for a summer fellowship.

Ethan and I keep in touch with phone calls because, as he says, "Why can't we still be friends and draw this lack of resolution out as long as possible?" Future Me would say: "I know why. Is trash can stink idea!" Then one day, Ethan tells me too many things: he realizes he's made a huge mistake; he's moving to DC to pursue his interest in politics; and we, of course, need to get right back together because, in a shocking twist, it turns out he's in love with me. At this point, I disagree. But because I am an accommodating slash easily manipulated person, I am guilt-tripped into letting him live in my parents' basement (in the house where I also live) until he finds his own place. This also means that sometimes my parents hear him loudly crying over my refusal to get back together with him. It isn't the crying that bothers me per se—I am all for emotional expression. It is all the everything about the situation. In short, we do not get back together, but I do find out he dates another South Asian woman right after me. And then moves to India. Very, very awesome information for me. I wish him the best.

If anyone ever says they miss their twenties, I refer them to this story. I also owe a big apology to understanding and patient Fred, who really gets caught in the middle of all this and who deserves better than an almost twenty-three-year-old acting, well, twenty-three.

If you didn't see it coming with my Victorian-level correspondence and web mingling, I am first in line for early vestiges of internet dating services like LavaLife (don't look it up; a delirious, weathered single will crawl out of your screen like the girl in *The Ring*) and Match.com. This is the closest thing I ever have to a "wild" phase. My most out-of-character hookup is with a douchey law student I meet in a club who is puzzled I ask him to put on a condom but keeps his socks on the whole time. I'm glad he isn't in med school, because that's not where the razzmatazz (scientific term) comes out, my man!

I know this guy was only interested in hooking up with me, but his choosing me over the next gal is what bowled me and my ego right over. Yes, he looked like a bully in an '80s movie and was probably going to end up working for a firm that defended Big Oil, but he chose me! The attention felt intoxicating. I existed!

Whaddaya Know, Another Box: Discovery

My first truly mature, long-term relationship is with a comedian—ironic since we spend most of it acting like buffoons and both of us still live with our parents for three years of it (I wish I could blame the 2008 recession, but that happened after we started dating). But it feels very secure and reliable and comfortable, and I don't feel the fickle ups and downs I've experienced when I've been interested in other male comics. We both say "I love you" a few months into the relationship. He makes me music mixes and writes me hilariously sweet letters to take on the road when we are apart for work. What can I say, I am a sucker for the written word.

There are some professional comparison issues—I feel he is superior to me as a writer and performer, but I try to not let it get to me. We eventually move to LA together to "pursue our dreams." Our rapport is very silly and fun, and it's like hanging out with my best friend all the time, but I quickly learn our compatibility is not synced up in terms of physical urges. I already have the suspicion sex isn't that important to me, but it doesn't really affect your life when no one else is invested in your having sex with them regularly. While his drive is like a hot-wired alarm clock, mine is more like a sloth who's going through something. I partly blame this on antidepressants, but I also realize it doesn't so much bother me. I like occasionally pleasuring myself, but the idea of sex is always preferable to the actual thing. Plus, I don't really want another person coming between me and the vibrator. Yes, fine, straight cis men, it's true: robots have stolen your jobs.

This relationship falls apart when I move to New York for a comedy job. He ends it, but the writing had been on the wall for a while. Fittingly, he says it feels like we are very, very good friends rather than in a relationship. Hey, me too! Except I liked that! One dream unlocked, another deferred. I find a new therapist. I am relieved nobody is dependent on my libido anymore. We do conduct an extremely drawn-out wake for the corpse of the relationship in that we take a road trip, attend a wedding together, and have a one-night fling when he's in town. You know, the trifecta of recent breakups where one person is still not over it?

Later, I date a very courteous gentleman who doesn't care that much about sex either, for his own reasons, so that part works at least. He's also an aspiring comedian because, well, I guess I am a dreamer. But whereas my career is in medias res, he is just starting out, and it creates something of a strange dynamic. Similar to my last relationship, there is a lot of goofing around and entertaining inside jokes, but I have an overall feeling we are not at the same stage in our lives. But it is easier to stay in the relationship than not because I do genuinely enjoy his company and he's basically a manic pixie dream boy. He does things like leave me little secret notes in my purse that I find when I'm randomly going about my day. I mean, come on! My Achilles' heel is clearly penmanship! But eventually, I end the relationship. Un-end the relationship. Then re-end the relationship. At the time, my mental health is zigzagging. In other words, I don't feel great, and my ongoing erratic choices indicate I am correct!

Tiny Box I Didn't Notice
at First: Embarrassment

I should admit that the vast majority of men I've been involved with and even those I've merely coveted from afar have been . . . bing bing bing . . . you guessed it, white! I cringe at the realization that I'm essentially a colonialist groupie. There's also the flip side of having crucial backstage VIP info on how South Asian men are often raised and, on some level, being on constant guard for a whole host of tendencies. Subjecting an entire group to a huge broad-stroke generalization? Hey, I learned from the best.

I have had crushes and dates across the racial and ethnic spectrum, but none of them led to anything serious. So often, we don't question our attractions or desires, and only now have I begun to look closer, eschewing defensiveness, at where I have most often tended and why. Luckily, like sex, this is work I can embark on internally. I will likely be excavating the true depths of this programming my entire life. But I'll cut to the chase—I do end up with a white guy, well, sort of—he's Jewish (not even going to touch that can of political worms). Date what you know. Cue the think pieces!

Looking at All the Open Boxes
and Considering the Haul: Acceptance

That's right—I meet THE ONE on Tinder. Just kidding. I hate the idea of THE ONE, but Gabe is definitely THE GABE. We're both now inductees to our forties, though he's three weeks younger than me and helpfully reminds me I am a cougar every chance he gets. But we're at a point in our lives where we know what our deals are in terms of what we want, what we'll put up with and what we won't (the relief of being too tired to pretend). The relationship feels easy in ways that are invaluable: he's reliable, trustworthy, and kind; he cooks; he cleans; he's funny, but doesn't feel the need to monetize it, which is incredible; he is able to support me through my mental health struggles; he's good with my family and his family; he's good with people in general. He does the heavy lifting at social events, even when they're my work events, and I quite literally play the silent partner. It's not too perfect—we have our disagreements and our personality clashes, but we can talk about scary things like the future because we're on the same page. We don't want kids and mainly got married for joint health insurance among other dreamy reasons. I know, it's like a fairy tale!

We move in together, adopt cats, and co-parent an air fryer, so I think in NYC terms, we have been, by and large, married for years now. We own more books than any other possession. We constantly make each other laugh and are both obsessed with absurdity. The other day I asked him a question in nonsense words and without missing a beat he responded correctly also in nonsense words, and I said, "It's a good thing we found each other." And I meant it.

He understands how I feel about sex, and he's the first person I have been able to explain it to without shame. It's an ongoing conversation, but it involves two people, so that's healthy. There are certain other topics to bridge like race and class and gender, but he views the world in an expansive, no-bullshit way, and he is fundamentally a good, no, a great egg. He is undoubtedly the person I am closest to in the world, with whom I am most often and most unguardedly myself, for better and for worse. Yes, he is my best friend, but he is also more than that. He feels like home.

I'm looking forward to our playing Memory in the not-so-distant future.

Because, in the end, I found someone I can be quiet with. And, you know, piss myself in the library next to without hesitation.

No Comment

A few years ago, I stopped checking social media. It happened with no send-off party or Viking funeral, despite all the mental hemming and hawing and hedging that led up to it. One afternoon, I deleted all the apps off my phone and had a surrogate change all my passwords and, if I had to, I posted through them. I essentially hired a hapless crony to do my dirty work.

The change was a long time coming. My relationship with the platforms had well-past soured, but I couldn't summon the courage to jump out of the moving car that is scrolling. There were countless reasons to stay on and in the loop—everything moves so fast. Was it even legal to "opt out" of the conversation when part of my job description is social commentary?

But my mind had fractured. I wanted to see if I could glue the pieces back together into something cohesive.

At the whim of the information torrent, I realized that as soon as I've formulated even the mildest of stances on something, an automatic reflex in me opens Google to find out what everyone else is saying. It's like the little window that pops up before you delete an entire folder of email like, "You sure about that, ding-dong?!" I need to cross-verify that at least some others agree with me, that my feelings on the America-China trade war and NFTs are in line with the "correct" attitude (laced with notes of cool remove because otherwise the whole thing rings desperate). Never mind it will all be ancient history within a week, if not days, and even that's generous.

Everything reeks of FONK—the fear of not knowing. It's not enough to be up on all the information; I also notice some underlying internal pressure to have processed it the right way in the timeliest fashion possible. I need to know what's a priority and what isn't, who's a good or a bad guy and who isn't, who or what the latest viral flavor of the week is, where I stand on this, that, and the other thing. It's not just that I need to know what something is, I need to know how I feel about it and update my feelings in real time with whatever is happening.

Consider the case of undecided voter Ken Bone, whom the internet fell in love with after his question at one of the 2016 presidential debates, that old cesspool of chestnuts. It wasn't just his reasonable question about energy policy that won everyone over during an otherwise unpleasant affair, it was his whole deal: glasses, red sweater, unassuming balding middle-aged man, and that name, that trusty Subaru of a name! A superhero for our times! We love Ken Bone! Welcome to the #BoneZone (real hashtag)! And then, four days later, the very same all-knowing, bountiful internet who giveth, vengefully tooketh away. After he did a Reddit AMA courtesy of his newfound adulation, Ken Bone's unsavory NSFW Reddit comment history came to light, including icky morsels such as admitting to looking at Jennifer Lawrence's leaked nude photos and arguing Trayvon Martin's death was justified, and this one is more just for wowzers, but in a group he frequented with pictures of pregnant people in bathing suits, he referred to them as "beautiful human submarines." Suddenly, we didn't know how we felt about Ken Bone, but it wasn't great. In the end, of course, none of it affected anything in the slightest, but the whole thing was born of me watching the 2016 presidential debates to be an informed citizen. I felt like a fool when Ken Bone was revealed to be not exactly who we thought he was. And that's how I generally feel regarding the internet these days: like a big old blockhead.

Here's the thing: Opinions are showboats. Any that I come up with present themselves like "the greatest hits" of my thoughts. Self-important, they carry themselves like a character witness in a trial, which is hardly surprising given the weight their testimony has in the court of public . . . opinion (sigh). Of course, that's very much the megaphone of an individualistic society blaring, where hierarchy rules and my place in it needs constant justification. Simple is the world where everything is understood in binaries: good versus bad, better versus worse, for versus against. Delicious exception: the black-and-white cookie.

This precarious intersection of commerce and criticism—that is, how we, as a society, "feel" about things—reveals a conflict of interest. Just look at all the expensive billboards dotting said intersection. Marketing wrests control of what we pay attention to and holds us captive. How can I honestly stand by my ideas or taste when so much of what shapes them is influenced by powerful, external, self-interested forces? And no, I'm not just talking about my deep-seated predilection for all-male folk-rock bands, in which every member looks like he grew up in the rough end of the gated community.

But, of course, "the greatest trick the devil ever pulled was convincing the world he doesn't exist." (Understated nods to both *The Usual Suspects* and Baudelaire for that one.) Rather than considering the systems that got us here, we remain in thrall to every individual's latest feelings (mine very much included) on this and that and the other thing too, as if the sun rises and sets on hashing out consensus. And by consensus, I mean, on who is the wrongest.

How often do I walk away from the internet more informed and connected?

Usually, I am only more agitated, irritated, and disoriented (an emotional triple threat I prefer to reserve for when I feel like some creep is staring at me and then I look and it's just a mannequin torso without a head). The worst part is I've been manipulated into believing it's extremely important to define how I feel in comparison with how everyone else feels, despite having also been told forty bajillion times that the "everyone" in question is selectively based on an algorithm. It's as if we're stuck in an involuntary high-stakes version of HotOrNot.com. And yes, that was the gist of Mark Zuckerberg's first go at a social network, so I'm guessing the metaverse may feel oddly familiar.

I watched a darkly cynical movie critiquing humanity and society at large and unequivocally loved it—so much so that before the movie was even over, I was already anticipating the glowing reviews online. (Yes, I read the reviews *after* I see a movie. I'm what you might call a maverick, if you actually had no idea what that word means and were just using it to impress me.) But when I did, the internet smugly told me how many critics hated it. I felt betrayed. I read one slam after the other in total disbelief until I finally concluded maybe that was the point. The movie skewered cultural conversation, so of course critics hated it. For once, they weren't in on the joke. They were the joke. That's what I told myself, anyway. Because the alternative—having questionable, unevolved taste—was too threatening to my sense of self.

Much later, I talked to two friends who saw the movie, and neither of them had any idea reviewers didn't like it. They both assumed it had done very well since so many people watched it and it even got nominated for a big, shiny film prize (the one from the Muppet who lives in a trash can). They entirely missed the critical backlash and then the online backlash to the backlash, which did beg the question "Was any of that necessary?"

I used to think opinions about art were less indicative of the same obstacle course of virtue. I thought they were all simply a matter of subjective, random taste, divorced from the world of principle and closer to the ineffable. But now every opinion of mine faces the same litmus test: What's the most balanced, empathic, worldly stance? Great question! I think it's a #5 combo of perceived progressivism filtered through the cheese cloth of an openness to being wrong with a side of fries. I've somehow become a robot whose default setting is to "avoid cancellation," whatever that means.

"Cancel culture" has become a pejorative catchall term for any type of online pile on, though its original intent rang more vital—calling those in power to account, most often regarding their abuse of said power. I agree it doesn't exist in the literal sense in that most of these perpetrators are never ultimately "canceled" in any meaningful way—none of them are in dire financial straits or lacking for opportunities after being called out. On the contrary, many of their supporters double down. Their "sabbaticals of conscience" typically amount to a weekend getaway full of detoxing and recharging (with, I'm guessing, their PR and brand management teams).

However, here's the more shameful part. If I am to be perfectly frank, as a fragile little husk of a performer, I still deeply care about what others think. And I also worry about being very wrong in the eyes of a bunch of strangers or letting people down, especially to the tune of "I used to think she was OK! Now I know better!" I am embarrassed to write this, because I know I sound like I'm aligning myself with the people who claim everything is now a witch hunt, even though you know they would be the very same people insisting so-and-so is a witch back in 1600s Salem. But I just don't like making people mad. I'm eternally convinced somehow, somewhere, my web presence has spinach in its teeth, and I do not even realize it. I wish I didn't revert to my thirteen-year-old self when it comes to prizing the favor of others, but alas, here we are.

Even admitting these hesitations feels dicey, as if I'm trying to divest myself of responsibility and accountability. The whole dance of "being right" online implies your world formulation is unimpeachable. You did your own research (the version of that before it became a misinformation catchphrase), your sources come vetted, and your resulting views are cut from the same sustainable, ethically sourced cloth. My initial impulse is to listen rather than assert or talk over, to make sure I'm not overlooking something, but I have taken this to an extreme. I operate from a defensive stance riddled with fear—the fear of ostracism; the fear of being a "bad" person; the fear of not getting it, whatever "it" is. Messing up online feels less like you gently transgressed and more like your entire existence is a mistake. Actually, it's a reasonable reaction when people are only too eager to toss a "kill yourself" every which way, like it's a beach ball at a music festival.

Here's the dirt: I've been "wrong" online before. And here's the stunning takeaway: I did not care for it.

Wait. Do you promise not to make fun of me? You don't? Ah well, I had to ask.

A legion of Swifties—that's Taylor Swift fans, in case you're staunchly Team Jonathan—came for me. I tweeted a dumb joke, a signature move ever since joining the platform in 2008. It was the free-content equivalent of "Nothing [approaching original thought] to see here. Keep it moving!" The joke went, "Taylor Swift's new single is called Me, which ironically, is also what she calls most of her relationships." The idea is an unimaginative snooze, the joke equivalent of sitting your kids in front of the TV so they will stop bothering you. And, sure, I'm giving Taylor some tossed-off shade, but as far as hateful, it's hardly that. When she's openly admitted to writing a good number of songs about her past relationships, I am not so out of line in supposing she "controls the narrative" in how these relationships play out in her work. If anything, she's owning and subverting it with that song title. I would make this argument of any artist, including myself, who uses their personal life as a muse. Anyway, I didn't really think about it more critically than that before smashing the post button, and that, good peoples, is how I "boop-booped" my key fob and obliviously walked away from a burning car (a small one, like a Jetta).

They hate me! They really hate me! [Credit: Personal screenshots.]

Taylor Swift's online representation consists of an extinction of superfans (like a "murder of crows" but more terrifying). Something like the bat signal must go up whenever a pop star's reputation is sullied to any degree, summoning anyone with a conscience to spring to action. I suspect there was some Black Swan version of myself in that mob. Also, I am guessing Ms. Swift (may I still call her that?) has worshippers of all stripes, but because they all use her image as their profile picture, it appeared I was being attacked by a poreless army of blonde white women demanding to speak to my manager. One of them dug up a *HuffPost* interview I did five years earlier and then questioned how I could call myself a feminist. Excuse me, ma'am, why are you even reading my old interviews? The only person who is allowed to do that is me at rock-bottom. Another one cited my avatar and said anything I wrote was inconsequential since I looked like shit. Now *there's* a feminist!

According to a great deal of the feedback, which of course I read line by painstaking line like I was auditing my reputation's bankruptcy filing, my joke was out of date? We're not allowed to make fun of you-know-who's relationships since 2012 or something? I am not sure what happened in 2012 in the T. Swift timeline; I tried to look up what it was, but halfway through, my brain informed me I had no more storage space for celebrity facts, unless I wanted to try deleting a bunch of family photos.

Guess what this brave societal truth teller did? I took the tweet down. I couldn't handle the onslaught. With each new verbal attack that came my way, I became further convinced I was a misogynist monster. I did not die on that one sacred hill of comedy—which is not backing down from a joke no matter whom it offends. I decided to just stop making fun of high-profile types, especially those with tween death squads. Amazing what one little Saturday afternoon verbal tarring and feathering can do for your sense of conviction! As soon as the joke was removed, a silver-tongued Swiftie tweeted at me, "good little bitch." And don't you forget it!

I feel so seen. [Credit: Personal screenshot.]

My defenses went straight up, and because I knew none of these people personally, I assumed they would stop at nothing to destroy me. (I have this same fear about my nearest and dearest, but at least I'm more well versed in their methods of attack.) The rub is that I am so often asked to be on panels defending the side of "intersectional wokeness and punching up" versus that of "equal-opportunity offending and PC culture have gone too far." To be accused of being on the side harboring the alt-right was a grim reality check. I laid low on the internet for a while after that, pulling my hoodie up and eating lunch in the bathroom. Judging by tone and content, I wasn't being attacked by belligerent, hateful, misogynist trolls, who in my thankfully limited experience are overwhelmingly clumsy, brutish, and derivative in their barbs. But rather, it was mostly snarky adolescents, which only clinched the issue for me. No group scares me more with their lethal combination of just-hatched hormones and bottomless capacity to pick you apart.

I've not only been shamed but, putting all my cards on the table, I have also shamed others. I've made plenty of jokes about public figures catching heat, even for transgressions fresh off the press—but when I do it, it's OK, right? Because I'm on the *good* side! Before social media, when I was in college (the year is 1312), I helped run our school satire rag for a spell. In one issue, we poked fun at a student who had plagiarized parts of a political science thesis. We wrote a top-ten joke list of other things in his life he plagiarized, accompanied by a sketch of him wearing very little, by which I mean nothing. The drawing wasn't at all graphic, but it was indicative (of the fact he wasn't wearing clothes). And here's the kicker: we ran it on the back page of the magazine, so you would see it even if you didn't plan on reading the cursed thing.

The backlash was immediate and cited the insensitivity of mocking a student, even if he had committed a transgression. In retrospect, I am deeply mortified I didn't flag this as incredibly uncalled for. I recall having a pang of hesitation upon seeing the image, and then thinking, *Well, it's just a silly list!* I was so eager to fill space (oh, print deadlines), it didn't even occur to me to think of him as a fellow student who had made an ill-conceived choice. Singling someone out to publicly ridicule them is inappropriate in many environments, a small college campus definitely being one of them. After all, he had already been found guilty of the offense and was suspended from school—there was no need to rub in the shame. He wasn't a public figure aiming to represent a segment of people like, say, a politician.

I see the same impulse we had at that magazine being carried out now, on the internet, where every transgression is magnified, and rather than a few hundred copies of a college satire rag, the reach is potentially infinite. Often a shaming pile-on can occur before any "real life" punishment has been meted out and, in many cases, before the accused has a chance to contextualize their misstep or take accountability for it. Anyone can be targeted for making an unfortunate decision—yes, in some cases, it can be purposely ill-intentioned behavior that should be called out, but sometimes, it's just an unfortunate mistake. (The journalist Jon Ronson wrote an entire book about it, *So You've Been Publicly Shamed*, a thorough examination of the cycle, which offered more time spent with the targets of the shaming and made me realize how differently actions can be perceived on a public stage versus a private one.) How many people have conversations with their friends that, taken out of context, might not paint them in the best light? Our more intimate social interactions and communities are where we try to make sense of ourselves, and we're messy creatures. It's easy to forget, especially if you are not a public figure, that everyone can see what you're posting, unless you make your account private. The internet becomes the town square, and people are made into examples. They are handled with such immediate condemnation and vitriol, there is almost never any room left for dialogue.

Nobody is being censored or irrevocably "canceled," but at the same time, split-second reactions and opinions are the fuel that keeps social media addictive and profitable, and there is collateral damage to all the finger-pointing.

In a *Vox* article entitled "Everyone Wants Forgiveness, but No One Is Being Forgiven," Aja Romano writes, "If we applied a positive road map to a typical outrage cycle, what we would hope to find after that initial period of outrage is discussion, apology, atonement, and forgiveness. That process almost never happens on the modern public stage." Romano posits that part of the problem is that there is now a blanket assumption that any opposition to one's stance is bad-faith engagement, and we need to amend this fallacy. She clarifies, "That doesn't mean, necessarily, that we must wind up dealing in good faith with extremists, conspiracists, disinformation agents, and other bad actors. It might mean that we stop assuming everyone who says anything with which we disagree falls into one of those categories."

When I was actively checking Twitter, I wasn't under the illusion that my followers were bound to me in any way. For better or for worse, my readership was not all Stancherlas (shhhh, it's a work in progress). The more followers I got, the more feedback I got. And for all the kindness and enthusiasm and sincerity, of which there was plenty, that's never what stuck out. It was the negative responses to material I created, mind you, to entertain people for free. I questioned myself before the medium because the algorithm never lies, right? It's always the contradictory—the "um, actually" and the one-upmanship. I once got the response "Your tweets aren't as funny anymore." Thank you for this valuable feedback, I will for sure bring it up at the next board meeting. Let's see if we can get some fresh blood in here!

On Twitter, I, true rebel out of a spaghetti Western, most enjoy the company of others who agree with me and, as Romano would assume, try to categorically dismiss those who do not (to varying degrees of success), because I am so painfully on guard against willful misreading. Regardless of however many other "views" seem to be involved in the conversation, it always boils down to me and my own agenda in big lights. After all, my account is not a democracy—it's a dictatorship with random listening sessions. I've even found myself defensively reacting to someone who's on the same side as me! More than once, I've thought someone was trying to troll me when they were just trying to be funny or "in on the joke" by negging me. (No doubt Mystery the pickup artist is due for his Nobel Prize any day now for his groundbreaking work.) For all these reasons (and more, if you order now), I inherently mistrust my ability to suss out a valid opinion from a well-meaning stranger that I should consider versus "noise." The easiest, safest, most self-preserving course of action is to hold my own opinions close to the vest and regard those of others with oceans of salt.

Yet I'm embarrassed at how thin my skin has gotten, especially when I've been growing it out for years. As a stand-up comedian, I've opened myself up to other people's opinions by trade. On a regular basis, I survey a random focus group for approval of my ideas IRL, though clips of my stand-up performances get plenty of uncensored comments online as well. One of the most common slams is "You should quit" or some variation on that theme. This dig, it amuses me. Comedians regularly experience rejection, whether we're trying a newer, half-baked idea or trying to win over a tough crowd. While we are hugely sensitive creatures with consistently raw senses of self, you're going to have to come at me with something way more original than "You should quit" to stand out. I have that thought multiple times a week. Write your own material!

My bigger fear with opinions is knowing how to feel about everything because I have never been good at keeping up on trends or gossip, especially those of the "Can you believe so-and-so did such-and-such?" variety. There is now a quick-working internet tribunal that decides "we all hate Mr. Clean now" or whoever or whatever it is. (Legal disclaimer: I do not, nor have I ever, had a problem with Mr. Clean. No, not even the self-congratulatory earring.) It's not just negative spin either; there are those who shine with the light of a thousand suns for but an instant. Must I bring up Ken Bone again? Every time I get online now, I am so behind on the reading and the watching and the listening and the scrolling that I feel immediate dread. I show up as if to a dance class that has already started. I try to jump in, but I can't follow the choreography. How does one know everything that's important to take in, and how does one know where to stop? If I gorge myself on too much of the hypnotic infinitude, I feel sick and unfocused and blurry, but if I don't check in on the larger conversation, I feel selfish and checked out and guilty for not being culturally, socially, and politically informed. And I feel that way every time despite knowing it's precisely by design—marketing and capitalism keep us coming back because they're set up that way. And this coming back leaves us hungrier than we were before. So, on we go, perpetually dissatisfied, craving something, anything, to fill the emptiness: Here! Maybe it's this web-exclusive asymmetrical pair of pants you abandoned in a cart last week! There is no "there" there, by which I mean an unbiased, contextualized, and non-incentivized way of getting information. In other words, how can we be a part of a dialogue that was never an honest conversation to begin with?

Of course, I've also read my share of social media slam pieces and literature dissecting the corrosive rot of Big Tech, nodding furiously in recognition. If anything, in terms of Peak Content and with the still-unprocessed perspective of a global pandemic, we've reached a saturation of thoughtful work cataloging the dangers of being extremely online, and yet like every good capitalist enterprise, the internet has absorbed this argument too and added it to its vast Cheesecake Factory menu for every taste and inclination. That's right! Now you can stay on the internet even if your whole deal is how you're sick of the internet! I guess you can have it all. And by "all," I mean the void.

Stepping away from my online social life reminded me of how I connected with others before, by engaging with them more personally, whether
on a phone call or face-to-face or even writing a long letter or email (alas,
completely removing the digital element of communication gets harder and
harder). I have missed this more human, less optimized level, as antiquated
and Luddite as it now seems. Before so much of our social lives became
transacted via app or platform, I recall lingering hangouts with friends
where we were just bored together, which, funnily enough, makes for great
bonding. Or even the mystique of other people when I didn't know what
they were up to every minute of the day, and finding out was a joyous, anti-
climactic mystery in and of itself. Yes, I know, deciding you would love more
in-person social contact during a global pandemic is a fool's errand but, as
I've said before, I am a ~~visionary~~ fool. I organized virtual game nights and
attended Zoom reunions with friends I hadn't spoken to in years. And every
time, the conversation would eventually turn to internet tidbits. The group
would enthusiastically bond over single dad TikTok, the YouTube makeup
artist who reports on true crimes, or the dog typing on the computer, and I
would have no idea what people were talking about. I would smile and nod
along, watching links as they were sent to me—and remembering when I
too spent large amounts of time on these platforms—feeling both slightly
superior and lonely.

When I first stopped checking social media, friends would ask, "Does it
help? Is your brain better?" I tried to explain the spaciousness I felt when my
sense of self was so much less at the whim of what everyone else was thinking, doing, or liking. But no, it doesn't fix all your problems. And I am
pained to say it creates new ones, like the aforementioned "feeling out of the
loop." I think that's exactly what they needed to hear to confirm they
shouldn't leave the platforms themselves. After all, nobody wants to feel like
they are no longer "in" on the joke, the joke being what everyone else is

talking about all the time. It's like when I tried to cut back on eating sugar because diabetes runs in my family; it's still annoying to mention. *I'm not weird about my diet, it's a medical thing!*

But even the pangs of alienation don't tempt me to go back. Because the small blips of it I do take in now immediately induce mild panic, by which I mean when someone sends me a tweet to read or an Instagram video to watch. I read the tweet, I watch the gram, but I feel like I am under siege, about to be ambushed by information I can't unsee. The idea of logging in to to these platforms myself or even looking at my profile page gives me hives, specifically one big one over each eye. A friend of mine recently told me she knows TikTok is a nightmare with privacy issues, but she loves it too much to give it up. Her blunt worship made the platform sound worse to me than it did before. No matter how good it might make people feel, the fact we're all being manipulated is too loud for me to ignore. And I know I too would readily embrace it, so I keep that door locked. And sure, maybe I sound like a monk proudly sporting iron underwear, but listen, it's *surprisingly breathable*.

What does give me pause is how to keep up with what is going on—in news, in culture, in my community. How do I stay current not only as a citizen of planet Earth but, just as important, as a comedian? It feels irresponsible as a verbal gut check to not have my finger on the throbbing pulse of culture. I don't want to stop reading the news or stop getting the most important goss, but at the same time, I realized once my main line was gone, I didn't really miss it. All you really need to have commentary is to live a life. Guess what? The information still finds you. People talk. Yes, I may be putting myself at risk of falling behind on timely touchstones, but the nice thing is a friend will tell you when you do that. If I hated being wrong or not knowing before, it turns out I am getting very good at both now. I guess I could go even more extreme and become the comic of recluses and off-the-grid types, the Howard Hughes of observation. But even in that scenario, I still can't convince myself that fully deleting my accounts won't tank my career. I guess the alternative would be switching to some kind of "follow the bread crumbs to my next gig!" model.

Thus far, I've been conflating the internet and social media, and I realize they're not quite the same thing. But it's rarer these days to get information directly by combing a home page or a blog or a website versus alerts, social media posts, or someone else passing along a link. Since I have stopped scrolling on social media, my latest compromise—besides compulsively doing the crossword, scouring restaurant menus, and, longest sigh, checking my email like someone playing the slots—is newsletters. The platform du jour is Substack. Everyone has one these days. They are like podcasts but for inboxes. (The worst comparison I've ever made? Sure. Print it!)

I subscribe to journalists and artists and scientists who write about their thoughts and lives and curate timely links to content that they find insightful or important. Yes, just tell me what to look at to stay "informed," whatever that even means anymore. And, why not, feel free to "trigger" me every now and again by embedding a viral tweet just to keep the dread fresh. I realize I've simply outsourced my content curation to an elite, arbitrary oligarchy, but got any better ideas? Even this approach has diminishing returns, though, because in reading one article, I open six hyperlinks embedded in that one, and end up even more overwhelmed. Should I just not click on any of them? Then why are they *there*?! My mind ends up so diffracted from the original source, I am unsure whether any information is retained in my brain, and if so, how it's interpreted. If someone were to ask me what I'd consumed during a given day, all that would come up would be a dull humming sound. It's all a blur of careful critique, self-help articles, secret sales, topical updates, sloths doing anything,* and assorted media sent via friends

---

* Animal content is my one exception for links I will indulge without question. Looking forward to being disavowed of my belief they're conflict-free and having to gently toss them too into the pit.

(led by aforementioned sloths). Still, I'm not even remotely tempted to stop. I continue to cram information in, putting on a news podcast within minutes of waking each morning (right after checking my email, vomit emoji). To what end? You got me.

The information I consume can be filed into a few different categories: (1) cute or funny, (2) purchasable, (3) distantly upsetting or concerning, (4) immediately upsetting or concerning, and (5) irrelevant to me. There are myriad overlaps between categories. For example, four and five are besties on Instagram. On a given morning, I skim a story about a geopolitically fraught incident in Kyrgyzstan, because it registers as important that I know something is happening there. I would rank Kyrgyzstan as a three. I don't know more than the basics about it (I hope the UN is reading this top-notch analysis), but at the same time, I'm not an international relations wonk. At most, I will tangentially refer to the situation there to my partner at dinner, and we will both comment on the state of the world for about fifteen minutes. Spoiler alert: it's never positive, though America gets the brunt of the dish flinging. I will sometimes "amplify" some dire situation or world event out of my own sheer helplessness. If I step back, there is no rhyme or reason to a comedian signal boosting a faraway conflict to their fans, whether it's just more information I found elucidating or the flimsy Band-Aid "ways to help," and yet I still do it. The other fallacy of the internet I often fall prey to is "If you don't weigh in, even indirectly, you don't care."

Weighing in directly on everything, on the other hand, is where people start getting in trouble and, frequently, never stop. Take the incident at the 2022 Oscars heretofore known as The Slap™. In case you decided to cryogenically sit out that year, in short, during the awards ceremony, Will Smith walked onstage unprompted and open-hand whacked presenter Chris Rock cleanly across the face for telling a joke that insulted Jada Pinkett Smith's hair. After sitting back down, Smith then twice yelled at Rock, "Keep my wife's name out of your fucking mouth!" In the history of events affecting the tilt of the online poles, this was certainly way up there. For days, there were takes on takes on takes and updates on updates, coming from every angle and agenda, infinite dissection and polarization and foofaraw. The Slap™ itself encapsulated a delectable cocktail of elements the internet delights in unpacking: celebrity, wealth, race, messy drama, and snappy sound and video to play on a loop. It was also a blessed reprieve amid a still-ticking plague, a nuclear-threat-tinged war between Russia and Ukraine, the latest Washington scandal—in this case, the wife of Supreme Court Justice Clarence Thomas apparently having encouraged overturning the 2020 election results— and the latest climate change report that we have no time left to prevent insurmountable global disaster.

All that said, what I ultimately found most fascinating wasn't the event itself, but the way it played out exactly how every other "Mass Attentional Event" plays out. I am borrowing that term from *Atlantic* internet journalist Charlie Warzel, who wrote a piece in the ongoing wake of Slapgate called "The Predictability of a Social-Media Discourse." In it, he details just how by the book the timeline and rhythm of reactions to Mass Attentional Events online have become. With this tedious monotony comes a sense of futility in its users who can't help but realize they've all essentially become conflict pawns. And yet. Still we participate. Writes Warzel, "Maybe we retreat into these predictable cycles because they're a way of exercising a bit of agency during these moments. But I'm guessing it's simpler than that—we've all just got lizard brains that seek affirmation and belonging, and we've outsourced a lot of our public communication to platforms that exploit those natural urges by offering short-term engagement reward incentives." After extracting myself from social media, I did see more clearly the confines of the stage upon which everyone is performing, and I realized the show was no longer worth the hype.

To the best of my ability, I still want to be informed and engaged. I want to be able to converse about the state of our world and discuss inspired, pitch-perfect memes during a podcast taping or at a dinner party (I have visual proof I've been to at least two). I want to revel and delight in the fever dream of online culture and to know what is happening in the larger snow globe that holds my smaller bubbles in which I live, work, and love. I want to show up and support in whatever small ways I can. Instead, I more often wonder how I have become so bad at stringing a basic sentence together, even if provided the buzzwords with which to compose it. Best-case scenario, it comes out bot-like: "Polarized bears the melting midterms I can't!" And while I can half regurgitate information, I can't form my own opinions anymore, not without trace elements of "Is this OK?" and "How about now?"

I guess that's the biggest lie of the internet—that I am the only one adrift in a sea of content, while everyone else knows exactly where they are going on the information superhighway (Who still calls it this? Me and one cell phone–holstered dad as my second, ready to duel?) and at which exit to get off. But how can any of us extrapolate anything with any nuance when we're all waiting for the next unpinned hand grenade to tumble down the road, demanding we run and shield ourselves with as much information as possible about how to feel and why? If you don't have a strong stance on, well, everything, the internet has this to say to you: "How can you not?! What's wrong with you!?!!"

It's not just that I no longer know how to form an opinion, it's that I don't know if I even want to. For a long time, I assumed opting out meant ignorance and apathy, and so I stayed in the game, shining a light into every dark, obscure corner, stumbling down rabbit holes I knew would inevitably make me feel worse. But the one thing being online all the time can't give me is breathing room. Or perspective. Or a moment to consider: What is the point of knowing all the things? Where does this constant churning drone of subjective information leave me?

If you've read this far, which is the writer's equivalent of a self-deprecating joke, I should qualify that the opinions that trip me up most aren't the big ones. I unequivocally know how I feel about, for example, Nazis. Bad!

It's the opinions that don't exactly affect everyone's right to pursue an autonomous life; these are the ones with which I struggle and can't keep up. For example, if almond milk is as bad for the environment as drinking cow's milk (you're very welcome if I just unnecessarily complicated your life), or where everyone stands on the white influencer who did the thing, but then apologized, but wait, the apology was maybe worse? Then again, there are no small ideas on the internet. Everything is huge and loud and incontrovertible evidence. And yes, I'll be the straw man that broke the camel's back and remind everyone that so many of these brave culture wars are frequently being hashed out on devices still made with slave labor.

We live in the era of the infinite take. There are so many voices and stances and fresh-off-the-press quick-draw POVs out there, and most of them come within hours or minutes, if not *seconds*, of news breaking. I wouldn't be surprised if they start coming out before the thing happens. Opinions are spread and then consumed so quickly en masse, ensuring they're less about depth and more about rate of propagation. Both on and off the web, so many things go the way of groupthink. The nonfiction essay collections I most often read cite multiple sources and end with bibliographies, and I find comfort in this. It's the author suggesting, "See? I'm not the only person who feels this way. So did this seventeenth-century French icon." That's one way to give heft to an argument, to include others in your idea salon. I do it myself plenty in this book; see if you caught it. Blink once if you agree. Burn the book if you don't.*

Across the internet, but most especially on social media, everything is

---

* By God, I meant metaphorically!

black-and-white. You're either the literal worst or you give people life. To-day, justice better go viral, or did the incident even happen, and leave out any complicating details please. (Save it for, I don't know, your chatbot.) On the internet, each of us is more a product or an idea than a human being with all the chaos that entails. The language itself trends hyperbolic be-cause digital performance works best when the stakes are high.

To put it too lightly, there will always be a horrible range of misinformation-spouting wellness influencers to Harvey Weinsteins, both running around doing unspeakable things to plants and even worse things to people. All of these bad actors and powerful entities must be held to account. And. Most humans aren't all good or all bad. Most of us are a mix, most likely a remix of some ancestor(s) of ours, just doing our best, but still screwing up on the reg. We've all had a year or a relationship or a deadly pathogen we wish we could strike from the record. Most of us are just trying to mitigate our own cycles of pain, so what is the point of constantly accusing each other no matter the stakes, insisting everyone else is the woefully misguided problem?

A world of absolutes might be easier to live in, but it's not real. Being alive means shuffling from one gray area to the next, tracking mud wherever we go, no matter how many times we try to argue otherwise. That's the tragic beauty of being human—as a species, we're well-intentioned but poorly ex-ecuted. And no, I'm not a centrist, but I do believe in nuance. There is al-ways some degree of complicity, regardless of our best intentions. This is not an argument for jaded apathy. On the contrary, it's a reminder that none of us is ever 100 percent right 100 percent of the time. And yet, here we are. We keep on showing up. Sometimes, especially when I am online, I forget that a measure of hope can be enough. That I can read *some* of the internet's words and find some salvation there instead of all of them and find nothing.

I guess my strongest opinion is one for ambiguity—am I a snake eating its own tail? To that I would say nothing because my mouth is full. I no longer believe in the pressure to take in boundless information. In fact, I openly reject it the best I can. Who likes a know-it-all anyway (not to be confused with an "intellectual elite")? I know what I know, but I don't question whether I am prioritizing the right things to know or whether I know all the right things at all the right times. I remind myself I am one person and try to take in as many different perspectives as I can, aware my worldview is limited. It is so easy to get caught up in bullshit on the internet, and sometimes, yes, there is escapist joy in it, but more often, it's a trap. I sense that I'm being made to feel like I should care about something irrefutable and urgent, when the truth is it might be more powerful to walk away.

I'm still not checking social media—I know, I know, I am a poster child at the intersection of FOMO and FONK, but the worthwhile trade-off is I get to choose what I pay attention to with a degree more independence in this overcommodified world. If the internet got a tattoo, it might read JUST SAYIN' in cursive rhinestone font, and I'm no longer here for it. I'd rather go stare at a waterfall. The reason we have to feel strongly about everything, including how we feel *about* feeling strongly, is that when we're online, we're all performance artists. When you're performing, you have to have a strong point of view. If you don't, the only thing you're communicating to the audience is you don't deserve their attention.

Of course, this begs the question of why bother staying on Twitter at all, especially since it's now owned by a misguided, mess-obsessed Tesla? Why not delete my account entirely, if I'm only going to very occasionally post anyway? I have never directly made money off my account. I have essentially put out free content to bankroll huge tech corporations that have not only profited from my brain without me seeing a cent but also refused to regulate the proliferation of misinformation, targeted abuse, and extremist propaganda on their sites. Plus, I am essentially keeping people on the sites longer by posting material on them that they might read. So, for what it's worth, I don't have an answer, have no plans to delete my account, and, yes, am a hypocrite (deep curtsy). I wish I knew what long-term social media use will do to my brain, having used it for over seventeen years (MySpace, never forget), but so far I can just make out the "now" effects and . . . they're not great.

We are, after all, human beings. Our perspectives and values are going to shift over the course of our lives as we evolve and intersect with others—hopefully in the direction of more grace and expansiveness. The culture of social media proclaims there is a right way to feel about everything and a wrong way, and independent of which "team" you're on, you could have your "fifteen minutes of shame" at any given moment. I personally don't align with the "we've gotten overly PC" camp, which seems to equate causing offense, if not outright harm, with a badge of honor, nor do I agree with the puritanism of woke* watchdogs, in which my spouting of progressivism is touted as evidence of my inability to ever cause harm. We're all composed of contradictions and limits. We all still have plenty of room to grow for lack of exposure. It's an impossible task to be perfectly positioned with regard to everything—that is a politician's tactic, and, as far as I know, nobody values politicians as moral compasses. At best, they are spokespeople for the closest audience to which they stand, purported river guides of the rapids of societal improvement, even when that so often proves to be an empty gesture. I'd sooner trust a bobblehead doll for moral guidance.

Unlike politicians, I've learned to embrace being wrong. The past half century, at least, has shown just how easily most of us can and will be mistaken. When I spent more time on Twitter, being wrong felt like the worst

---

* I resent even using this word, which has been, as is tradition, co-opted and flattened of all meaning.

crime: *How stupid could I be to post a joke like that?* Yes, it's uncomfortable and embarrassing, and who wants to be the one with a three-egg omelet on their face? But mistakes are the can openers of the conversations we most need to have. And hey, maybe some of them will have those fun snakes inside! There is harmony in agreement, sure, but it can also so quickly devolve into an orgy of back-patting. Around and around we go on the carousel of shared views, riding the highest of horses. Growth and change are often born from disagreement, but only if you're willing to have a face-to-face conversation—offline, when possible.

I am happy to own how I feel about things now given where I've come from and where I'm headed, but I also hold space for feeling differently in the future. We are lucky to have opportunities to evolve and hopefully can surround ourselves with people who are open to hearing us out—which, of course, means we are prepared to return the favor. These changes will show up in different ways: in talking less, in listening more, in sharing differently, and in amplifying with purpose. As a comedian, I know it's my job to hold a microphone of opinion, but I've divorced myself from the need to do that all day, every day, about everything. Sometimes "no comment" is the best response, should you even have to voice one.

Confessions:
The Brains of the Bunch

I don't know how planes stay up in the sky. I mean, I have a vague idea, but barely. . . . If you asked me in an interview, I'd look out the window, pause for a measure, and venture, "A good attitude?"

When I want to run errands but in an epic way, I put on the *Lord of the Rings* trilogy soundtrack. I highly recommend it, especially if you want buying stamps to feel sweeping and triumphant, against all odds.

Every time I hear a conspiracy theory,* I do have at least a moment where I'm like, "I mean, maybe???"

---

* No, no, no, not one of the QAnon-flavored or outright bigoted ones, I'm talking classics like the JFK assassination, Bigfoot, Area 51, etc. Sign me the hell up!

Talking about Nothing

In the dawn of my pursuit of stand-up, I read an interview with an East Asian comic in which she said she had to address what she looked like within the first few minutes of her set. If she didn't, the audience wouldn't "accept" her or any of her jokes. It was necessary to name the loaded obvious—her racialized identity—or the audience, whether consciously or unconsciously, would spend the whole set waiting for her to get to it. It was a preemptive strike. I'll other me before you can other me. But it's a joke, so it's fine, right? [Pause for effect.] Am I right?

While I didn't like what she was insinuating, you could argue her instincts were to reclaim ownership of the space. After all, stand-up is an art of control. The audience is putting their assumptions on you, so you're telling them, "I'm naming it so that *you* know that *I* know *I'm different*. I am still in charge. Annnnd now we're going to talk about my annoying neighbor."

In my own act, my move used to be telling audiences that I was going to go ahead and name the elephant in the room—with the caveat that it was racist it had to be an elephant. People laughed because people laugh when you point out ethnic differences in a palatable, lowest-common-denominator kind of way. It wasn't the most original joke, but maybe that's part of why it felt safe. There are elephants in India! Don't your people sometimes ride elephants? Most of them don't, by the way, and that's most out of a billion. *We see you, but only in the most generic, clumsiest strokes.* I am exotic, but I'm giving you permission to laugh about that. I soon dropped the elephant line, though, because I felt dirty using it, like I was turning the pen on myself in a lazy, thoughtless way. In today's climate, I doubt most audiences would even laugh at that line, and they shouldn't. Back then, I might have been to blame for setting the crowd up, but I was still disappointed when they laughed. It felt like a test that all of us failed.

For a while, I opened with: "It's OK, I'm surprised I'm a comedian, too." The hidden double entendre was that when I said I was surprised I was a comedian, I meant because I wasn't the most boisterous personality. *I wear my giant foam finger on the inside.* Meanwhile, to an audience, I was addressing how I didn't "present" like a typical comedian for any number of reasons—in ethnicity, in volume, in general vibe. The line was a way for us to meet in the middle. I even used it to open my first late-night set on *Conan*, incidentally the first US late-night set ever by a South Asian woman (in 2013, yay but also yikes). At that time, whenever I got onstage, I knew what most of the audience was thinking: *Wait, you're the comedian?* I was giving them permission to laugh at the incongruity. I was saying, "It's OK, I don't get it either. You're right. I'm wrong, as in *all of me* is wrong. Showing up in a package that isn't a cishet, white, neurotypical male with no visible disabilities sure is weird, isn't it? Haha! What a relief you said it. For us mostly, the majority! Feel free to laugh along with us, as otherwise, we *will* take it personally."

I was aiding and abetting my own difference. But it's fine, we tell ourselves (and each other), because comedy often comes from self-deprecation. I'm not punching up or punching down, I'm punching the mirror. Nobody gets hurt—except me. Luckily, comedians don't feel anything because we're dead inside. That's supposed to be our whole bag.

It's a well-played ruse. Comics are some of the most sensitive people alive, hiding behind this idea that nothing gets to us by constantly deflecting and dodging. But that same sensitivity is what gives us the ability to so acutely observe everything around us, a trait on which professional funny people pride themselves. We're lint rollers for society, picking up every stray bit of fluff and dust that accumulates in the vicissitudes of life, things no one else thinks twice about. Our minds turn in an endless "why, why, why" of face value. People mostly put up with the incessant questions of small children because they're cute—the only reason stand-ups get away with shitting on everything is that we spin our endless cynicism into something you can laugh at.

I had a "joke" when I was starting out about how "being brown" can be an umbrella term when it comes to race. The setup was about how sometimes I was misidentified as ethnicities other than my own (true), whether that was Latinx or Indigenous or some wild card third option (I once convinced a date I was Italian). And how I would lean into ill-informed white colleagues' questions of "What are you?" by wearing a dot on my forehead but also a feather in my hair and bringing taquitos for lunch (all cringingly false). It's very superficial Comedy 101 "ethnicity and race in the most broad, problematic terms." I would be mortified to tell that joke now. In terms of both the current comedic and cultural bar, it's not saying anything new or nuanced about the state of identity, let alone intersectionality. Nor is it doing anything subversive to dismantle tolerated white ignorance. At the same time, I'm pretty sure that joke helped get me picked for the NBC Stand-up for Diversity national talent search in 2007 (now called StandUp NBC) and the *Last Comic Standing* NYC showcase in 2008 (blink and you'll miss me in that season).

Sure, the butt of the joke is technically white people's cluelessness about minorities rather than my own understanding of them, but wearing a feather and eating taquitos, which are already careless depictions of two vast ethno-graphic identities, are not my stereotypes to subvert or appropriate. The Latinx and Indigenous populations are far more vulnerable in many ways than a large swath of South Asian immigrants (though not all) who have settled in America, and my full understanding of that is a constant evo-lution.

White ignorance is, of course, an umbrella term for an attitude that stems from appeasing American white supremacy. I can be just as complicit in it as the next person. Plenty of non-white people have crumpled my identity in the same way. Months before I even did that bit, a Black comic saw me per-form and decided I was squandering the treasure trove of material that was my ethnicity. Lucky for me, he worked pro bono. He took it upon himself to write some jokes for me about being South Asian. Here's one: "Indian ste-reotypes almost got me killed. Yeah, I had a sniper stalking me for six months, but nobody said anything because they thought the red dot on my forehead was supposed to be there." (Cue an orchestra of sad trombones.)

Don't worry, it gets better! I did tell his jokes onstage! But wait, before you ban this book, I did it with the full context of how they didn't come with a gift receipt, and so the audience had to sit in the awkwardness with me. Not only were all his jokes playing on tired tropes, but I never wanted to let my ethnic identity take up that much room in my set. Yes, there was the aforementioned joke about being brown, but if anything, I wrote that one to check off the box about what I looked like and move on. I wanted to talk about *me* and how I saw things, not about how other people saw me. For once, I had the microphone, and no one else was going to steal focus.

While this wasn't a conscious political choice on my part, well-intentioned interviewers would later assume it was. "We notice you don't overtly talk much about your race in your act. Care to comment?" Standing out because of this supposed decision also implied I had made the "correct" choice. It was the "good" way to set myself apart. In stand-up, certain jokes are seen as "easy," and pointing out your identity is often considered well-trod territory by those who have come before you. I didn't want to be pigeonholed.※ A better comic is at least expected to approach the topic from a fresh perspective. If you don't have that, then best to steer clear.

And right from the start of my career, my peers approved of my doing just that. I was doubly praised by men in comedy, who said it was cool that I didn't do "hacky" jokes about being a woman or being South Asian. And even now, I still find myself partly springing to their defense. *They just meant I was being refreshing and original.* I absorbed the positive feedback and worked to make my outer identity smaller and my inner identity bigger, like the newest iPhone model.

This, in and of itself, was a form of privilege, and one that is clearly affected by the gray areas of intersectionality. Not everyone has this luxury to the same degree. The tricky thing about privilege is realizing your inability to ever comprehend fully what a life might be like without the benefits you have in yours. One of the most invaluable goals of art is to try to bridge that divide. Stand-up is often about closing the gap between what people expect when they see you, and where you decide to take them once you have their attention. Ultimately, the choice is yours, but it does feel as though audiences, depending on their makeup, believe some performers are more capable of having a life they can relate to than others. I too have been guilty of seeing a stand-up for the first time and assuming I know what their set will be about based on what they look and sound like, cishet white males very much included. Get ready for a groundbreaking sermon on the ins and outs of porn! (C'mon, it writes itself.)

I didn't notice the heavy omission of my race and ethnicity in my act

---

※ I suspect where this expression comes from, but haven't pigeons been through enough?

until others pointed it out to me. But I doubt it was a coincidence. Growing up South Asian, I stuck out among my majority white peers. So it makes sense that I shied away from making that part of myself my "whole deal" onstage. And even with non-white-of-other-ethnicities peers, I worried my background and home life wouldn't make sense to them. But I also didn't feel like I blended in enough at cultural and community events among my fellow South Asian Americans either. I spent so much of my life trying to seamlessly toggle between my Western surroundings and my Eastern roots that it felt impossible to determine my lane as a comic onstage. When I thought of my place in the world, the safest route was suppressing the racial aspects of identity altogether. Instead, I led with my interiority, which no one could call my bluff on. In that sense, my humor was generated as an outsider from every group.

Like many people in comedy, I was first attracted to it as a way of belonging. Subcultures and cultural scenes are like jackets you can throw on to explain who you are and who your people are. It's amazing how hard we will work to make it seem like those jackets are custom made, as opposed to desperately coveted and then covertly purchased in the off-brand version. Throughout elementary school, I wanted nothing more than a jean jacket. I thought it was the coolest status item, though my entire point of reference was seeing a Muppet wear one on an episode of *Sesame Street* while performing a variation of a Bruce Springsteen song. Muppets: they're just like us!

My cultural references as a sheltered immigrant kid were frequently missing due to lack of exposure. I mostly hung out with my family. I didn't watch the cool movies or TV shows or play the latest video games (or any for that matter) or wear the trendy clothes. Everything was slightly off. And so, I inhabited an identity that was more observer than participant, rendering myself more invisible than visible. In my head, I could be whoever I wanted, especially if no one else was bothering to label me. This is perhaps still a sign of whitewashing, but it's near impossible to be an immigrant child trying to assimilate (since this was the only strategy on offer) and not participate in some form of erasure as a means of self-preservation.

This of course influenced my point of view in stand-up, though I didn't make that connection right away. A lifelong misfit, I felt so cool to be invited into the boys' club of comedy in DC, where I slipped into a kid sister role. I could be "special" but only by partially erasing any vestige of my cultural dichotomy. Perhaps I intrinsically knew that talking about my background would automatically brand me as niche—in an inauthentic way.

As a performer, I can speak only to my own experience, and whoever relates to that experience is more than welcome to. I never felt the same amount of ownership over my South Asian identity as, say, my sibling, Bhav, who has spent long periods of time in India for work and proficiently speaks Telugu, my family's native language. I was the only one in my family born here in America, and I leaned into that technicality hard. I was playing at whiteness and cishet maleness, albeit through my own filter. I was performing the idea of neutrality to others.

Around this same time, a comedian peer of mine, whom, full disclosure, I ended up dating for a long time, told me, "You do stand-up like someone who's never seen stand-up before." He clarified that this was a compliment, but his comment emphasized how I started stand-up as a tabula rasa. I had no preconceived notions about what was expected of me or what had preceded me. Little did I know how particular was the box in which I fit for others.

ONE OF MY first big breaks came when I did the aforementioned program, NBC Stand-up for Diversity, a comprehensive search across the US for acts from groups underrepresented in the industry. "Diversity" was used in the vague, inclusive, feel-good way it's always used. They might as well have said NBC Stand-up for You People. And it wasn't a search limited to race—they were also seeking a wide range of sexual orientations and gender identities, neurodiversity, and people with disabilities. Basically, if you stuck out in any way in which people could be like, "So cool of us to be helping you."

I was chosen as one of the ten finalists flown to Los Angeles, where we performed four-minute sets for a gathering of suits, who received our contact information in case they saw little dollar signs over our heads. As far as the internet tells me, the last time the competition was conducted was 2020, shortly before the pandemic.

This is typical of my experience with corporate diversity programs. Hey, you, you count as diverse. Now join us as we take some credit and, maybe, sure, you might also benefit. Obviously, that's inherently part of show business no matter who you are, but if marginalization is already part of your daily reality, it's that much worse.

In an acting class I once took in Los Angeles, we did an exercise in which our classmates named actors or actresses who reminded them of us. It was supposed to help each of us figure out our "type" and what kinds of roles we might be cast for. It was an unimaginative exercise to begin with, made worse by the excruciating results.

The first answer I got was "Oh! That one girl from *The Office*!" Bzz. Sorry, the answer we were looking for is Mindy Kaling. She had her own show by that point, I think you can figure out her name. It's like calling Barack Obama "that one Black guy from the White House." Then there was some hesitation, after which the second pick arrived: "Aziz Ansari!" Gender identity aside, our energies are as far apart as they come. He's more "kinetic energy" while I am more "potential energy" slash "inert." Which brings me to the last one I got, and don't worry, they really went out with a bang: "Science." That's right, the last one wasn't even a person, it was a concept. At least they could have said "cloud" or "saudade" (a Portuguese word for a feeling of longing or melancholy), which would have at least been ballpark for my demeanor. In my classmates' defense, I get it. I'm hard to pin down. I'm a shape-shifter, which I also, by the way, would have accepted as a third choice.

For example, my sense of humor was the epitome of basic when I started stand-up. My favorite comedy movie when I was a kid was *Weekend at Bernie's II* and, before that, *The Gods Must Be Crazy II* (in retrospect, dated and offensive!). The only thing I loved more than screwball was sequels. Ellen DeGeneres is the only comedian I recall performing on TV, and I didn't even know she was doing something called stand-up. As far as I could tell, show business was not a career just anyone could go into. I figured it was like the circus; your family had to be born into the trade, going from town to town with red noses and enviable timing.

When I first began to delve seriously into the world and history of comedy, I was drawn to the comedians who did tightly crafted, setup-punchline stand-up. Whether it was Jim Gaffigan, Wanda Sykes, or Mitch Hedberg, their perspectives on being a human alive in the world were specific to them and pitch perfect.

But gradually, I began idolizing comics who were more expansive in their styles and harder to categorize. Maria Bamford was a singular favorite with her endless world building via voice and mannerisms alone, as was Tig Notaro in her unassuming brilliance and willingness to play in the moment. Kristen Schaal and Chelsea Peretti were both joyfully inventive, toying with form and substance, and Janeane Garofalo came through town once and blew me away with her stream-of-consciousness oratory.

It wasn't all women breaking boundaries, though. Yep, believe it or not, men are sometimes also creative, and good for them. They're doing their best. When I first saw Brent Weinbach, a half-Filipino, half-Jewish comic, I saw something utterly new and different and hard to describe, in the best way. He uses his entire self as an instrument—integrating faces, movements, voices, tics, and non sequiturs that make you laugh at a primal level. I felt a similar way when I first saw Taiwanese American comic Sheng Wang—his stage presence is so laidback and easy, it's like you're hanging out with your chillest friend, who is effortlessly hilarious and philosophical on everything from avocados to automatic hand dryers. He manages to elevate the everyday situations of life into absurd genius. As with all great comedians, they lead with their personalities first. This approach was what called to me the loudest.

While all comedians have a joke or two referencing their identity, a few make it more of a mainstay of their act, unpacking the political nature of it. Though I greatly respect and look up to many comics who talk about their identities and social justice in compelling ways—Hari Kondabolu, for example, has been very outspoken on race and progressive politics in his act, as has W. Kamau Bell—I have never thought I was qualified to do the same.

It's also no coincidence that to speak about the complexities of marginalized identity at any length is to automatically be political within the infrastructures of capitalism and ableist heteropatriarchy and white supremacy that silently underpin all our institutions. You can feel certain audiences' tolerances shrivel up when they hear these topics. They don't want their own assumptions challenged and are looking to "laugh to forget." Even liberals prefer back-patting political comedy rather than any indication they can be as complicit as radical right-wingers. It's why it's so ludicrous to me that people lump all stand-ups together, when so many different performers have vastly divergent goals with their material.

Ever the humble dinner party guest, I didn't feel politically conscious or worldly enough on anything when I started. Topics exploring race and gender and institutional shortcomings were outside my wheelhouse. As someone decidedly focused on not rocking the boat, I found it inconceivable to attempt broaching any big, thorny issues. I didn't always trust my own instincts about the larger world around me. The only thing I felt sure of was taking shots within safer territory, making sure to frame everything within the subtext of "But maybe it's just me!"

SOMETIMES I WISH I didn't have to address my identity at all. It's not like when I wake up in the morning, I think, *Ah, just another day being* a quiet South Asian American woman *in a culture dominated by whiteness. Better live my truth!* It is the lens through which others may often view me, but it's not the one at the forefront of my mind when I'm looking out at everyone else. The counterpoint to that might be that people are watching, especially those who share my identity. When you are participating in an art form where there aren't a lot of people who look like you, whether you want to or not, you represent more than just yourself.

At multiple points in my career, I've been advised to either drop my last name or change it. Every time, the person would helpfully note my last name is not intuitive to know how to pronounce or spell. *People use stage names all the time—why not just make it easier on everyone?* Let's all take a second and imagine if I were an Aparna Jones. There's a tiny part of me that recognizes the upgrade, the part of me that felt embarrassed every time my name got butchered since roll call immemorial.

But despite the countless times it's been dismembered beyond recognition or dropped without my permission, I've never considered changing my last name. It felt like the bare minimum of representing some part of my identity. To this day, it's still regularly misspelled and mispronounced, sometimes even when I am being sought out for a job! It's a constant reminder that "one of these things is not like the other." Cue musical sting: It's me! [Sheepishly shrug to camera.]

At the same time, I have always held a deep pride in being South Asian so close to the vest that I couldn't quite articulate it to myself, let alone anyone else. It's a sense of being part of something much bigger, something that enveloped me without question or accreditation, an escape hatch from playing at whiteface. The automatic acceptance has felt equal parts precious and tenuous. I didn't want to then mock that belonging in front of a mixed audience. They wouldn't be laughing with me, they'd be laughing at me! It would be yet another way for the crowd to think, *Told you! Different!* But more than that, taking the incredible warmth of fitting in and disparaging it in front of many who barely understood in the first place struck me as dangerous. Mockery presumed an overconfidence in the strength of my relationship with this sense of pride—one that I did not have.

Unsurprisingly, I've frequently been offered shows that catered to a mostly South Asian audience, but I've often found myself uncomfortable in those environments. Because it feels like I'm not doing the material that the audience wants to see. If it's a younger crowd, they are generally OK with it (though I still fear some implicit judgment on my level of internalized self-loathing), but older crowds have often stared blankly at my cerebral, quasi-absurdist me-specific observations. On more than one occasion, my mom has told me that she and my dad don't fully understand my jokes, but they enjoy the fact that other people around them seem to be having a good time. Classic.

When I was younger, I didn't relate to being a brown-skinned person in that same nonelective way that is forced upon Black people as well as many other demographics within the minority umbrella. I knew I had brown skin, but I didn't connect to it deeply, frequently forgetting I had it at all. My mother is fairer skinned than I am, and Bhav and I both fall closer to my dad's shade of milky coffee. I was so often in a sea of eggshell and salmon swatches that I conveniently forgot I wasn't a distant subset of beige. Unless, that is, I was in majority South Asian–people environments, where it became the default again. I didn't even think my parents spoke English with Indian accents. I thought they were the only two older Indian immigrants I knew who just happened not to have them.

It's almost as if in white environments, I thought I somehow trended white, or at the very least, adjacent. I knew I wasn't, but the fact that no one called me out on it if I kept a low enough profile made me think of it as something I could get away with. If South Asian Americans stayed in line and kept our heads down, we could benefit from some of the privileges of whiteness that weren't afforded to other disenfranchised groups, with class and status being an important, often overlooked element to include here. To that point, my parents were both doctors, and we were raised upper-middle class, with benefits that many working-class or financially insecure Americans—of all races and ethnicities—are denied. In witnessing the benefits of assimilation, I thought I could play along.

It was also no small coincidence that I very much identified as a tomboy growing up and loved consuming books about little Caucasian scamp-dudes and their dogs getting into mischief. *Henry and Ribsy* over *Beezus and Ramona*, anyone? *Where the Red Fern Grows* over *Anne of Green Gables*? *The Outsiders* over *Little Women*? All the spoils went to the white man, so, little go-getter that I was, I figured I'd be one of those when I grew up. And, duh, we all know the ultimate hype "person" is a dog.

Growing up, I had South Asian friends and extended family with whom I was very close, and those relationships felt magical to me. But that part of my life was completely cloistered and compartmentalized from my school life. I would meet these friends when my parents took us to their friends' parties on the weekends, or when we started going to Hinduism Sunday school. It felt like you had to pick a side, and the white one felt like the safer bet. The reality is that these white-dominant environments (school, work, etc.) were the ones in which I had to spend the majority of my time fitting in. Even when some of my peers were also children of immigrants or non-white, we were still subsumed by the aspirational suburban white hierarchy. Mathematically, it made more sense to focus on fitting into these places, and no, I am not going to make a nerd joke, because I am better than that and so are you, reader. Add to that my own hesitation in navigating South Asian–skewed environments because I had fewer opportunities to figure them out, and the die was cast. The fun thing with assimilation is that no matter how much you think you've done the assignment, it's still returned to you with the words "Needs work, please see me" scribbled in red across the top.

WOMAN. WOMAN OF COLOR. Upper-middle-class immigrant. Creative. Lived experience with mental illness. These are all considered niche identities. To add to the perversity of flattening my entire experience in this way, these identities have also become "hot" in the marketplace. Who even knows if that will be the case when this screed goes to print, but there's still, despite the magnanimous moment we're in, a very real part of me that sees my story as tokenized. I'm sure many would immediately scoff, hold up their hands, and beg to differ at the progressive community meeting, but the depth with which internalized self-loathing is branded into you as reflected by the media and culture is not undone overnight, neither by one Black president nor by one groundbreaking TV show where you are finally represented. In a world where whiteness and lightness are still very much the default, even within the skin tones of minority communities, and there are countless stories and memoirs of young cis heterosexual white men (*and* women) being told, why does it still feel like my story gets one shot and one shot only?

When you're a woman of color, the tokenism can double. Instead of taking up twice as much room at the table you aren't always sure you deserve a

seat at, you barely give yourself any space to sit at all. Eager to accommodate, you insist, "I'll just stand in the doorway!" Not only do you undervalue
your own worth, but everyone who looks like you or might have a similar
experience also becomes an opponent, and not because you feel any ill will
toward them or their work. But because to a tribunal of white tastemakers,
consciously or not, "You are all the same. Your stories are all the same.
They need to be told only once, and whoever tells it first dictates what comes
after that, if anything." The liberal white gaze has only so much tolerance
for hearing about "your authentic experience" before it gets restless, shifting
its feet, moving on to the next benevolent enterprise. And by virtue of not
being as well versed or assured in my South Asian identity as others, I feel
like my value goes down; I somehow offer a less worthwhile minority perspective.

Immigrant stories sweep the gamut of age, gender identity, race, class,
ethnicity, sexual orientation, presumed disability, neurodiversity—and that's
before taking into account the subtler qualities of personality and human
nature. And yet they are still considered niche in comparison with so many
standard depictions of American whiteness, which get told and retold countless ways without once stopping to ask, *Why is this important? Why does this
matter? And to whom?*

It matters because this person is allowed to exist regardless of their
identity—their humanity is considered first. Being reduced to what you look
like and what you represent demographically eats away at you, forcing you
to consider yourself the way others do, as a box to be checked off before
moving on to the next. For example, I am constantly paranoid that being a
woman of color has done the heavy lifting on opening the door to every
writers' room for me, but who knows how many have been likewise closed?

Now, thankfully, things are evolving, due to demographic shifts as well
as the boom in streaming platforms and content, which are more dependent

on paid subscribers than the traditional broadcast and cable network advertising-based models.

Minorities now make up roughly 43 percent of the US population, on track to become the largest US demographic within the next twenty years, and, good news, our numbers are showing. We consume disproportionately more media than white households; shows with majority minority casts performed extremely well with adults eighteen to forty-nine, a demographic that is now 53 percent non-white and growing.

In the 2022 *Hollywood Diversity Report* for film, movies with more diverse casts grossed more money, due in no small part to theatergoing audiences being more diverse. And while gains have been made for people of color in front of the camera—for example, by maintaining proportionate representation as leads on-screen—they still remain underrepresented as both film directors and film writers, as do women.

According to the 2022 *Hollywood Diversity Report* for television, while there have been steady gains in representation across the board for both women and minority talent, there are still noticeable gaps. For example, Latinx talent still remains woefully underrepresented on-screen across broadcast, streaming, and cable shows. Another finding was that women and minority show creators often receive smaller budgets compared with their white male counterparts. As categorized in the report, the BIPOC demographic is nearing proportionate representation in lead acting, directing, and writing for cable programs, as well as lead acting for digital programs, it remained underrepresented otherwise in digital and broadcast spaces for the 2020–2021 television season. There was no update on the previous year's finding that there has been no expansion in opening studio and network C-level positions to BIPOC and women, and these are the suits who continue to make all the green-lighting decisions.

I participated in a union meeting over Zoom at which writers of color convened with leadership to discuss their experiences in late-night writing rooms to work toward making these environments more inclusive and accountable. Even in this "safe space," I was nervous to speak up, but after seeing so many others vulnerably share, I decided to say something as well. While I was relating my story, the highest person in leadership in the meeting (a white man) got up to go do something else. AT A MEETING ABOUT LISTENING TO WRITERS OF COLOR.

Experiences like these make me wonder, if a white person tries to lead reform for non-white people within a white-dominated system, is it really changing the system, or is it further entrenching it? Ceding that power and decentering oneself isn't easy, but it is necessary. Building structures that aren't mere offshoots of the existing paradigms is important work that takes time to sustain itself. No, it's not going to be easy or smooth, but considering the end goal is to build an alternative to a system whose entire purpose is meant to swallow any opposition, that is by design.

At its best, representation is about allowing the inherent three-dimensionality that accompanies being a person alive on this earth ahead of any other labels put on top of that humanity. Unfortunately, that doesn't always fit into society's rigid expectations of diverse content. This explains to me why a show like *Insecure* got parsed and slammed in real time online for its depiction of Black culture—while simultaneously being very popular. Since it was one of the few highly visible mainstream shows of its time depicting modern-day Black women in America through the lens of friendship, *Insecure* was under impossible pressure to be everything to everyone. It got picked through with a fine-tooth comb for accuracy and how it might come across to the white gaze, when it was speaking only for the experiences of those in its writers' room and could never speak for all Black women or people. That shouldn't have to be its job.

I've often wondered how critical I'm allowed to be of minority-helmed art when there are comparatively less options available. If I respond to something particularly negatively, I question whether I'm enforcing unreasonable standards. But when I automatically embrace another work wholeheartedly, I wonder if I am being too feel-good. I never trust my instincts in the same way, muddied as they are with considerations I don't apply elsewhere. Ultimately, a group should be well-enough represented that they are allowed the same chances to fail as other groups. Artists need to be able to take risks, and with risks always come the possibility of a flop or, *gasp*, something that's fine, I guess. But that should not be a bad thing. My underlying hope is the chance to be just so-so for all.

In "The Privilege of Mediocrity," a piece for *T: The New York Times Style Magazine*, Adam Bradley writes, "Mediocrity is a creative resource for minority artists in at least two ways. First, as a barometer: when a critical mass of opportunity means that no one work is taken as predictive. Second, as an imaginative resource: When mediocrity can be safely thematized in characters, when ambitious art is made about unambitious or even deeply flawed people, creatives of color wrest control from the narrow confines of others' projections." The burden of creating only critically infallible work, often about exceptional specimens, cannot be placed on groups that already spend so much time having to explain their existences to others.

I grew up in the 1990s, when there was a boom in shows depicting Black people, like *Living Single*, *Moesha*, and *Family Matters*, and then with Margaret Cho starring in the short-lived *All-American Girl*, it was one giant step forward for Asian Americans. But the needle has moved much more since then. Culturally, visibility is now becoming a "must-have" rather than a "nice-to-have." There is clearly an appetite for more diverse stories being told, as reflected by my own experience in Hollywood—yet the viability of these projects remains at the whim of white gatekeepers. There are still reductionist minority stories that are more palatable to a white audience (for example, *Green Book* and *The Help*). But now there are also minority stories that push the envelope beyond relatable to irreverent (*Ramy* and *Atlanta* and *A Black Lady Sketch Show* and *Beef*) and minority stories that highlight universal themes in their specificity (*The Farewell* and *Moonlight*). But knowing how hard it is to get something made, it does seem like the emphasis now is on "authentic" minority stories, which means still getting the progressive credit, whether through pathos, sneaky shoehorning, or classic feel-goodism. I'm not arguing this step doesn't need to exist on the path to progress, but we need to see people of color as more than just a market trend. Our stories are not niche. Or, if we're going to play that game, I want to see a Netflix category called Same Old Status Quo.

At least in the realm of stand-up, one would assume there's more of an impetus to champion systemic change. After all, comics often stake their claim on saying what other people are afraid to and being truth tellers who are willing to hold an unflattering light up to society. It would follow that such an art form would welcome with open arms, even seek out, those who may suffer a sense of "otherness." Specifically, those who stand on the margins of society, voicing uncomfortable truths about what we believe versus how we act, the nexus of which holds the majority of us complicit. Yet only recently have any spaces in comedy become more inclusive—and largely only as a by-product of the democratization of online exposure.

IT TOOK A LONG TIME before I was routinely exposed to comics who were radically outspoken in their stand-up. I got my first taste of this in college when I saw Margaret Cho perform, with her complete destruction of the submissive Asian woman stereotype. I couldn't even believe she and I were the same species. In DC, I was lucky to get to know comics like Erin Jackson and Diana Saez, who were also unapologetic about being women of color.

Years later, I had the same feeling when I saw Ali Wong perform. I've been further influenced by so many peers. To name just a few, the experimental stream-of-consciousness styles of Jacqueline Novak and Kate Berlant; the incredible ease of Michelle Buteau, Beth Stelling, and Naomi Ekperigin; and the no-fucks-given approach of comics like Yamaneika Saunders, Sabrina Jalees, Emily Heller, Gina Yashere, and Lizzy Cooperman—I was constantly enchanted.

I didn't think I was capable of taking such a stand on any issues until I saw that just about anyone could. I was the poster child of waiting for permission. I clocked that saying "Well-behaved women rarely make history" and thought, *Well, there goes my spot in the books*. I have strong self-preservation-at-any-cost instincts, and I guess that's always going to be my main problem. Our culture rewards game changers and rebels, and while you could argue I challenged the establishment on my own terms, sometimes it feels like if you quietly do the work, did you do it at all? Not in this attention economy.

It was an indelible step forward, albeit an embarrassingly late one, when I began to understand intersectional feminism and the extent of institutionalized racism that lives and breathes in our society. Once I saw the injustices, I couldn't unsee them. Stepping out of my protective bubble, I both was horrified at my extended ignorance and felt duplicitous speaking to these issues with any confidence. I was also acutely aware that a lot of comedy audiences want to hear only what they already believe, just phrased in a way that catches them off guard. This is not the same as considering someone else's point of view, which takes patience and a willingness to be uncomfortable. It certainly explains the divide between—ugh, for lack of a better term— "woke" comedy and "PC culture is ruining everything" comedy. (There are, of course, eager audiences for both, so, not to worry, the execs are still happy!)

But then I was hired as a writer-performer on *Totally Biased with W. Kamau Bell*, which was very much a sociopolitical comedy show. I remember

Kamau told me that even if I wasn't an overtly political comic, my very identity was a political statement. I tried to absorb these words as I wrote and performed on the show, and I further learned from coworkers and friends who were also stand-ups, like Hari, Kamau, Janine Brito, Eliza Skinner, Guy Branum, Kevin Avery, Kevin Kataoka, Louis Katz, and the incomparable Dwayne Kennedy. They taught me that anyone could take a stance on something they felt strongly about. At first, I wanted to make my platform the mundane, the trivial, the oft overlooked, but slowly I learned to weave in my own larger views in nuanced ways. It's a sneak attack—making the micro the macro.

But as my profile has risen in comedy, I've felt more pressure to be every-thing to everyone. With increased exposure came increased opportunities, and I worried about letting people down more than ever before, which is really saying something! At first, I worried because I couldn't fulfill all the requests I was getting. That worry soon branched out into not being able to meet people's expectations even when I was able to participate. My fear that I was more symbol than person ate away at me and my sense of what my comedic voice should even be.

At stand-up shows, I began to feel as if I were disappointing the audi-ence. No matter what I talked about it, it never felt like the "correct" choice for what I was supposed to represent. There were still some jokes I wrote that tickled me, but it became harder and harder to take pleasure in performing. It felt like no matter who I was, I wasn't the right version of me. Without the ability to be flawed and three-dimensional, I couldn't be any-one at all. When kind people came up to me on the street and said they en-joyed my work and how important it was to them, I couldn't fathom which work they were referring to, and it felt tacky to ask.

I still get crowds who don't want to hear a minority woman talk about anything beyond the obvious. Yet I am humbled to frequently hear from younger women of color, "I started comedy because of you. You made me realize I want to do it, too." I'd also be lying if I didn't acknowledge that I still feel conflicted hearing these words. At least I've learned to deconstruct the reasons why.

When I started comedy, I didn't see many people like me, and thus identified as a token aka one of the lucky few. In fact, soon after I started in the DC scene, another small South Asian woman in the area began performing stand-up, too. My peers secretly referred to her as Aparna 2.0. It was a joke (it's always a joke, right?) but one that felt mean-spirited, though I couldn't tell whom it was undermining. Me? Her? Both of us? No matter how far I get with my career, I feel as though at any moment the ground beneath my feet will fall away, and my place will be given to someone more deserving.

Of course, solidarity comes part and parcel with any coalition building, especially among members of the same group. That's why when I feel natural impulses like envy or comparison with my peers, the shame cuts even deeper. In the midst of writing this, I stumbled upon a book by a young—it turns out anybody younger than you is *shockingly young*—first-generation-immigrant South Asian author. It was razor-sharp and insubordinate in both humor and its social commentary, but also genuinely moving. I'm ashamed to say a part of me crumpled. The grotesque thing is you can probably figure out which book I'm talking about without my even having to name it, because your options are limited in that regard. Hence my spiral!

When pitting your laurels against someone else progressing your entire group forward, it feels less like you're just "comparing and despairing" and more like you're a traitor to the movement. After all, yes, we're allowed to be unpredictable, imperfect humans—that is the point of the movement—but since we operate within the bounds of a system that inherently flattens us as "others," the scarcity mentality courses *strong*. It's critical to have these conversations unpacking some of the "uglier" feelings that come up around intersectional identity. The truth is that colorism, gender identity, pretty privilege, classism, ableism, and ageism, to name a few, are still very much at play, and the system may well value a peer over you, even though neither of you is part of the majority. The shame of talking about it becomes further entrenched because it feels as though it might weaken the power of your group as a whole. But not talking about it inevitably does the same thing.

I try to remind myself constantly there's room for all of us. I have peers, especially those of a younger generation, who embrace this progressive and forward-thinking ethos with open arms, which I find incredible. But I also know this may not tell the full story. Reducing our humanity to either "gets it" or "does not" undoes the complicated work that actual progress requires. It takes having compassion for less palatable parts of myself, sorting through all of the emotions evoked by race and gender and class and power and who gets to call the shots when, where, and how. The only way to move through those knee-jerk reactions of fear, envy, and shame is to admit I have internalized some of the self-loathing that is inculcated early on when you are female and a minority and an immigrant.

An interviewer once asked me why I'm so much more politically strident online than in my act onstage, and I have no idea what I answered, because I was so caught off guard. The truth is I still haven't given myself permission to convey the same amount of rage out loud as I can on a page, and that is something I'm continuing to figure out for myself. Is not explicitly talking about the political nature of identity undercutting how it's received? On the other hand, does that burden always need to be on the artist?

When I first started doing stand-up, I wanted to talk about nothing, because that's what felt "natural." I have seen countless cis, straight white male comics talk about nothing, whether that's an outlandish pot story or another super-crucial observation about women as a species—it's the freedom to exist as a fresh canvas first. There's a smooth-ride ease to the SUV commercial of genetic phenotypes. It's the all-purpose-terrain horsepower of being the default option. Even a comedy audience frequently senses the well-worn "favorite pair of jeans" comfort of a white man's confidence. Stand-up comedy is all about observation, and it's easy to be an observer on the sidelines when you know you were never actually on the sidelines to begin with. The coach was always going to put you in the game.

These guys have the privilege of keeping it light because the "entire costume" they're wearing is in line with the dominant structure of society. The whole stance of "I'm not afraid to make fun of any group" is inherently alpha. The rest of us, even in avoiding overt identity topics, become political statements by virtue of existing at all. Looking ahead, I will find the most delight where I have from the beginning—in the minutiae, the absurdly banal, the sublime of life's quotidian moments, but I can do that without trying to erase my identity. I may never be a megaphone of a political comic, but since I am more aware and informed than when I started stand-up, that mindset now finds its way into the work. I hope I can own that more— mostly for myself. Stand-ups loosely believe it takes ten years to find your real voice as a performer, so it's only natural that I have a different perspective than before. But negotiating identity was something that I had to work through both onstage and off. It was to be expected that it took me so long to find my way out of the Kafkaesque hall of mirrors. That's the gradual realization of talking about nothing—you may be saying far more than you originally fathomed.

Distant Dispatches from the Land of Virtual Interaction

To the Other Four Friends on the Group Text Thread Who Went Radio Silent after I Wrote What I Thought Was a Great Joke Response:

It's not what you didn't say, it's how you didn't say it.

Warmly,
Aparna

To All My Professional Colleagues on the Zoom Meeting Who Clicked "Leave Meeting" So Fast That for Three Whole Seconds I Was Forced to Stare at My Own Face Alone:

I promise you I also live a full and active life.

Best,
Aparna

To the Barely-Even-an-Acquaintance Who Somehow Got My Number and Called Me for No Reason and Then I Foolishly Picked Up because It Was a Local Area Code and Then I Didn't Know How to Get Out of the Conversation:

You made me wish you were a robocall. There's no coming back from that.

Respectfully,
Aparna

To the Perpetrator of the Butt Dial That Goes to Voicemail:

Way to see it through. Your commitment is admirable.

Ever yours,
Aparna

To the "Fan" Who Emailed Me to Ask for Advice about Pursuing a Career in Comedy because "If You Can Do It, Anyone Can!":

Congratulations, I died. I'm a ghost now.

Boo,
Aparna

PS: My only advice is don't. Look what happened to me.

Standing Up on My Own Terms

I am neither a storied veteran nor a singular savant of comedy. I am not well-known enough that I am the face of, say, a frozen potpie company or a new app that's like Shazam for whether someone is actually listening to you. I've had some success and recognition, and yes, it's an accomplishment to "make it" as a professional stand-up comedian, in that I can support myself through my work and I get paid to write and perform my own jokes, supplemented with other writing and acting opportunities that arrived after I established myself as a stand-up. But how to prove I'm really *in* the fraternity? Because if I were in it, I would get it. Mic drop. (Standing ovation of crickets.)

I show up to the meetings, hovering near the door. Make sure enough people see I'm there, grab a cookie, and peace out. It's very lonely to be in an art form where you can speak truth to power about everything except your inherent reservations with what it means to identify as a member of that group.

But I still can't stop questioning the institution of stand-up comedy. I don't question it as a medium of art and self-expression, but rather, the pervasive, undisputed messaging I've witnessed within its culture. And no, I'm not talking about the blatant misogyny, homophobia, bigotry, and sexual misconduct, if not outright violence, that marks the territory. While each of those topics merit their own essays, what I'm referring to is subtler than that, more inside baseball. I'm talking about the entrenched expectations of what it means to call yourself a bona fide stand-up comedian. (Warning: I'm now going to be somber about comedy. If you prefer a lighter read, feel free to add your own laugh track.)

Perhaps my skepticism persists because, like most things in my life, my comedy journey has been a slow burn, frequently leaving me wondering when or if there would be a payoff. My stand-up career has moved at a steady plod, but for the first few years, I hesitated to tell people I was a comedian at all. It wasn't just because I didn't think I had earned the right to call myself one. There was an underlying, not entirely conscious hesitation I had with claiming the identity. I arrived amped for the mix-and-mingle but refused to fill out one of those "Hello, I am . . ." stickers.

I've always had a love-hate relationship with performing. Full stop. I guess this is one of the multiple-choice selections when you decide the specific type of tortured artist you want to be. Or perhaps, it's just a not-so-unusual consequence of how strange a feat performing often is. Some performers are functional people who treat it as one aspect of their well-balanced lives. I mean, I guess . . . I can't be entirely sure since I've rarely had more than a short conversation with one of these human sunflowers before my shadow self starts bleeding out of my haunted eyeballs. I, as I think we've well established at this point in our relationship, am one of the oversensitive overthinkers with an anxious-depressive cherry on top. No, that's not a brag—I know there's a lot of generalized romanticism behind the mentally crumbling jester—but it is true. And, yes, should I ever pivot and go full party clown, you can bet good money that Crumbles would be my name. I'd mostly play wakes and heated divorce trials.

Of the comedic performance genres, stand-up tends to attract a type of personality that operates as a dubious eyewitness to reality, questioning all of it, wondering why things have to be a given way, forever unable to take anything solely on a surface level. Not that these tendencies can't also be found in humor writers or, say, improvisers and sketch comedians, but with stand-up, there's a particular trial-by-jury element. A stand-up faces the crowd alone, time and again, generally as a heightened version of themselves, with a permanently shattered fourth wall, daring anyone to disagree.

When I first landed among other comics, it was like coming home, a bunch of punchy misanthropes eager to reframe their lifelong sense of alienation into the verbal embrace of a laugh. There is a natural rapport between comedians, a sly marriage of world-weariness and instinctive playfulness that is tricky to imagine and even trickier to execute. But it proliferates among a certain set. That's the thread that binds us all together—outsiders who have developed a language to get back in—one that's charming, seductive, and full of delightful surprises. What a relief it is then to finally find others who are also fluent.

But the longer I did stand-up, the more suspicious I grew of this newfound homeland. It's one thing to flock to an art form because you feel like you don't quite fit in anywhere else, another to realize maybe you don't fit in there either. To question stand-up comedy as often as I do feels like walking on a tightrope that is burning at both ends. Where can you go after stand-up, an industry built on skewering everything and everyone else? Once you've self-excommunicated from the too-cool-for-society lunch table, you look around and realize there's nowhere left to sit. Time to go woefully impale your Capri Sun open in the bathroom.

If you're a comic, the answer to any career existential crisis is always more stage time. More is unequivocally better. Obviously. That's the American way. You like this sassy shirt? Buy five of it in every color, even though shoulder cutouts are a microaggression.

The logic is certainly there. Stage time is how you hone your act and get more comfortable talking to a crowd. It is where you learn how to crush and, far more important, how to tank. Stage time is the compulsion of every good, if not great, performer. Stand-up without an audience is like the old tree-falling-in-a-forest riddle: Who cares?

The common belief is there's never a downside to more sets, especially when you're a greener comic looking to cut your teeth. Even though, for many new comics, the stage time opportunities can be empirically bad. *Such as?* I'm so glad you asked. Allow me: A bringer show at a comedy club where you're responsible for packing the audience—asking (soon-to-be-ex-) friends and acquaintances or barking in sorry saps from the street with promises of seeing "Tina Fey" and "Steve Carell" (neither of whom are stand-ups nor have they ever stepped foot inside that venue, but hey, whatever gets tourist butts in seats). Or, it's a pay-to-play situation, where, you guessed it, the co-median pays money in exchange for stage time. I once paid five dollars to perform five minutes at an open mic in Los Angeles. My only audience? Two other comedians who also paid five dollars. In those situations, the comics are not so much getting an eager, hot crowd as much as a roomful of bemused suckers. Of course, there are far more than just these two options, with a plethora of independent shows these days, but the wonderful thing about comedy is that every kind of show can still be very bad and absolutely not what you thought you signed up for.

Because I started stand-up in a non-showbiz town with a smaller scene, Washington, DC (politics: the other hot mess), I did a lot of shows at alterna-tive venues. And yes, there were still plenty of nights of performing for seven people—all of whom were on their laptops, no doubt googling "How do I get rid of this weird skin rash while also crushing someone's dreams?"

But even then, when I was coming up, the creed in stand-up was very much "Get up there and start verbally soft shoeing, no matter how ambushed the crowd or inappropriate the venue! If you're good, you'll get their attention. And hey, if you don't, there's always next time, and it'll toughen you up." It was and is an inelegant but clear-cut formula where more time equals more laughs equals more eventual work equals hopefully more money and opportunities. Keep your eye on the prize and your dignity in a panic room at all times.

I remember peers telling me they were doing five or six open mics or shows a night or about how they never, ever took a night off, with the implication that they were more dedicated and harder-working. They were aspirational heroes. At open mics in places like New York City and Los Angeles, you wait hours to go up and then typically get only a few minutes of stage time, so I still have no idea how those time travelers did it.

As with any craft or skill, the idea was that to be good, you had to struggle, you had to be relentless. The reward was in the discomfort, the glory was in the dead-eyed stares, the psyche-detonating fails. I wouldn't wish the pain of a three-hour-plus open mic with only comedians in attendance on anyone. Somehow an art form directly tied to joy and laughter generates the grimmest basement black holes of empathy, where you will hear ideas that were offensive in 1974, frequently paired with an unbridled confidence and genuine disbelief that said ideas might not be warmly received.

Every institution has its handbook, and stand-ups, like so many others, are all about the hustle. Because of the simplicity of the medium and setup, it's possible to perform multiple times a night much easier than, say, a Polyphonic Spree cover band. No matter what, you can always tack on one more show. And there are certainly those who are paying rent by doing a certain number of paid spots a week (generally at comedy clubs, though sometimes at independently produced shows)—but the mentality is about more than just the paycheck. It's an ethos of "Take every opportunity or maybe you don't want to be a stand-up badly enough?"

It's taken me a long time and a lot of shame to admit it, but that model doesn't work for me. I found I could healthily do one or two spots a night max, with regular nights off. And now I definitely don't drop everything for the chance of more stage time because I am lucky enough to be at a point in my career where I can get the stage time when and where I need it.

When stand-up dominates too much of my life, I forget how to be a person. There's an obsessive mentality that can come with it that addictively feeds on itself, and the toll it takes, the price you pay, can be exorbitant to your state of mind. I've had to draw a boundary. A little voice in me protests, *Yes, but a real stand-up would never say no to another spot,* and to that I say, *Well, who made up that rule?* That's not the life I want to live. I'd rather live enough of a life outside of stand-up to have something to write about that doesn't solely revolve around how an audience receives it.

There will always be purists who argue I would be better if I doubled down on performing, and hey, maybe I would be, but I'd also be miserable. It's a disservice to perpetuate the myth that everyone can fit into a single prototype. If art is supposed to be far-reaching, shouldn't the terms of making art be as well?

The ten thousand hours rule—the precept that putting in ten thousand hours of practice at something will make you a master, popularized by Malcolm Gladwell in his book *Outliers*—is hardly limited to stand-up. It's also been debunked. Multiple studies have found increased practice correlates less to performance ability than initially thought across fields as diverse as chess, music, and athletics. Factors such as age when a skill was taken up as well as genes and innate ability play, quelle surprise,* important roles. With the crucial caveat that these variations in ability occur at an individual level,

---

* Pardon my French.

not at a group level, which clears us of that toxic remnant of assuming the genetic predisposition of entire identity groups to certain traits.

While some might consider this information demoralizing and fatalistic, I find it liberating. It completely supplants the idea that if you work hard enough at something, you will receive the same level of achievement as the next person. And if you don't, you just didn't work hard enough. Meritocracy is its own prison because it feeds into the idea that everything is your fault rather than that of the entrenched systems that don't have to be held to account while you're beating yourself up.

Nobody has ever heralded the entertainment industry as a bastion of fairness, so of course it's easier to control what you can by working harder and harder. The alternative is acknowledging that your fate comes down to sheer chance, no matter how talented you are. And yet, there's nothing our culture loves more than a "she never stopped trying" story, and look at her now! It all fell into place! It's because she earned it!

"Ambition isn't the sole measure of a life" is a message I'd sure love to hear every now and again, if not all the time. My whole life I've been compelled to do more and more with no sense of my own well-being, forever trying to reach some arbitrary goalpost that keeps moving. And show business constantly finds seductive new ways to remind its players of their dispensability. I often wonder how I could have been the millionth chump to fall for it.

The Spanish philosopher José Ortega y Gasset said, "Tell me to what you pay attention and I will tell you who you are." To which a stand-up might answer, "Me? Are you paying attention to me?" That's the standard idée fixe* that comes along with being a stand-up. (Though, these days, the pondering has scaled up to anyone with a modicum of web presence.

---

* I guess I speak French now?

Congrats! We're all working performers now—and so many unpaid!) If the answer is no, a stand-up is forced to blame themselves, as they are, after all, the CEO of the company.

When I first got on Twitter, it felt like a magical break from the more cloying parts of stand-up culture. It was play! I loved writing jokes, bantering with other people, and forming a small community. This was 2008, mind you, before the darkness descended. I could do it on my own terms without anyone telling me what a "real" Twitter user did. But even then, right from the start, it was hard not to get caught up in things like how many likes did a tweet get? Who retweeted me?

I was still chasing the same dragon, wanting quantified approval as much I wanted laughs onstage, except now the lines were open anywhere and everywhere 24/7. As I gained more Twitter followers, I started getting more job leads, and the pressure to produce kept going up. Suddenly, it didn't feel so fun anymore. It felt just like the battle for stage time, one unwinnable, unending race for quantity and immediacy with no room for consideration or patience or thoughtfulness. Just so long as you keep putting out new, new, new and more, more, more, you will "earn" a piece of the attention pie.

I understand the appeal of this approach. Social media has helped to engender the obsolescence of old power structures, and this development is strategically filtered through the expanding lens of representation and opportunities. The internet has revolutionized the possibility of finding one's own audience and has, in many ways, made traditional gatekeepers antiquated.

But until the top-down structures significantly shift, the availability of opportunity won't ever be as plentiful as it could. I see more women of color getting their due in this moment. As I write this book, two eponymous comedic talk shows on air right now are *The Amber Ruffin Show* on Peacock and

Ziwe on Showtime (alas, the latter has since been canceled by the time this went to press), though it's hard to decouple that both shows came out in the wake of the protests surrounding the murders of George Floyd, Breonna Taylor, and Ahmaud Arbery and the long overdue cultural shift in acknowledging "racism is totally still a thing, y'all." Both these women very much deserve their own shows, but there have been Black women deserving their own shows as long as racism has been around (say it with me, everyone, *forever*). Having diverse voices at the table doesn't matter if the implicit agenda never changes; the onus is still on individuals to excel so that they can reform from within. The reality, though, is they remain embedded in the same system that incessantly demands they justify their worth in the eyes of the market.

Stand-up, like all show business, rewards exceptionalism vis-à-vis the meritocracy myth, and especially among groups that lack equity. Multihyphenate and multitalent Issa Rae is trying to push the industry to take a more collective approach to success with her media label, Hoorae, and a sister company ColorCreative, a pipeline for underrepresented writers. She once said in an interview with *Variety*, "It's about rooting our place within this industry, establishing longevity, building the platforms, because I've seen it all disappear. I've seen us bc hot. I've seen us be a trend for years, and it's frustrating to know what we're capable of but then constantly see it be ripped from under us because we don't have the control."

It's vitally important that these efforts to usher in change are led by those in historically underrepresented groups—and yet the responsibility still falls on a handful of individuals, rather than part of a clear and committed mindset for sweeping, collective change across Hollywood. When I was coming up, I often witnessed male comedians championing each other and lifting each other up—a bigger headliner asking an up-and-comer to open for him, etc. Among female headliners, however, I noticed somewhat more hesitation in featuring other female acts on their tour, with notable exceptions like

Maria Bamford and Margaret Cho. For us, belonging, power, and access that male (and majority white) comedians enjoyed among themselves was not as free flowing a resource. The tide has shifted for the better, but the decades that preceded it have cast a long shadow.

For what it's worth, I do see far more independent live shows celebrating a range of voices now. The longtime comedy producer and booker Marianne Ways books the weekly Brooklyn show Butterboy that I used to cohost alongside comedians Maeve Higgins and Jo Firestone, and the lineups have a minority of cis, straight, white men. If anyone feels the show is discriminatory, they could always go to, hmm, let's see, any other comedy show in the city. Some of the most welcoming shows I've done happened to have all-women/queer/otherwise diverse lineups. Part of their accomplishment is eliminating the idea that inviting a non–status quo individual to perform is an automatic statement. This is true not only for the comedians but also for the crowd. Audience members may feel more welcome in these spaces, too. For once, they know their identity isn't likely to be thrown under the bus by any of the stand-ups performing.

Of course, this evolution has gotten pushback. There are plenty of comedians (I'll let you guess their dominant identities) who decry the popularity of cancel culture and the rise of MeToo. I've heard strange arguments like "Wow, I wish I was Black and trans, then maybe I'd get my own show." This sentence uttered in the same world in which there are still an untoward number of crimes perpetrated against trans women of color. Yet again, the individual example overshadows the reality of the group.

It's the same reason, even knee-deep into the twenty-first century, audience members will still come up to me after shows and say, "I don't usually think women are funny, but you were great," as if that's a compliment, to be singled out as deserving, as compared with the rest of your kind.

———

ONE OF THE most panic-inducing facets of being new to comedy and try-ing to gain a foothold in a slippery, nebulous industry was being surrounded by comics who were constantly overidentifying with being a "real" come-dian. Along with the infinite stage-time credo, there were other unspoken bylaws for those who really belonged. For instance, you had to be a precise combination of impermeable and charismatic. Vulnerability was a liability. Yes, there were people seemingly getting vulnerable onstage, but since ev-erything is turned into a joke, they were still maintaining the upper hand. You can laugh at me, but it's because I made you do it.

Being a "real" comedian is not an exact formula. A stand-up might quote Supreme Court Justice Potter Stewart and say, "I know it when I see it," even though Judgy McJudgerson was talking about hard-core pornography. Same difference. It comes down to dedication, talent, and singularity, and like any art form, there are the dilettantes and hobbyists. Ideally, if you're deemed funny enough (a subjective standard but one that requires quorum), you will be welcomed into the flock. But the price of entry is having your entire identity subsumed by this one thing. That's how the club works. It makes you question yourself deeply before it ever occurs to you to question the expectations and why they must look the same for everyone.

The resistance that reared its stubborn head in me early on and only grew over time resulted from the pressure to conform among a group that claims to embrace nonconformists. I had spent a lifetime cultivating a moon-eyed, fish-out-of-water perspective. Both my senses of self and humor are built on this foundation. So to find my place in a community, no matter how fringe, threatened to dilute my point of view. Who would I even be then? A sheep in a meadow shrugging with sarcasm? There was no way it was going to work, which isn't a hugely revolutionary statement coming from a cynic.

Not that I wasn't ecstatic to be admitted. It felt like a hiccup in reality, a glitch in the fabric of the universe. There was a quiet magic in continuing to show up, in getting to be a part of this special club. But internally, I knew I didn't buy into the vaulted expectations that came with my stand-up bona fides—neither the insatiable hunger for getting onstage nor the "burn it all down" mentality when it came to any life outside of comedy. Was this yet another space in which I could never ultimately feel worthy?

One might think the solution was right in front of my face or, rather, microphone. Why worry about my peers? The reason I do comedy at all is to find a way to connect. And, most of the time, at least, what I say does somehow seem to get through to the audience. Maybe those are my actual people, right? HA! Now *that's* funny. This is the ever-present contradiction of being a comedian: you make others laugh to win them over, but ultimately, you still never feel like you fit in because it's all a performance. You're never dropping the mask. Ultimately, your professional peers are the ones you really want to win over. Audiences come and go, but it's your fellow comedians whose respect gives you the real golden ticket.

The most clarity I've ever gained around stand-up's cultural tenets has been when I stepped away from it for a prolonged period of time. Immersed in any experience, our minds find ways to justify what we're dealing with, especially if it isn't working for us and hasn't been for a long time. Any fixation renders your world smaller and through a skewed lens. Head and heart buried in stand-up for many years, I forgot that its markers of value were hardly universal and that there's so much more to life.

Of course I don't feel like I fit in with other stand-ups. The odd-person-out mentality was what drove me here in the first place. Yes, there are still status hierarchies and cliques because we're still simple primates who happen to hold microphones. Deep down, I'd bet even my peers who appear to have the most social ease and cachet often feel off in comparison with everyone else. Their masks are just more intriguing. Mine, meanwhile, is a Scream mask.

That stand-ups can get so dogmatic is fascinating to me, given that our whole brand is being independent thinkers. Maybe that's the crux of the solution. To put on my comedian cap and not accept any of it wholesale. Questioning why anything is accepted—but without further investigation or comment—is the lifeblood of the form. Therefore, challenging an outdated set of proscribed values might just be the most "real" comedian response of all.

I'll be an outsider. And an insider. An inside outsider. At the risk of navel-gazing, an innie outie. Wait, scratch that. Have you ever tried looking into your belly button? It's terrifying and undoes years of emotional work. Perhaps my way of doing stand-up is not letting it define everything I am, because all that does is inhibit my ability to be a stand-up in the first place. Plus, every social media bio these days is a collage of identities paper-doll linked together by slashes—à la sister/wife/sister wife/working mom/working mime. Maybe it's shortsighted to think you're just the one thing. We all contain multitudes, even the bots.

The curse of stand-up for me is that as much as I might shine one day, I will flounder another, and never will the gap fully be closed between the audience and me. There will be moments of communion and even states of rapture, but ultimately, I will see myself as far, far away from those I most want to connect with—both the crowd and my peers. Therein lies the contradiction. Embrace the paradox, kiddo! The terms are mine to set, like a joke coming together, a lightness where once there was only dark.

Imagined Reviews
for, Ahem, This Book

I liked the part where she wasn't sure she knew what she was talking about because I really agreed with those parts.　　　—*The Guardian*

I actually haven't read it yet, but the cover is cute. You can use that for now if you want?　　　—My mom

This author says she's a comedian, but I've never heard of her???
　　　—Stephen King (not that one)

I'm normally someone who never leaves reviews, but I just had to say I really enjoyed the acknowledgments section. Hands down favorite part.
　　　—My mom (again)

Why are ebooks so hard to load? One star.　　　—Malala

I once read the comments on a recipe in the *New York Times* Cooking app for a vaguely ethnic stew that had been reimagined by a white person. I only mention that part to explain how popular the recipe was (very).

You could almost hear how authentically the proud chef pronounced paprika—a "very brave" spice for any culinary colonizer. Anyway, most of the comments on the recipes were to the tune of "I tried this, but used broccoli instead of spinach, and served with a side salad" or "If you prep it early, it heats up great and is even better the next day." But there was one comment that stood out to me. It simply said: "Michael didn't like this." Now, I have no idea who Michael is because that wasn't the name of the commenter who posted it, but I like that this information felt crucial to share with everyone else looking up recipes. This book feels like that comment—did it really need to be written? Alas, in both cases, it still was. And here we are. Also, I think it's safe to assume Michael wouldn't like this book either. —My inner critic

I got about halfway through and then I learned my book club changed books for this month. Thanks a lot!!! —God

I Tried: An Epilogue

For some reason, I still remember that my college application essay prompt was to write about an experience that changed how you thought about the world. Fittingly vague, but also vaguely poignant, the catnip of admissions committees. I, and I'm sure I'm not alone in this, felt as though nothing had happened to me in my entire life. So that's what I wrote about. I described a three-week outdoor wilderness survival trip I had gone on to try to change my life. It wasn't the first or the last time I've tried to force my own world-shifting experiences, but epiphanies are not poker hands. They're not a lot of things. It's hard to describe them really, hence their mystery. I left that outdoor wilderness camp with some great anecdotes—like when a bee got in another camper's pants and when I peed myself during an endurance run. But did my life irrevocably change? No, no, it did not.*

Rinse and repeat. I wanted to write this book to fix my impostor syndrome. I assumed I could write my way out of it. But that's like saying I'm going to sleep my way through this plate of food. When you try to write

---

* I mean, sure, I did break out in hives every morning for like a month after I got back and sporadically ever since, but tuh-may-toe, tuh-mah-toe.

about your core insecurities, it turns out that sometimes they get louder. It's like all those horror movies where you're not supposed to touch the old relics. You touch the old relics? The spirits get pissed. You try to fix the mental demons? The demons create a mosh pit on your sense of self.

But there is something I learned in this whole process, an epiphany about epiphanies, if you will. And please don't, I implore you. They don't arrive on a schedule, and sometimes you're the last to know you're having one. Because epiphanies can take years to sink in. Yes, of course there are those moments that strike like a bolt of lightning with accompanying thunderclap, but more often there is no fanfare. And usually, you still end up needing to relearn the lesson again. But, hey, at least you remember it better the next time around, what with everything looking so familiar, like a dream you've had many times before.

That's what I've learned about my own impostor syndrome. It's probably never going to really go away, but I can remember I've been here before. I'm late to most things in life, my own self-discovery had to be one of them, if we're being on-brand. This entire book has been an exercise in hesitation. I frequently felt as though the more of it that came together, the more of me that came apart. Yet, here we are, at the end somehow. Only there are no tidy conclusions, are there? Most everything I've written about remains open-ended in my own life, ongoing battles that must be faced and negotiated without fanfare. I wish I knew another way to do it, but this looks like it's it.

You hear that vague advice that no one really knows what they're doing, and you should fake it till you make it. But some of us have been steeped in uncertainty since birth and may never convince ourselves of our own performance, even if we manage to convince others along the way.

I struggle. I overthink. I find my limitations. And the beautiful thing is, I realize maybe they aren't as scary and damning as I thought. It's OK to not be exceptional, or genius, or unstoppable. Goals don't have to always look like superlatives.

And as often as I forget these things, I keep finding ways to remember. We forget. We remember. We forget. We remember. What's important is not the forgetting or even the remembering. It's what happens in the space between, that imperceptible shift, that I find is enough.

Acknowledgments

I can't even tell you what the process of writing this book was like because I already did that several times throughout these pieces. That's the thing with detailing one's suffering: you have to dole it out in manageable portions or you lose your audience, not out of boredom but because they start to think, *What about* my *suffering?!*

But, in terms of writing this "thing," let's just say the difficulty level was higher than a mountaintop on 4/20. Suffice to say there are a lot of book doulas who had to show up to get it out of me.

I've always been bad at thank-yous because I never feel like I can adequately express how much gratitude I have for anyone helping me in any way. Yet here I go, still showing up with my glistening brow and overeager, floppy smile, attempting to puzzle together the words.

I've noticed other people do their acknowledgments in reverse order of intimacy and it starts to feel like a countdown as to WHO REALLY MATTERS in this person's life. And, as with most matters, I don't want to deal with that, nor do I want to name names because the stress of someone being left out is so great, I can't even handle it.

In that sense, I would like to thank my depression and anxiety for never taking a day off, and for showing up for a job they were never hired for and yet continue to give their all. In that regard, thank you to anyone (pills included) who has ever tasked themselves with my mental health.

And, of course, thank you to everyone at Penguin Random House and Viking for taking a chance on me and this haunted manuscript, which took close to a presidential term to conjure. But what even are presidents anymore? (You know I was going to go political here.) To my editors—Georgia Bodnar, Gretchen Schmidt, and Emily Wunderlich—all the doves. To Victoria Loustalot, who came in at the eleventh hour and truly was an oasis in the desert, a caravan of roses. To the entire production, editing, design, publicity, and marketing teams, thank you for honoring my vision and bearing my inability to answer an email on time.

Thank you to all my showbiz reps, past and present. Your willingness to work with someone whose willingness to work is often theoretical is admirable.

Next up: friends and family. I'm embarrassed to put everyone in a clump like this, but here's the thing: if I have to start narrowing down who deserves to be named specifically and who doesn't, I'll actually throw up and the smell will never come out. Let's say if we've confided in each other in the last six months to five years (scheduling is hard), you have no idea how much you mean to me because I'm not always great at expressing it. But being truly understood by anyone (no filter) is so rare anymore that I can't help but scream at how lucky I am to have those moments with all of you. And to Gabe, for you?, I will take out the poop, just ask me a third time. And to the kittos, for providing that poop that keeps the whole ecosystem running.

And thank you, brave reader, for spending some time in my brain with me. I don't know how you feel now, but I, for one, am a bit peckish. At the very least, grab a complimentary chocolate chip on your way out. Just a single one. For the road.

Notes

EPIGRAPHS

vii **That is the funny:** Jean Dawson, "Jean Dawson: My Sound Is 'Pop Music from Different Generations,'" interview by Elle Evans, *Notion*, February 5, 2021, notion.online/jean-dawson -my-sound-is-pop-music-from-different-generations.

vii **In the artist:** D. W. Winnicott, *The Collected Works of D. W. Winnicott: Volume 6, 1960–1963*, eds. Lesley Caldwell and Helen Taylor Robinson (New York: Oxford University Press, 2016), 433–36, sas.upenn.edu/~cavitch/pdf-library/Winnicott_Communicating_and_Not _Communicating.pdf.

NOW THAT I HAVE YOU HERE

2 **The term is derived:** Pauline Rose Clance and Suzanne Ament Imes, "The Impostor Phenomenon in High Achieving Women: Dynamics and Therapeutic Intervention," *Psychotherapy: Theory, Research and Practice* 15, no. 3 (Fall 1978): 241–47, doi.org/10.1037/h0086006.

2 **Not to brag:** Joe Langford and Pauline Rose Clance, "The Impostor Phenomenon: Recent Research Findings regarding Dynamics, Personality and Family Patterns and Their Implications for Treatment," *Psychotherapy: Theory, Research, Practice, Training* 30, no. 3 (Fall 1993): 495–501, doi.org/10.1037/0033-3204.30.3.495.

3 ***New York Times* writer:** Benedict Carey, "Feel like a Fraud? At Times, Maybe You Should," *New York Times*, February 5, 2008, nytimes.com/2008/02/05/health/05mind.html.

7 **Tina Fey (of all people):** Tina Fey, "Tina Fey—from Spoofer to Movie Stardom," interview by *The Independent*, *The Independent*, March 19, 2010, independent.co.uk/arts-entertainment /films/features/tina-fey-from-spoofer-to-movie-stardom-1923552.html.

8 **In 2015, Rannazzisi:** Serge F. Kovaleski, "Steve Rannazzisi, Comedian Who Told of 9/11 Escape, Admits He Lied," *New York Times*, September 16, 2015, nytimes.com/2015/09/17 /arts/television/steve-rannazzisi-comedian-who-told-of-9-11-escape-admits-he-lied.html.

8 While his starring role: Serge F. Kovaleski, "Steve Rannazzisi, Comedian Who Lied About 9/11, Loses Wild Wings Ad Campaign," *New York Times*, September 17, 2015, archive .nytimes.com/artsbeat.blogs.nytimes.com/2015/09/17/comedian-who-lied-about-911 -loses-wild-wings-ad-campaign.

14 In an op-ed for *JAMA*: Samyukta Mullangi and Reshma Jagsi, "Imposter Syndrome: Treat the Cause, Not the Symptom," *JAMA* 322, no. 5 (August 6, 2019): 403–4, jamanetwork.com /journals/jama/article-abstract/2740724.

14 "the impact of systemic": Ruchika Tulshyan and Jodi-Ann Burey, "Stop Telling Women They Have Imposter Syndrome," *Harvard Business Review*, February 11, 2021, hbr.org/2021 /02/stop-telling-women-they-have-imposter-syndrome.

15 "that the impostor phenomenon": Leslie Jamison, "Why Everyone Feels Like They're Faking It," *New Yorker*, February 6, 2023, newyorker.com/magazine/2023/02/13/the-dubious -rise-of-impostor-syndrome.

16 A 2019 University of Chicago: Lauren Eskreis-Winkler and Ayelet Fishbach, "Not Learning from Failure—the Greatest Failure of All," *Psychological Science* 30, no. 12 (December 2019): 1733–44, doi.org/10.1177/0956797619881133.

16 A different study used: Frederik Joelving, "How You Learn More from Success Than Failure," *Scientific American*, November 1, 2009, scientificamerican.com/article/why-success -breeds-success.

16 And if you thought: Janet Polivy, C. Peter Herman, and Rajbir Deo, "Getting a Bigger Slice of the Pie. Effects on Eating and Emotion in Restrained and Unrestrained Eaters," *Appetite* 55, no. 3 (December 2010): 426–30, doi.org/10.1016/j.appet.2010.07.015.

17 subjects learn just as much: Eskreis-Winkler and Fishbach, "Not Learning."

17 study where individuals in Japan: Eskreis-Winkler and Fishbach, "Not Learning."

17 Usually after the initial thrill: Arthur C. Brooks, "Why Success Can Feel So Bitter," *The Atlantic*, February 24, 2022, theatlantic.com/family/archive/2022/02/reaching-goals-doesnt -always-lead-to-happiness/622894.

BE FREE, YOU WRINKLY GHOST!

20 I already knew that working: Shelley Ortiz, "Essential," interview by Chana Joffe-Walt, August 13, 2021, in *This American Life*, produced by Bim Adewunmi, 67:33, thisamericanlife .org/744/essential/act-two-6.

22 In her essay: Janet Mock, "Being Pretty Is a Privilege, but We Refuse to Acknowledge It," *Allure*, June 18, 2017, allure.com/story/pretty-privilege.

22 Even the counter-wave: Virginia Sole-Smith, "The Food Movement Became the Wellness Culture, Which Is Just Diet Culture Rebranded by Gwyneth Paltrow," interview by Anne Helen Petersen, *Culture Study*, March 25, 2021, annehelen.substack.com/p/the-food -movement-became-the-wellness.

24 **As sociologist Tressie:** Tressie McMillan Cottom, "In the Name of Beauty," in *Thick: And Other Essays* (New York: New Press, 2019), 52.

24 **According to McMillan Cottom:** McMillan Cottom, "In the Name of Beauty," 58.

36 **When I was a year:** *Slate*, "Flutter: The New Twitter," April 8, 2009, produced by Andy Bouvé, YouTube video, 3:43, youtube.com/watch?v=BeLZCy-_m3s.

40 **Another small epiphany:** Elisa Gabbert, "Vanity Project," in *The Unreality of Memory: And Other Essays* (New York: FSG Originals, 2020), 114.

40 **In a study conducted at:** Lydia Rivers, "This Is Why the Inverted Filter on TikTok Makes Your Face Look Weird," *Discover*, May 7, 2021, discovermagazine.com/technology/this-is -why-the-inverted-filter-on-tiktok-makes-your-face-look-weird.

42 **As Akiko Busch writes:** Akiko Busch, introduction to *How to Disappear: Notes on Invisibility in a Time of Transparency* (New York: Penguin Press, 2019), 9.

FAILURE RÉSUMÉ

45 **When she was still:** Melanie Stefan, "A CV of Failures," *Nature* 468 (November 7, 2010): 467, doi.org/10.1038/nj7322-467a.

INSIDE VOICE

55 **postulates that valuing magnetic:** Susan Cain, "Susan Cain: 'Society Has a Cultural Bias Towards Extroverts,'" interview by Ian Tucker, *The Guardian*, March 31, 2012, theguardian .com/technology/2012/apr/01/susan-cain-extrovert-introvert-interview.

59 **though no longer:** Joseph Stromberg and Estelle Caswell, "Why the Myers-Briggs Test Is Totally Meaningless," *Vox*, October 8, 2015, vox.com/2014/7/15/5881947/myers-briggs -personality-test-meaningless.

60 **Also, despite introverts constituting:** Kendra Cherry, "8 Signs You're an Introvert: Understanding Introversion vs. Extroversion," VeryWellMind, May 13, 2022, verywellmind .com/signs-you-are-an-introvert-2795427.

60 **of our kind, ultra-introverts:** Faith Hill, "The Ultra-Introverts Who Live Nocturnally," *The Atlantic*, February 22, 2022, theatlantic.com/family/archive/2022/02/ultra-introverts -nocturnal-lives/622856.

63 **Research from the University of New Mexico:** Ewen Callaway, "Personality Tests Reveal the Flip Side of Comedy," *New Scientist*, March 16, 2009, newscientist.com/article /dn16766-personality-tests-reveal-the-flip-side-of-comedy.

63 **It helps to learn:** Laura Studarus, "Bridget Everett Is Coming of Age, Again," Shondaland, January 17, 2022, shondaland.com/inspire/a38771050/bridget-everett-is-coming-of-age-again.

64 **In an interview with *Billboard*:** Missy Elliott, "Billboard Cover: Missy Elliott on Her Comeback—'There Is Only One Missy,'" interview by Jonathan Ringen, *Billboard*, Nov-

ember 19, 2015, billboard.com/music/music-news/missy-elliott-comeback-wtf-new-album
-graves-disease-anxiety-super-bowl-6769236.

66 **For example, in 2011:** Jennifer O. Grimes, Jonathan M. Cheek, and Julie K. Norem,
"Four Meanings of Introversion: Social, Thinking, Anxious, and Inhibited Introversion,"
presented at the Society for Personality and Social Psychology Annual Meeting, San Anto-
nio, Texas, January 2011, researchgate.net/publication/263279416_Four_Meanings_of
_Introversion_Social_Thinking_Anxious_and_Inhibited_Introversion.

67 **There's even a whole school:** Amanda J. Minor, "Internal Family Systems Model," in
The SAGE Encyclopedia of Marriage, Family, and Couples Counseling, eds. Jon Carlson and Shan-
non B. Dermer (Los Angeles: SAGE Publications, 2016), 884–88.

71 **For too long:** Thomas Gilovich, Victoria Husted Medvec, and Kenneth Savitsky, "The
Spotlight Effect in Social Judgment: An Egocentric Bias in Estimates of the Salience of One's
Own Actions and Appearance," *Journal of Personality and Social Psychology* 78, no. 2 (2000):
211–22, doi.org/10.1037/0022-3514.78.2.211.

BEING WELL

75 **After a crucial internet deep dive:** "Major Depressive Disorder," Course Hero, accessed
February 27, 2023, coursehero.com/study-guides/abnormalpsychology/major-depressive
-disorder.

79 **There's an idea in psychology:** Lauren B. Alloy and Lyn Y. Abramson, "Depressive
Realism: Four Theoretical Perspectives," in *Cognitive Processes in Depression,* ed. Lauren B. Alloy
(New York: Guilford Press, 1988), 223–65, psycnet.apa.org/record/1988-98142-008.

79 **Social scientist Robert Weiss:** Robert S. Weiss, *Loneliness: the Experience of Emotional and
Social Isolation* (Cambridge, MA: MIT Press, 1975), 12.

82 **Then again, as Andrew Solomon:** Andrew Solomon, *The Noonday Demon: An Atlas of Depression* (New York: Scribner, 2001), 283.

82 **According to the site:** Debra Fulghum Bruce, "Dysthymia (Mild, Chronic Depression),"
WebMD, August 28, 2022, webmd.com/depression/guide/chronic-depression-dysthymia.

84 **According to the National Institute:** Katie Hurley, "Persistent Depressive Disorder
(Dysthymia)," Psycom, September 6, 2022, psycom.net/depression.central.dysthymia.html.

85 **The World Health Organization notes:** World Health Organization, "Depression,"
September 13, 2021, who.int/news-room/fact-sheets/detail/depression.

86 **"It makes a difference that":** Eva Meijer, *The Limits of My Language: Meditations on Depression* (London: Pushkin Press, 2021), 20–21.

87 **The possible causes:** "What Causes Depression?," Harvard Health Publishing, January
10, 2022, health.harvard.edu/mind-and-mood/what-causes-depression.

87 **"How much does my fear":** Arianna Rebolini, "How Do We Survive Suicide?," Cata-
pult, October 26, 2021, https://catapult.co/stories/arianna-rebolini-sylvia-plath-how-do-we
-survive-suicide.

89 **"Sad Girl culture grew up":** Jess Joho, "How Being Sad, Depressed, and Anxious Online
Became Trendy," Mashable, June 28, 2019, mashable.com/article/anxiety-depression-social
-media-sad-online.

89 **"The self-care narrative":** Amanda Hess, "How Social Media Turned 'Prioritizing
Mental Health' into a Trap," *New York Times Magazine*, October 27, 2021, nytimes.com/2021
/10/27/magazine/social-media-mental-health.html.

90 **findings by *The Wall Street Journal*:** Georgia Wells, Jeff Horwitz, and Deepa Seethara-
man, "Facebook Knows Instagram Is Toxic for Teen Girls, Company Documents Show,"
Wall Street Journal, September 14, 2021, wsj.com/articles/facebook-knows-instagram-is-toxic
-for-teen-girls-company-documents-show-11631620739.

90 **"The same consumerist culture":** Jake Bittle, "I Feel Better Now," *The Baffler*, July 11,
2019, thebaffler.com/latest/i-feel-better-now-bittle.

90 **"Wasn't it disrespectful":** Katy Waldman, "The Rise of Therapy-Speak," *New Yorker*,
March 26, 2021, newyorker.com/culture/cultural-comment/the-rise-of-therapy-speak.

91 **"people will use whatever":** Lisa Feldman Barrett, *How Emotions Are Made: The Secret Life
of the Brain* (Boston: Mariner Books, 2018), 214.

93 **Some are giving mental health:** Morgan Sung, "On TikTok, Mental Health Creators Are
Confused for Therapists. That's a Serious Problem," Mashable, March 10, 2021, mashable
.com/article/tiktok-mental-health-therapist-psychology.

93 **not to mention providing:** Rola Jadayel, Karim Medlej, and Jinan Jennifer Jadayel,
"Mental Disorders: A Glamorous Attraction on Social Media?," *Journal of Teaching and Education* 7, no. 1 (2017): 465–76, universitypublications.net/jte/0701/pdf/V7NA374.pdf.

93 **The teen suicide rate:** Laura Santhanam, "Youth Suicide Rates Are on the Rise in the
U.S.," *PBS NewsHour*, October 18, 2019, pbs.org/newshour/health/youth-suicide-rates-are-on
-the-rise-in-the-u-s.

93 **Similarly, a CDC study:** Derek Thompson, "Why American Teens Are So Sad," *The Atlantic*, April 11, 2022, theatlantic.com/newsletters/archive/2022/04/american-teens-sadness
-depression-anxiety/629524.

93 **"social media isn't like":** Thompson, "Why American Teens Are So Sad."

93 **However, it's important:** Matt Richtel, "'It's Life or Death': The Mental Health Crisis
among U.S. Teens," *New York Times*, April 23, 2022, nytimes.com/2022/04/23/health/mental
-health-crisis-teens.html.

94 **by-products of industrialization:** Seth J. Prins, Lisa M. Bates, Katherine M. Keyes,
and Carles Muntaner, "Anxious? Depressed? You Might Be Suffering from Capitalism:

Contradictory Class Locations and the Prevalence of Depression and Anxiety in the USA," *Sociology of Health & Illness* 37, no. 8 (November 2015): 1352–72, doi.org/10.1111/1467 -9566.12315.

94 **stressful conditions of modern life:** Mike Hidaka, "Depression as a Disease of Modernity: Explanations for Increasing Prevalence," *Journal of Affective Disorders* 140, no. 3 (November 2012): 205–14, doi.org/10.1016/j.jad.2011.12.036.

94 **"I want to make the work":** Sarah Schulman, "Transcript: Ezra Klein Interviews Sarah Schulman," interview by Ezra Klein, *The Ezra Klein Show, New York Times,* June 22, 2021, nytimes.com/2021/06/22/podcasts/transcript-ezra-klein-interviews-sarah-schulman .html.

96 **But health-care and emergency workers:** Allana Akhtar and Rebecca Aydin, "Some of the Jobs Most at Risk for Suicide and Depression Are the Most Important to Society. Here's a Rundown of Mental-Health Risks for Doctors, Childcare Workers, First Responders, and More," *Business Insider,* November 14, 2019, businessinsider.com/jobs-with-mental-health -risks-like-suicide-depression-2019-10.

96 **As Sigmund Freud:** Sigmund Freud, *Jokes and Their Relation to the Unconscious,* ed. James Strachey (New York: W. W. Norton, 1960), 9.

CONFESSIONS: THE BODY ELECTRIC

105 **It doesn't happen to everyone:** Jonathan Jarry, "The Unbearable Poopness of Bookstores," McGill University Office for Science and Society, January 22, 2022, mcgill.ca/oss /article/general-science/unbearable-poopness-bookstores.

TO DO OR NOT TO DO

106 **on the town dump:** Charles Simic, "Could This Be Me?," *New Yorker,* January 10, 2022, newyorker.com/magazine/2022/01/17/could-this-be-me.

107 **"Everywhere you look":** Rachel Syme, "What Deadlines Do to Lifetimes," *New Yorker,* June 28, 2021, newyorker.com/magazine/2021/07/05/what-deadlines-do-to-lifetimes.

110 **In her book *Do Nothing*:** Celeste Headlee, *Do Nothing: How to Break Away from Overworking, Overdoing, and Underliving* (New York: Harmony, 2021), 33–78.

114 **"Better to cherish":** Oliver Burkeman, *Four Thousand Weeks: Time Management for Mortals* (New York: Macmillan, 2021), 78–79.

116 **Toni Morrison used to:** Toni Morrison, "Toni Morrison, The Art of Fiction No. 134," interview by Elissa Schappell and Claudia Brodsky Lacour, *Paris Review,* no. 128 (Fall 1993), theparisreview.org/interviews/1888/the-art-of-fiction-no-134-toni-morrison.

116 **"Sleep is death":** Fran Lebowitz, "Why I Love Sleep," in *The Fran Lebowitz Reader* (New York: Vintage Books, 1994), 158.

117 **Sleep researchers have:** Katie Heaney, "When Stress Makes You Fall Asleep," *The Cut*, *New York*, July 11, 2017, thecut.com/2017/07/when-stress-makes-you-fall-asleep.html.

118 **"the only piece":** Adrian Horton, "How Bo Burnham's Netflix Special Inside Set the Bar for Quarantine Art," *The Guardian*, June 15, 2021, theguardian.com/stage/2021/jun/15/bo -burnham-inside-netflix-special-comedy.

122 **"irregular and unpredictable":** Joe Zadeh, "The Tyranny of Time," *Noēma*, June 3, 2021, noemamag.com/the-tyranny-of-time.

122 **I attended a Zoom:** Ruth Ozeki, "One-Time Intimate Talk," *The Seventh Wave*, March 7, 2022, Zoom, private access link.

123 **"Capitalism did not create":** Zadeh, "The Tyranny of Time."

123 **"You're obliged to deal":** Burkeman, *Four Thousand Weeks*, 106.

124 **"For someone in a":** Jenny Odell, *Inhabiting the Negative Space*, Virtual Commencement 2020 Harvard University Graduate School of Design (Cambridge, MA: Sternberg Press, 2021), 19.

124 **"Everything fell apart":** Anne Helen Petersen, "You're Still Exhausted," *Culture Study*, August 4, 2021, annehelen.substack.com/p/youre-still-exhausted.

126 **"We are resting simply":** Tricia Hersey, "Why Rest Is an Act of Resistance," interview by Shereen Marisol Maraji, October 13, 2022, *Life Kit* (podcast), NPR, transcript, npr.org /transcripts/1127470930?ft=nprml&f=510338.

126 *How to Do Nothing* **is:** Jenny Odell, *How to Do Nothing: Resisting the Attention Economy* (Brooklyn: Melville House, 2019).

126 **Odell's second book:** Jenny Odell, *Saving Time: Discovering a Life Beyond the Clock* (New York: Random House, 2023).

126 **In China, there:** Elsie Chen, "These Chinese Millennials Are 'Chilling,' and Beijing Isn't Happy," *New York Times*, July 3, 2021, nytimes.com/2021/07/03/world/asia/china-slackers -tangping.html.

A NIGHT IN THE LIFE OF REVENGE BEDTIME PROCRASTINATION (RBP)

128 **"Learned a very":** Daphne K. Lee (@daphnekylee), Twitter, June 28, 2020, 12:49 a.m., twitter.com/daphnekylee/status/1277101831693275136?s=20.

THE AGREEABILITY INDUSTRIAL COMPLEX

135 **"People pleasers crave":** Kelsey Borresen, "How to Stop Being a People Pleaser and Learn to Say No," *HuffPost*, April 9, 2021, huffpost.com/entry/how-to-stop-people-pleaser -say-no_l_606e2c65c5b6034a70844049.

135 **"Successful women of color":** Anna Holmes, "How about Never?," *The Atlantic*, November 5, 2021, theatlantic.com/ideas/archive/2021/11/liberating-power-no/620612.

139 **At best, humans:** Kiona N. Smith, "80,000-Year-Old Footprints Reveal Neanderthal Social Life," *Ars Technica*, September 10, 2019, arstechnica.com/science/2019/09/80000-year-old-footprints-reveal-neanderthal-social-life.

139 **"We shouldn't pretend":** Holmes, "How about Never?"

141 **According to the Rape, Abuse:** "Victims of Sexual Violence: Statistics," RAINN, accessed February 23, 2023, rainn.org/statistics/victims-sexual-violence.

141 **Globally, the problem:** World Health Organization, "Violence against Women," March 9, 2021, who.int/news-room/fact-sheets/detail/violence-against-women.

142 **"I wasn't at all surprised":** Melissa Febos, "Thank You for Taking Care of Yourself," in *Girlhood* (New York: Bloomsbury, 2021), 244.

146 **I do experience some:** Claire Gillespie, "What Does It Mean to be Graysexual?," Health, updated October 6, 2022, health.com/mind-body/lgbtq-health/graysexual.

147 **In *Ace: What Asexuality*:** Angela Chen, *Ace: What Asexuality Reveals about Desire, Society, and the Meaning of Sex* (Boston: Beacon Press, 2020), 34–40.

147 **"Life is a continuous process":** Chen, *Ace*, 71.

150 **"We go in":** Dave Itzkoff, "Michaela Coel Puts Herself Together in 'Misfits,'" *New York Times*, August 22, 2021, nytimes.com/2021/08/22/books/michaela-coel-misfits-book.html.

DON'T GET MAD, GET EVEN . . . MORE MAD

155 **It was then, of course:** Jeff Guo, "The Real Reasons the U.S. Became Less Racist toward Asian Americans," *Washington Post*, November 29, 2016, washingtonpost.com/news/wonk/wp/2016/11/29/the-real-reason-americans-stopped-spitting-on-asian-americans-and-started-praising-them.

156 **This rings even:** "S0201: Selected Population Profile in the United States," American Community Survey 2021, United States Census Bureau, accessed February 23, 2023, data.census.gov/table?t=013:014:015:016:017:018:019:020:021:022:023:024:026:027:028:029:032:033:034:035:036:037:038:039:040:041:042:043:045:046:047:048:081:084:073:076:Income+and+Poverty&g=0100000US&tid=ACSSPP1Y2021.S0201&moe=true.

156 **while the poorest Asian Americans:** Christian E. Weller and Jeffrey Thompson, "Wealth Inequality among Asian Americans Greater Than among Whites," Center for American Progress, December 20, 2016, americanprogress.org/article/wealth-inequality-among-asian-americans-greater-than-among-whites.

157 **Since then, it has come:** Maeve Sheehy, "Christine Blasey Ford Lawyers Call Kavanaugh Investigation a 'Sham' after New Details Emerge," *Politico*, July 23, 2021, politico.com

/news/2021/07/23/christine-blasey-ford-brett-kavanaugh-investigation-new-details
-500652.

157 **"I have learned":** Uma Thurman, "Uma Thurman Gets Emotional about Women Speaking Out on Sexual Harrassment in Hollywood," interview by *Access Hollywood*, YouTube video, 1:10, October 18, 2017, youtube.com/watch?v=Rs4gK8DuuWY, 0:29.

158 **"The truth is that Angry":** Brittney Cooper, "The Problem with Sass," in *Eloquent Rage: A Black Feminist Discovers Her Superpower* (New York: St. Martin's Press, 2018), 3.

159 **"Well, all comedy":** Jerry Seinfeld, "Takes One to Know One," interview by David Steinberg, *Los Angeles Times*, November 24, 2008, latimes.com/style/la-mag-nov302008-theear -story.html.

161 **In the video I forced:** "'Kramer's' Racist Tirade Caught on Tape," TMZ, November 20, 2006, video, 2:27, tmz.com/2006/11/20/kramers-racist-tirade-caught-on-tape.

161 **In his public apology:** Dan Glaister, "Seinfeld Actor Lets Fly with Racist Tirade," *The Guardian*, November 22, 2006, theguardian.com/world/2006/nov/22/usa.danglaister.

161 **Richards later cited:** Michael Richards, "It's Bubby Time, Jerry," September 27, 2012, in *Comedians in Cars Getting Coffee*, web series, Crackle, video, 17:07, web.archive.org/web/20121 002001805/http://www.comediansincarsgettingcoffee.com/michael-richards-its-bubbly -time-jerry.

162 **I strongly disagree, because comedy:** Tamara Markovic, Christian E. Pedersen, Nicolas Massaly, Yvan M. Vachez, Brian Ruyle, Caitlin A. Murphy, Kavitha Abiraman et al., "Pain Induces Adaptations in Ventral Tegmental Area Dopamine Neurons to Drive Anhedonia-like Behavior," *Nature Neuroscience* 24, no. 11 (November 2021): 1601–13, doi.org /10.1038/s41593-021-00924-3.

163 **"I wanted to distract":** Hannah Gadsby, *Ten Steps to Nanette: A Memoir Situation* (New York: Ballantine, 2022), 348.

ANXIETY IN THREE ACTS

179 **I did a joke:** *The Half Hour*, season 5, episode 5, "Comedy Central Presents: Aparna Nancherla," directed by Joe DeMaio and Ryan Polito, aired September 9, 2016, on Comedy Central, cc.com/episodes/5tspp9/the-half-hour-aparna-nancherla-season-5-ep-5.

186 **According to a 2020 article:** Caleb Warren, Adam Barsky, and A. Peter McGraw, "What Makes Things Funny? An Integrative Review of the Antecedents of Laughter and Amusement," *Personality and Social Psychology Review* 25, no. 1 (February 2021): 41–65, doi.org /10.1177/1088868320961909.

190 **"Insanity is doing":** Christina Sterbenz, "12 Famous Quotes That Always Get Misattributed," *Business Insider*, October 7, 2013, businessinsider.com/misattributed-quotes -2013-10.

NO COMMENT

209 **Consider the case:** Nico Lang, "The Rise and Fall of Ken Bone: This Is What Happens When Real Humans Become Internet Memes," *Salon*, October 15, 2016, salon.com/2016 /10/15/the-rise-and-fall-of-ken-bone-this-is-what-happens-when-real-humans-become -internet-memes.

210 **"the greatest trick":** "The Greatest Trick the Devil Ever Pulled Was Convincing the World He Didn't Exist," Quote Investigator, March 20, 2018, quoteinvestigator.com/2018 /03/20/devil.

218 **"If we applied":** Aja Romano, "Everyone Wants Forgiveness, but No One Is Being Forgiven," *Vox*, March 22, 2022, vox.com/22969804/forgiveness-gibson-logan-paul-jk-rowling.

218 **"That doesn't mean, necessarily":** Romano, "Everyone Wants Forgiveness."

224 **Take the incident:** Constance Grady, "Will Smith's Slap and Oscars Ban, Briefly Explained," *Vox*, updated April 8, 2022, vox.com/culture/22999328/will-smith-hit-chris-rock -oscars-best-actor.

225 **I am borrowing that term:** Charlie Warzel, "The Predictability of a Social-Media Discourse," *Galaxy Brain* newsletter, *The Atlantic*, March 29, 2022, newsletters.theatlantic.com /galaxy-brain/624231c1dc551a00208b6b8e/twitter-backlash-over-will-smith-oscars-slap.

225 **"Maybe we retreat":** Warzel, "The Predictability of a Social-Media Discourse."

227 **And yes, I'll:** Katie Canales, "7 Apple Suppliers in China Have Links to Forced Labor Programs, Including the Use of Uyghur Muslims from Xinjiang, According to a New Report," *Business Insider*, May 10, 2021, businessinsider.com/apple-china-suppliers-uyghur-muslims -forced-labor-report-2021-5.

TALKING ABOUT NOTHING

234 **I even used:** *Conan*, episode 475, "Aaron Aaronson and the First-in-the-Phonebook Caper," directed by Billy Bollotino, featuring Steven Yeun, Eric André, and Aparna Nancherla, aired October 14, 2013, on TBS.

234 **incidentally the first:** Erin Gloria Ryan, "Check Out the First Indian Woman to Perform Stand Up on Late Night TV," Jezebel, October 15, 2013, jezebel.com/check-out-the-first -indian-woman-to-perform-stand-up-on-1445843162.

240 **As far as the internet:** Kaitlin Milligan, "NBC's Diverse Stand-Up Competition Crowns Winners," BroadwayWorld, January 14, 2020, broadwayworld.com/bwwtv/article/NBCS -Diverse-StandUp-Competition-Crowns-Winners-20200114.

248 **Minorities now make:** Ana-Christina Ramón, Michael Tran, and Darnell Hunt, *Hollywood Diversity Report 2022: A New, Post-Pandemic Normal? Part 2: Television*, UCLA Institute for Research on Labor and Employment, October 27, 2022, socialsciences.ucla.edu/wp -content/uploads/2022/10/UCLA-Hollywood-Diversity-Report-2022-Television -10-27-2022.pdf, 2.

248 **We consume disproportionately:** Darnell Hunt and Ana-Christina Ramón, *Hollywood Diversity Report 2021: Pandemic in Progress, Part 2: Television*, UCLA Institute for Research on Labor and Employment, October 26, 2021, socialsciences.ucla.edu/wp-content/uploads /2021/10/UCLA-Hollywood-Diversity-Report-2021-Television-10-26-2021.pdf, 69–70.

248 **In the 2022 *Hollywood*:** Darnell Hunt and Ana-Christina Ramón, *Hollywood Diversity Report 2022: A New, Post-Pandemic Normal? Part 1: Film*, UCLA Institute for Research on Labor and Employment, March 24, 2022, socialsciences.ucla.edu/wp-content/uploads/2022/03 /UCLA-Hollywood-Diversity-Report-2022-Film-3-24-2022.pdf, 3–4.

248 **For example, Latinx:** Ramón, Tran, and Hunt, *Hollywood Diversity Report 2022*, 60–61.

248 **Another finding was:** Ramón, Tran, and Hunt, *Hollywood Diversity Report 2022*, 14–15.

248 **As categorized in the report:** Ramón, Tran, and Hunt, *Hollywood Diversity Report 2022*, 3.

248 **There was no update:** Hunt and Ramón, *Hollywood Diversity Report 2021*, 70.

250 **"Mediocrity is a creative resource":** Adam Bradley, "The Privilege of Mediocrity," *T: The New York Times Style Magazine*, September 30, 2021, nytimes.com/2021/09/30/t-magazine /mediocrity-people-of-color.html.

STANDING UP ON MY OWN TERMS

264 **It's also been debunked:** Brian Resnick, "The '10,000-Hour Rule' Was Debunked Again. That's a Relief," *Vox*, August 23, 2019, vox.com/science-and-health/2019/8/23/2082 8597/the-10000-hour-rule-debunked.

264 **Multiple studies have found:** David Z. Hambrick, Fernanda Ferreira, and John M. Henderson, "Practice Does Not Make Perfect," *Slate*, September 28, 2014, slate.com/technology /2014/09/malcolm-gladwells-10000-hour-rule-for-deliberate-practice-is-wrong-genes-for -music-iq-drawing-ability-and-other-skills.html.

265 **"Tell me to what":** José Ortega y Gasset, *Man and Crisis* (New York: W. W. Norton, 1962), 94.

267 **"It's about rooting":** Issa Rae, "Issa Rae's Next Chapter: How 'Insecure' Creator Is Becoming a Media Mogul with Production Banner Hoorae," interview by Angelique Jackson, *Variety*, March 24, 2021, variety.com/2021/tv/news/issa-rae-insecure-hbo-hoorae-1234936020.